INHUMANS
ATTILAN RISING

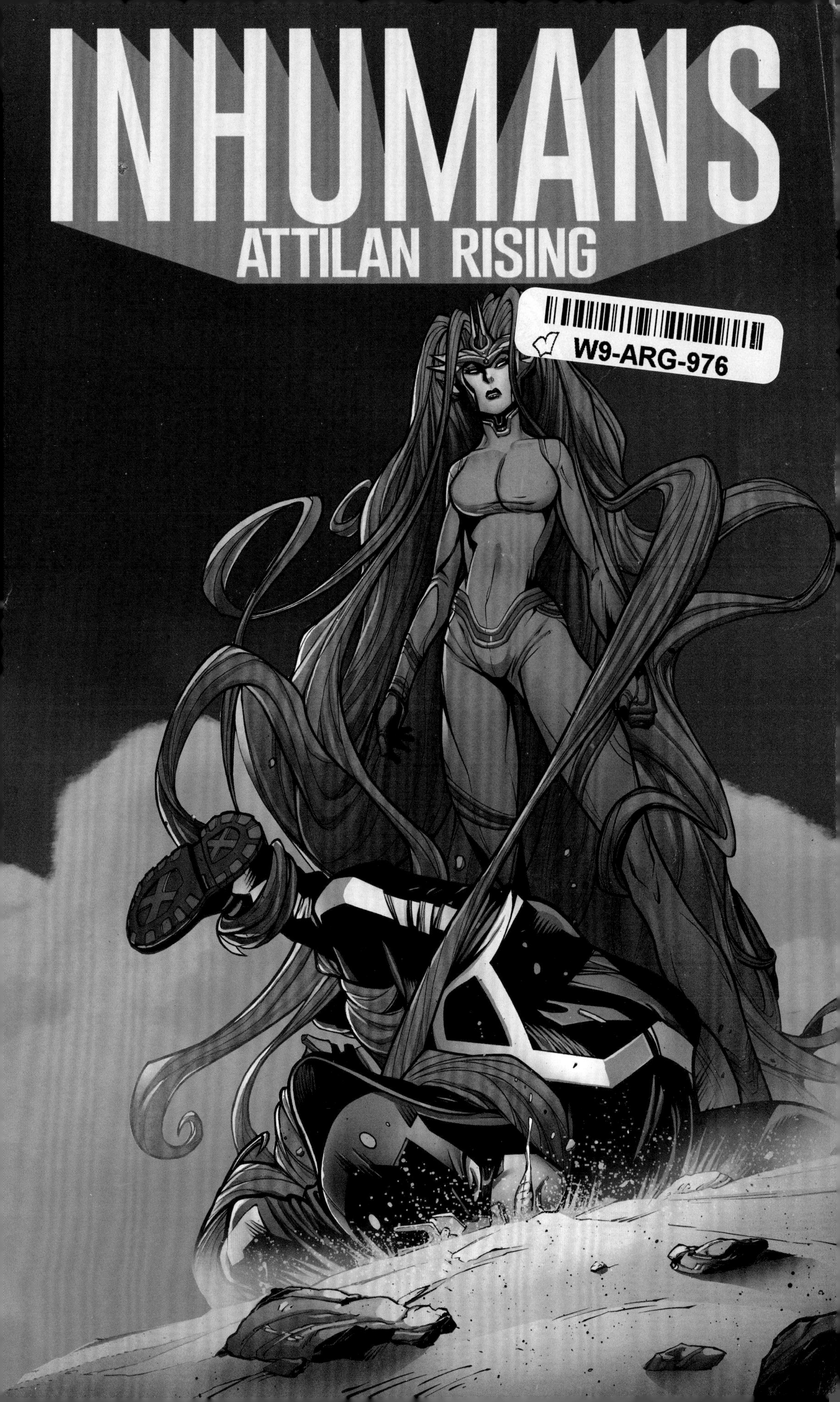

INHUMANS

ATTILAN RISING

WRITER:
CHARLES SOULE

ARTIST:
JOHN TIMMS

INKER: **ROBERTO POGGI**
COLORIST: **FRANK D'ARMATA**
LETTERER: **VC'S CLAYTON COWLES**
COVER ART: **DAVE JOHNSON**

ASSISTANT EDITOR: **CHARLES BEACHAM**
EDITOR: **NICK LOWE**

INHUMANS CREATED BY **STAN LEE** & **JACK KIRBY**

COLLECTION EDITOR: **SARAH BRUNSTAD**
ASSOCIATE MANAGING EDITOR: **ALEX STARBUCK**
EDITORS, SPECIAL PROJECTS: **JENNIFER GRÜNWALD** & **MARK D. BEAZLEY**
SENIOR EDITOR, SPECIAL PROJECTS: **JEFF YOUNGQUIST**
SVP PRINT, SALES & MARKETING: **DAVID GABRIEL**

EDITOR IN CHIEF: **AXEL ALONSO**   CHIEF CREATIVE OFFICER: **JOE QUESADA**
PUBLISHER: **DAN BUCKLEY**   EXECUTIVE PRODUCER: **ALAN FINE**

INHUMANS: ATTILAN RISING. Contains material originally published in magazine form as INHUMANS: ATTILAN RISING #1-5. First printing 2015. ISBN# 978-0-7851-9875-8. Published by MARVEL WORLDWIDE, INC., a subsidiary of MARVEL ENTERTAINMENT, LLC. OFFICE OF PUBLICATION: 135 West 50th Street, New York, NY 10020. Copyright © 2016 MARVEL No similarity between any of the names, characters, persons, and/or institutions in this magazine with those of any living or dead person or institution is intended, and any such similarity which may exist is purely coincidental. **Printed in Canada.** ALAN FINE, President, Marvel Entertainment; DAN BUCKLEY, President, TV, Publishing and Brand Management; JOE QUESADA, Chief Creative Officer; TOM BREVOORT, SVP of Publishing; DAVID BOGART, SVP of Operations & Procurement, Publishing; C.B. CEBULSKI, VP of International Development & Brand Management; DAVID GABRIEL, SVP Print, Sales & Marketing; JIM O'KEEFE, VP of Operations & Logistics; DAN CARR, Executive Director of Publishing Technology; SUSAN CRESPI, Editorial Operations Manager; ALEX MORALES, Publishing Operations Manager; STAN LEE, Chairman Emeritus. For information regarding advertising in Marvel Comics or on Marvel.com, please contact Jonathan Rheingold, VP of Custom Solutions & Ad Sales, at jrheingold@marvel.com. For Marvel subscription inquiries, please call 800-217-9158. **Manufactured between 12/9/2015 and 1/11/2016 by SOLISCO PRINTERS, SCOTT, QC, CANADA.**
10 9 8 7 6 5 4 3 2 1

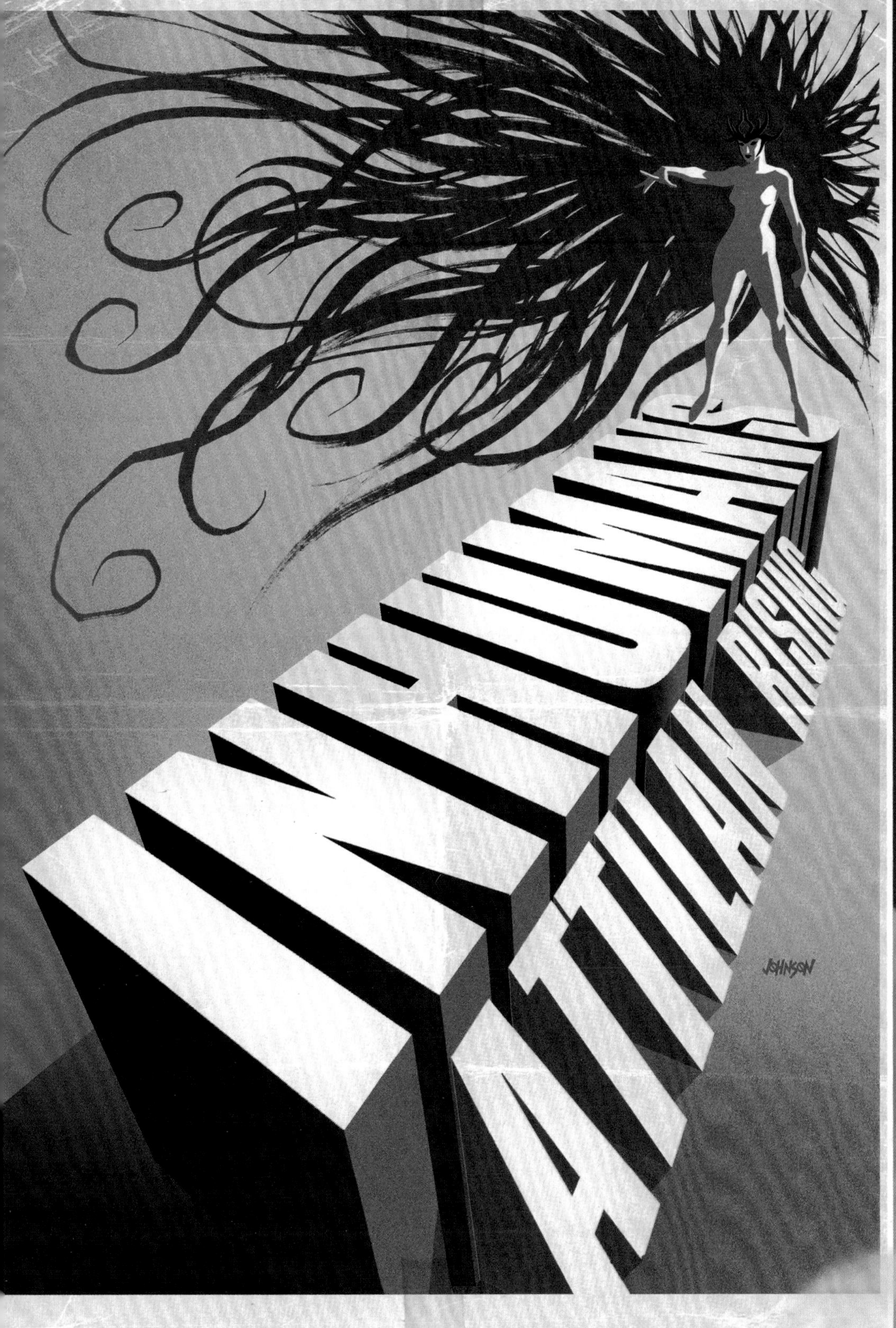
INHUMANS
ATTILAN RISING
JOHNSON

PART 1: THE VOICE UNHEARD

SECRET WARS

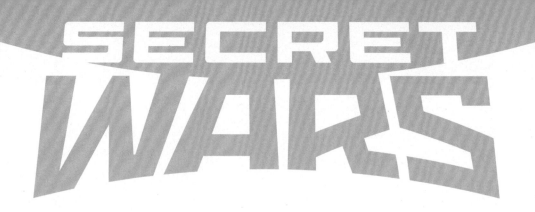

THE MULTIVERSE WAS DESTROYED!

THE HEROES OF EARTH-616 AND EARTH-1610
WERE POWERLESS TO SAVE IT!

NOW, ALL THAT REMAINS...IS **BATTLEWORLD**:

A MASSIVE, PATCHWORK PLANET COMPOSED OF THE FRAGMENTS OF WORLDS THAT NO LONGER EXIST, MAINTAINED BY THE IRON WILL OF ITS GOD AND MASTER, VICTOR VON DOOM!

EACH REGION IS A DOMAIN UNTO ITSELF!

INHUMANS
ATTILAN RISING

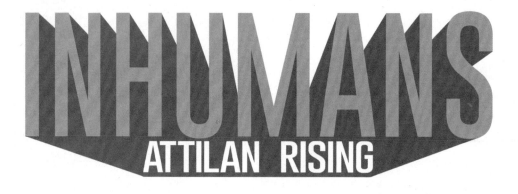

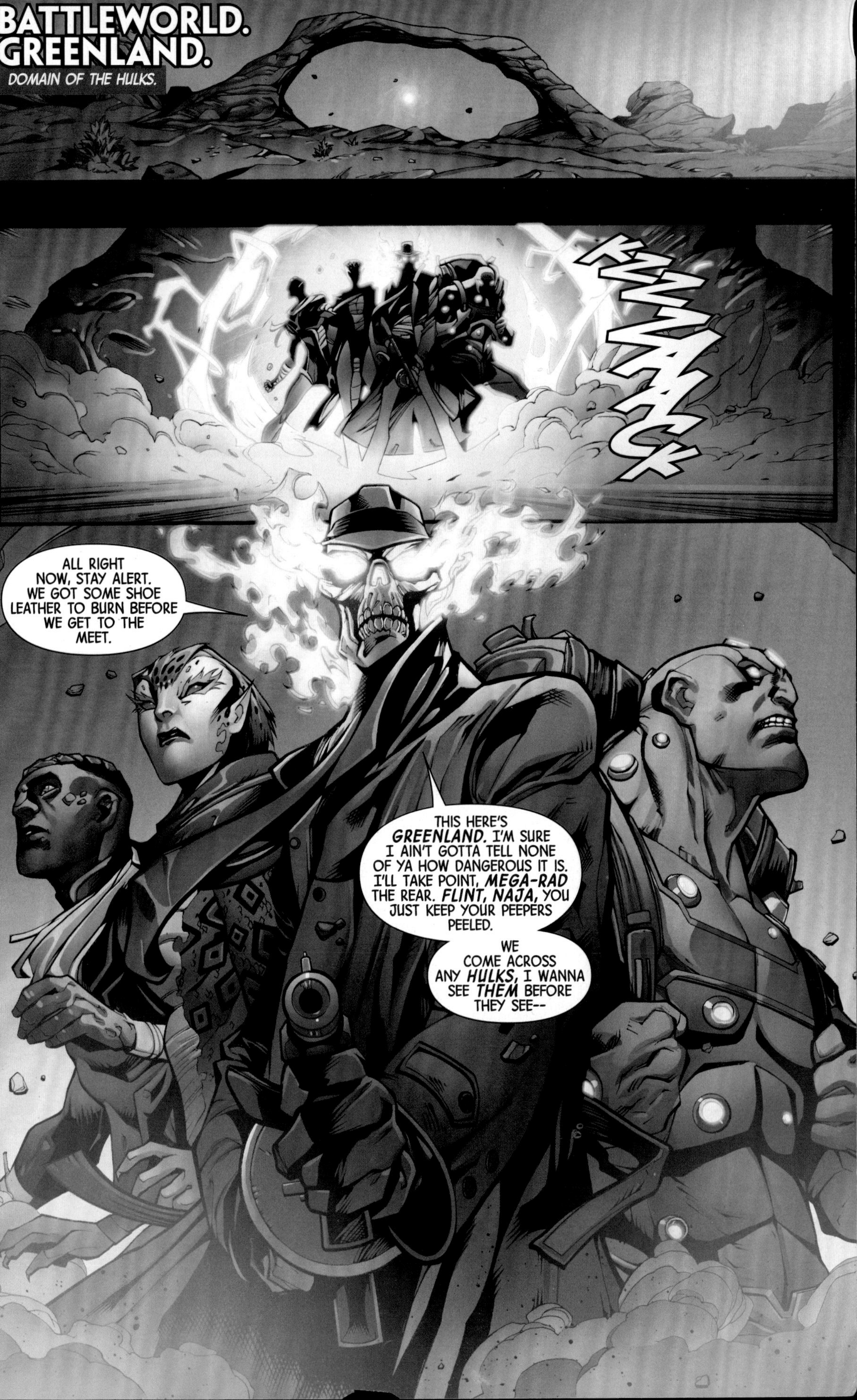

BATTLEWORLD. GREENLAND.
DOMAIN OF THE HULKS.
KZZAACK
ALL RIGHT NOW, STAY ALERT. WE GOT SOME SHOE LEATHER TO BURN BEFORE WE GET TO THE MEET.
THIS HERE'S GREENLAND. I'M SURE I AIN'T GOTTA TELL NONE OF YA HOW DANGEROUS IT IS. I'LL TAKE POINT, MEGA-RAD THE REAR. FLINT, NAJA, YOU JUST KEEP YOUR PEEPERS PEELED.
WE COME ACROSS ANY HULKS, I WANNA SEE THEM BEFORE THEY SEE--

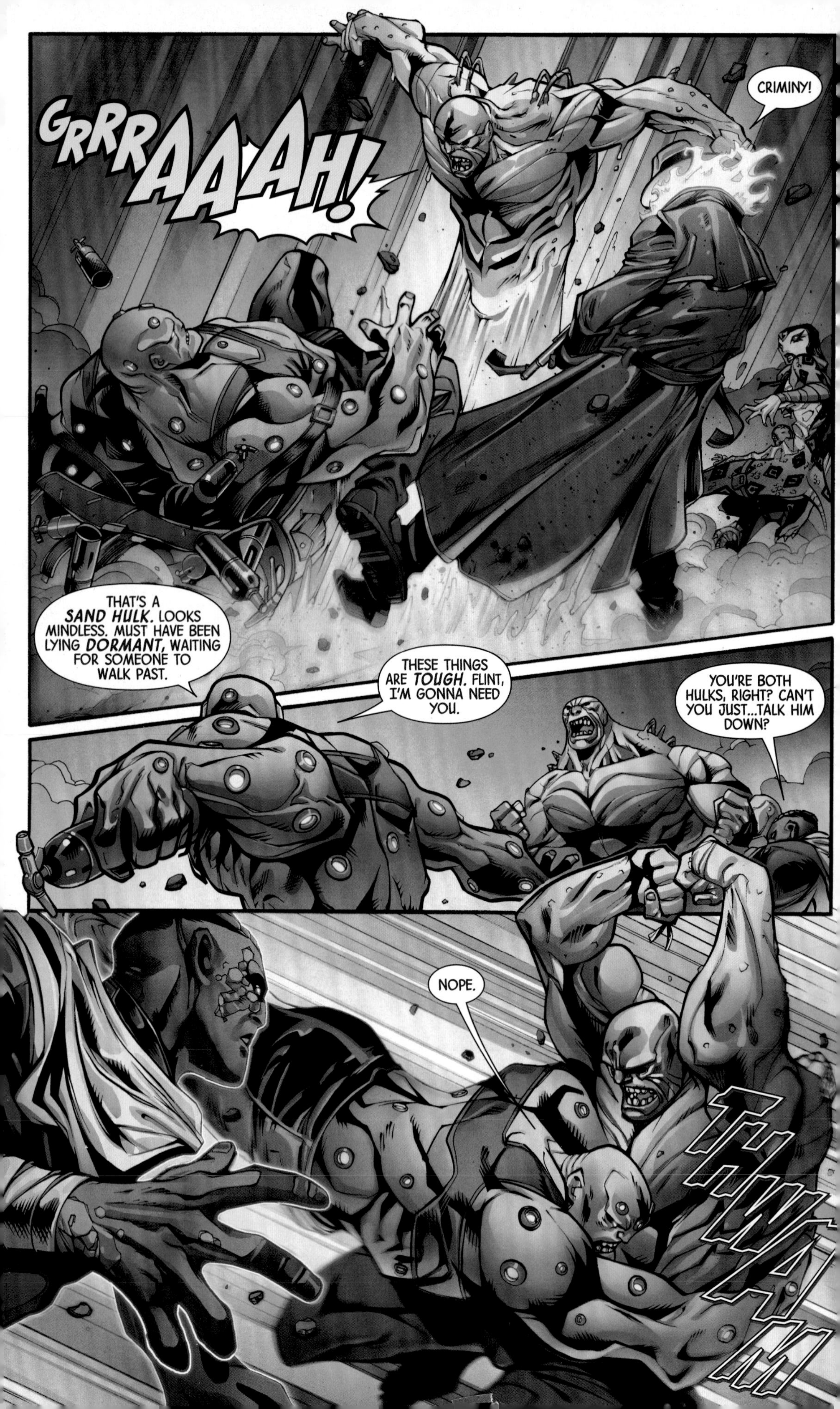
GRRRAAAAH!
CRIMINY!
THAT'S A SAND HULK. LOOKS MINDLESS. MUST HAVE BEEN LYING DORMANT, WAITING FOR SOMEONE TO WALK PAST.
THESE THINGS ARE TOUGH. FLINT, I'M GONNA NEED YOU.
YOU'RE BOTH HULKS, RIGHT? CAN'T YOU JUST...TALK HIM DOWN?
NOPE.

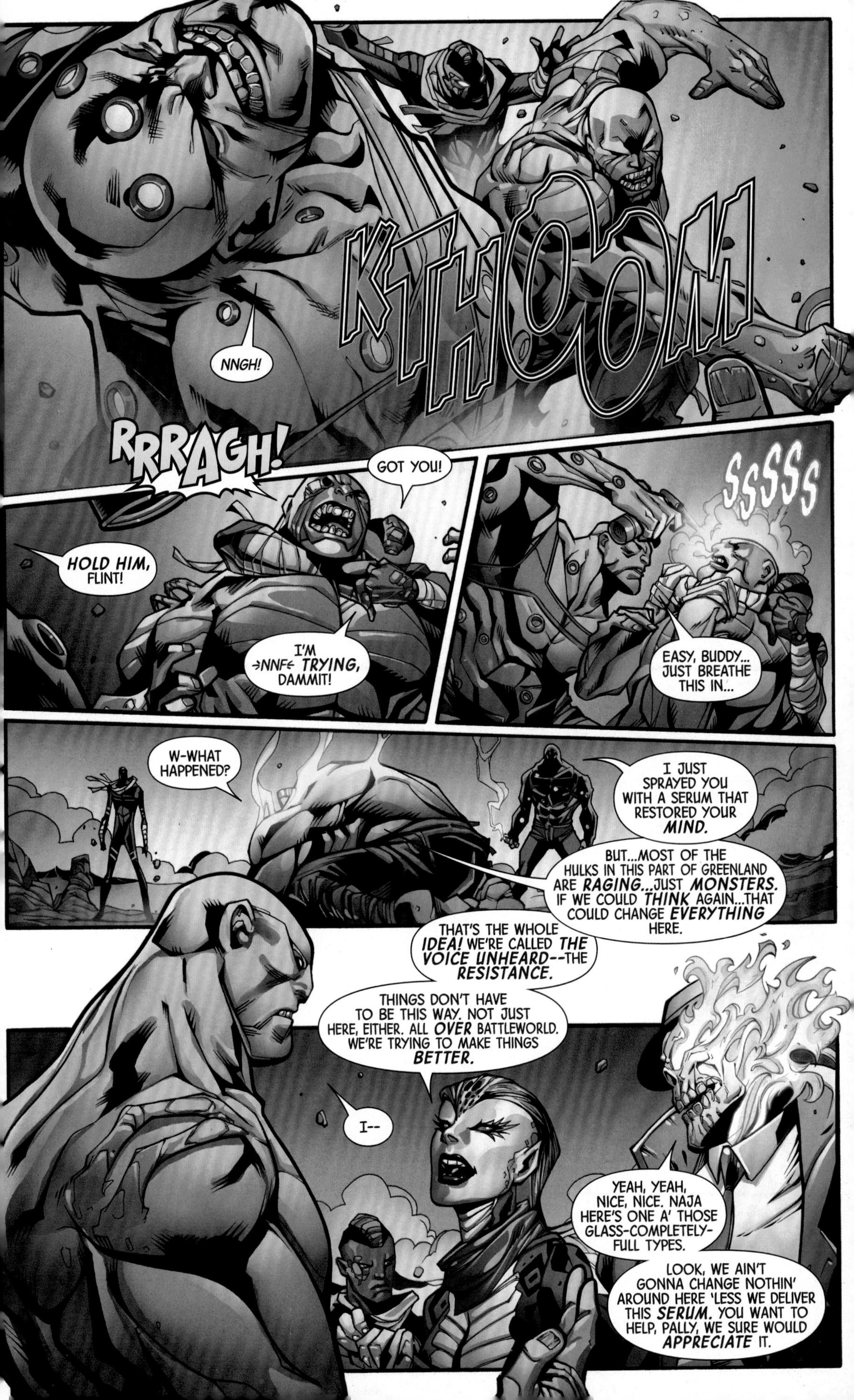
KTHOOOM
NNGH!
RRRAGH!
GOT YOU!
HOLD HIM, FLINT!
I'M ≯NNF≮ TRYING, DAMMIT!
SSSSS
EASY, BUDDY... JUST BREATHE THIS IN...
W-WHAT HAPPENED?
I JUST SPRAYED YOU WITH A SERUM THAT RESTORED YOUR MIND.
BUT...MOST OF THE HULKS IN THIS PART OF GREENLAND ARE RAGING...JUST MONSTERS. IF WE COULD THINK AGAIN...THAT COULD CHANGE EVERYTHING HERE.
THAT'S THE WHOLE IDEA! WE'RE CALLED THE VOICE UNHEARD--THE RESISTANCE.
THINGS DON'T HAVE TO BE THIS WAY. NOT JUST HERE, EITHER. ALL OVER BATTLEWORLD. WE'RE TRYING TO MAKE THINGS BETTER.
I--
YEAH, YEAH, NICE, NICE. NAJA HERE'S ONE A' THOSE GLASS-COMPLETELY-FULL TYPES.
LOOK, WE AIN'T GONNA CHANGE NOTHIN' AROUND HERE 'LESS WE DELIVER THIS SERUM. YOU WANT TO HELP, PALLY, WE SURE WOULD APPRECIATE IT.

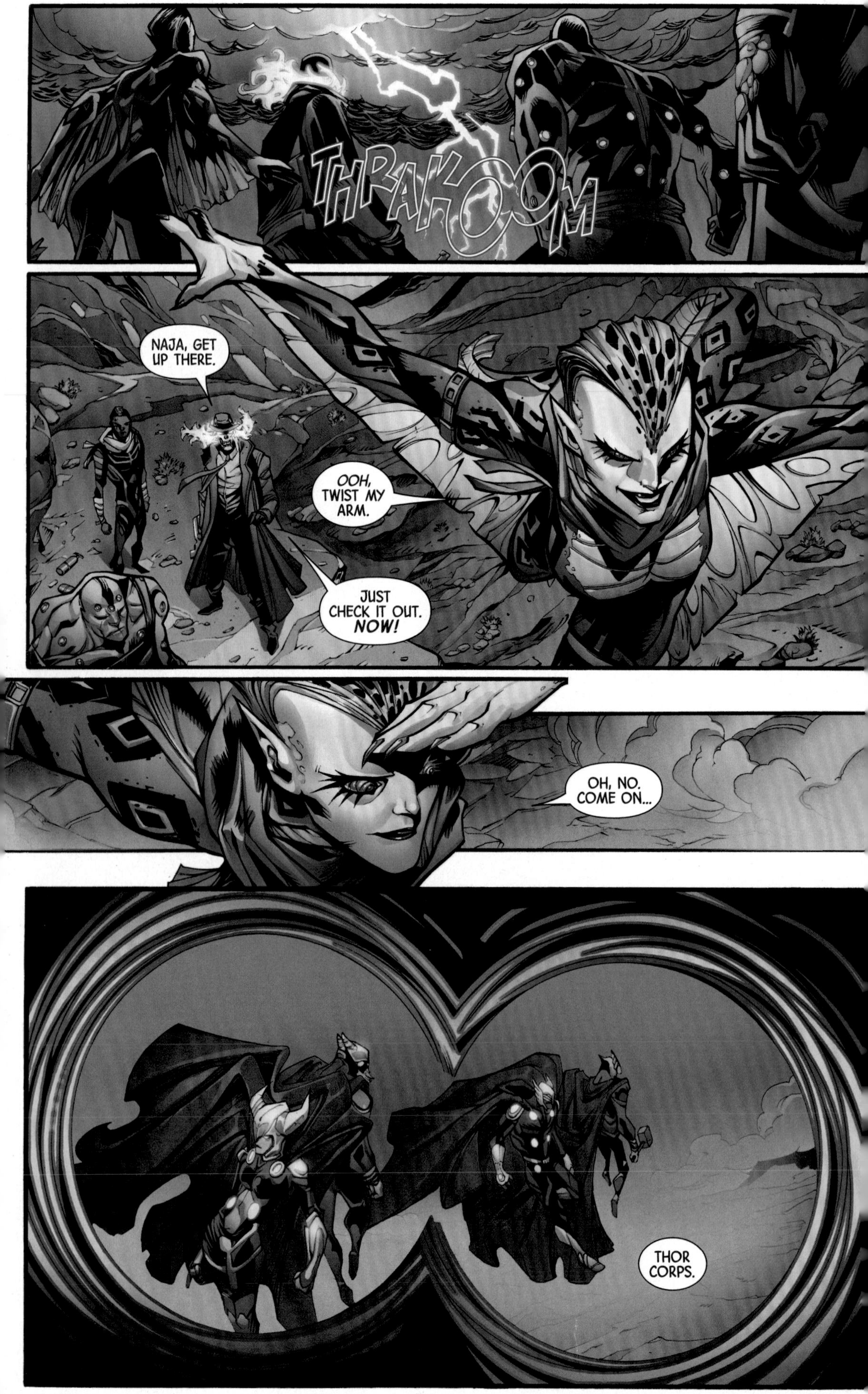
THRAKOOM
NAJA, GET UP THERE.
OOH, TWIST MY ARM.
JUST CHECK IT OUT. NOW!
OH, NO. COME ON...
THOR CORPS.

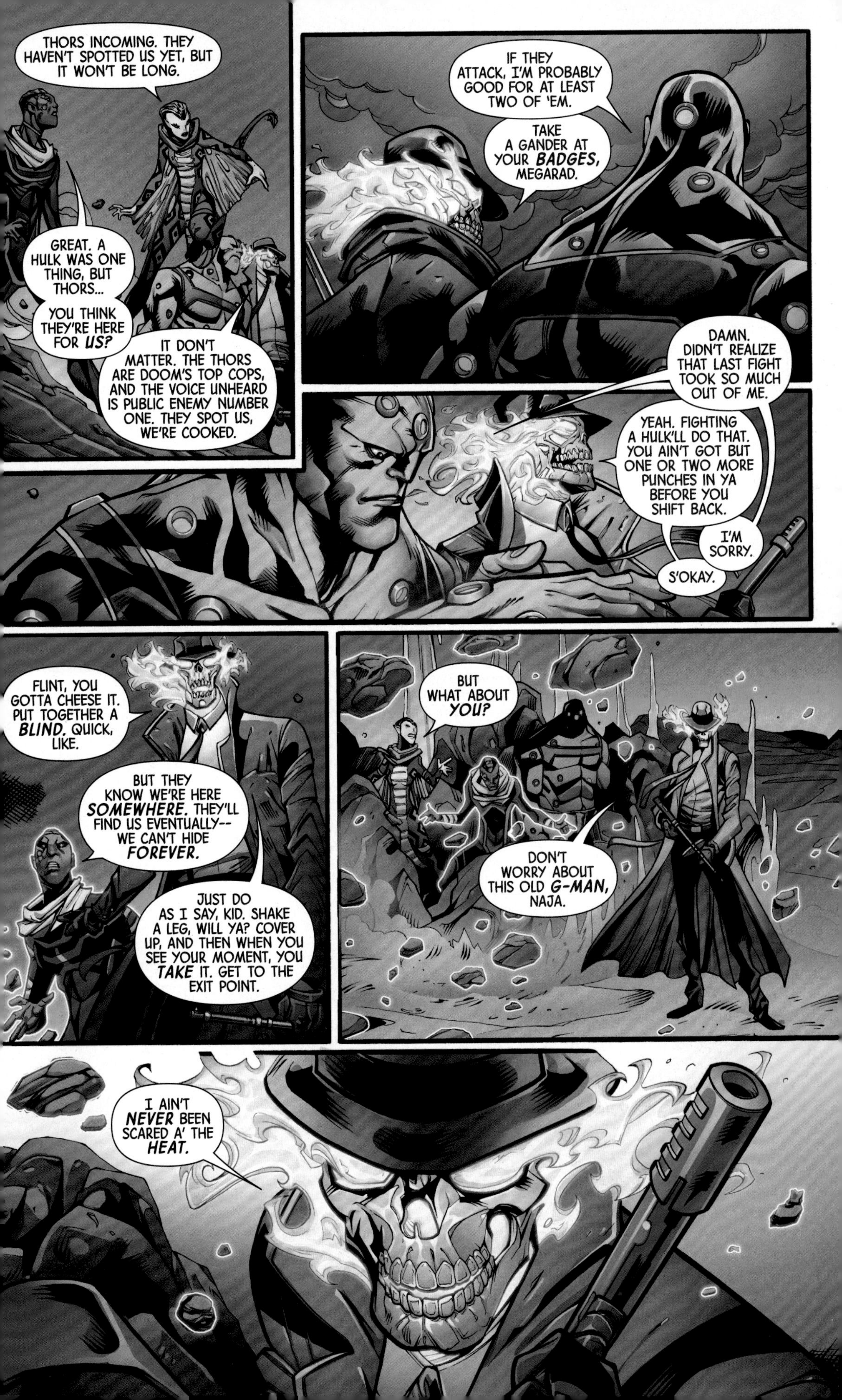
THORS INCOMING. THEY HAVEN'T SPOTTED US YET, BUT IT WON'T BE LONG.
GREAT. A HULK WAS ONE THING, BUT THORS...
YOU THINK THEY'RE HERE FOR *US?*
IT DON'T MATTER. THE THORS ARE DOOM'S TOP COPS, AND THE VOICE UNHEARD IS PUBLIC ENEMY NUMBER ONE. THEY SPOT US, WE'RE COOKED.
IF THEY ATTACK, I'M PROBABLY GOOD FOR AT LEAST TWO OF 'EM.
TAKE A GANDER AT YOUR *BADGES,* MEGARAD.
DAMN. DIDN'T REALIZE THAT LAST FIGHT TOOK SO MUCH OUT OF ME.
YEAH. FIGHTING A HULK'LL DO THAT. YOU AIN'T GOT BUT ONE OR TWO MORE PUNCHES IN YA BEFORE YOU SHIFT BACK.
I'M SORRY.
S'OKAY.
FLINT, YOU GOTTA CHEESE IT. PUT TOGETHER A *BLIND.* QUICK, LIKE.
BUT THEY KNOW WE'RE HERE *SOMEWHERE.* THEY'LL FIND US EVENTUALLY-- WE CAN'T HIDE *FOREVER.*
JUST DO AS I SAY, KID. SHAKE A LEG, WILL YA? COVER UP, AND THEN WHEN YOU SEE YOUR MOMENT, YOU *TAKE* IT. GET TO THE EXIT POINT.
BUT WHAT ABOUT *YOU?*
DON'T WORRY ABOUT THIS OLD *G-MAN,* NAJA.
I AIN'T *NEVER* BEEN SCARED A' THE *HEAT.*

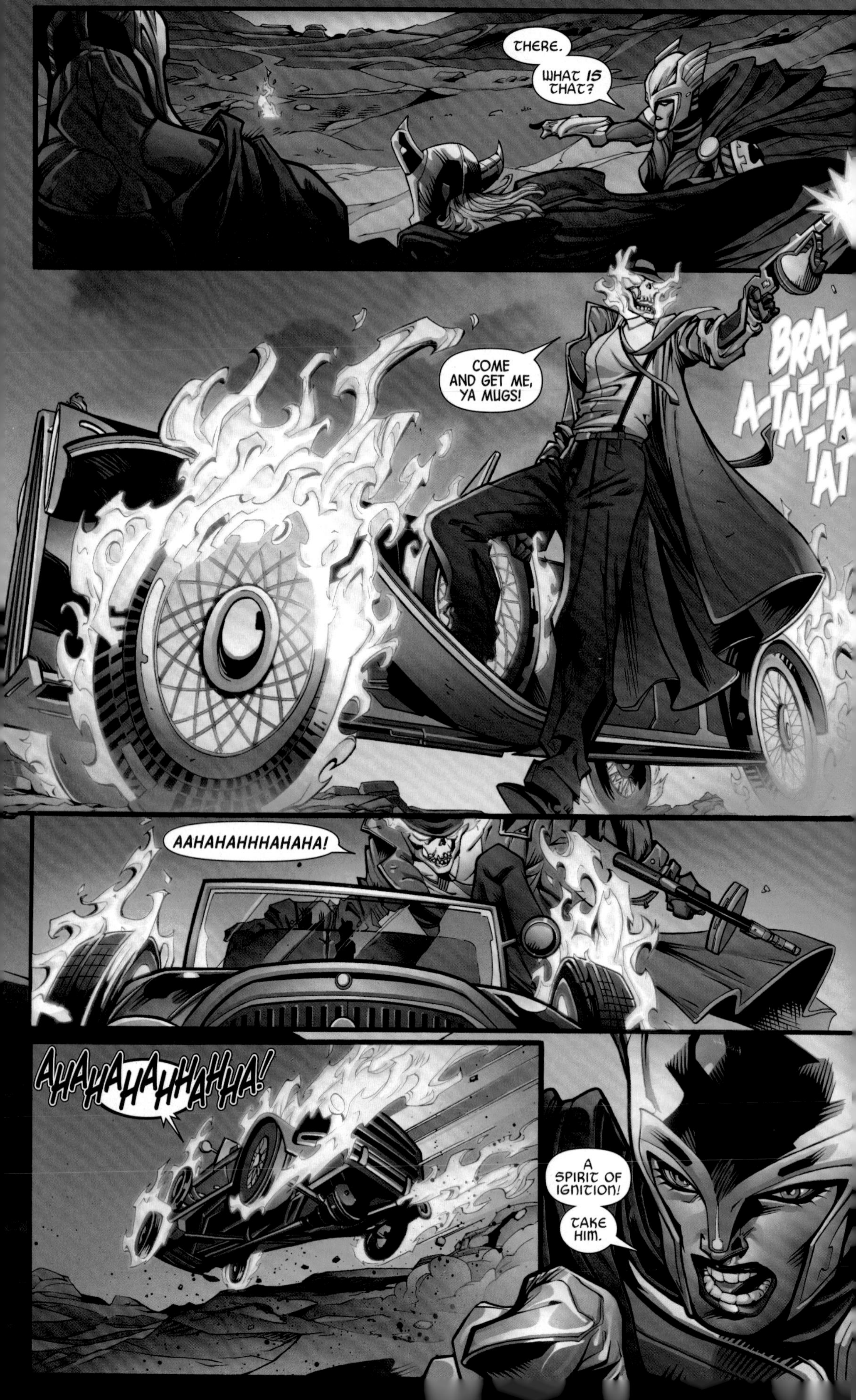
THERE.
WHAT IS THAT?
COME AND GET ME, YA MUGS!
BRAT-A-TAT-TAT-TAT
AAHAHAHHHAHAHA!
AHAHAHAHHAHHA!
A SPIRIT OF IGNITION!
TAKE HIM.

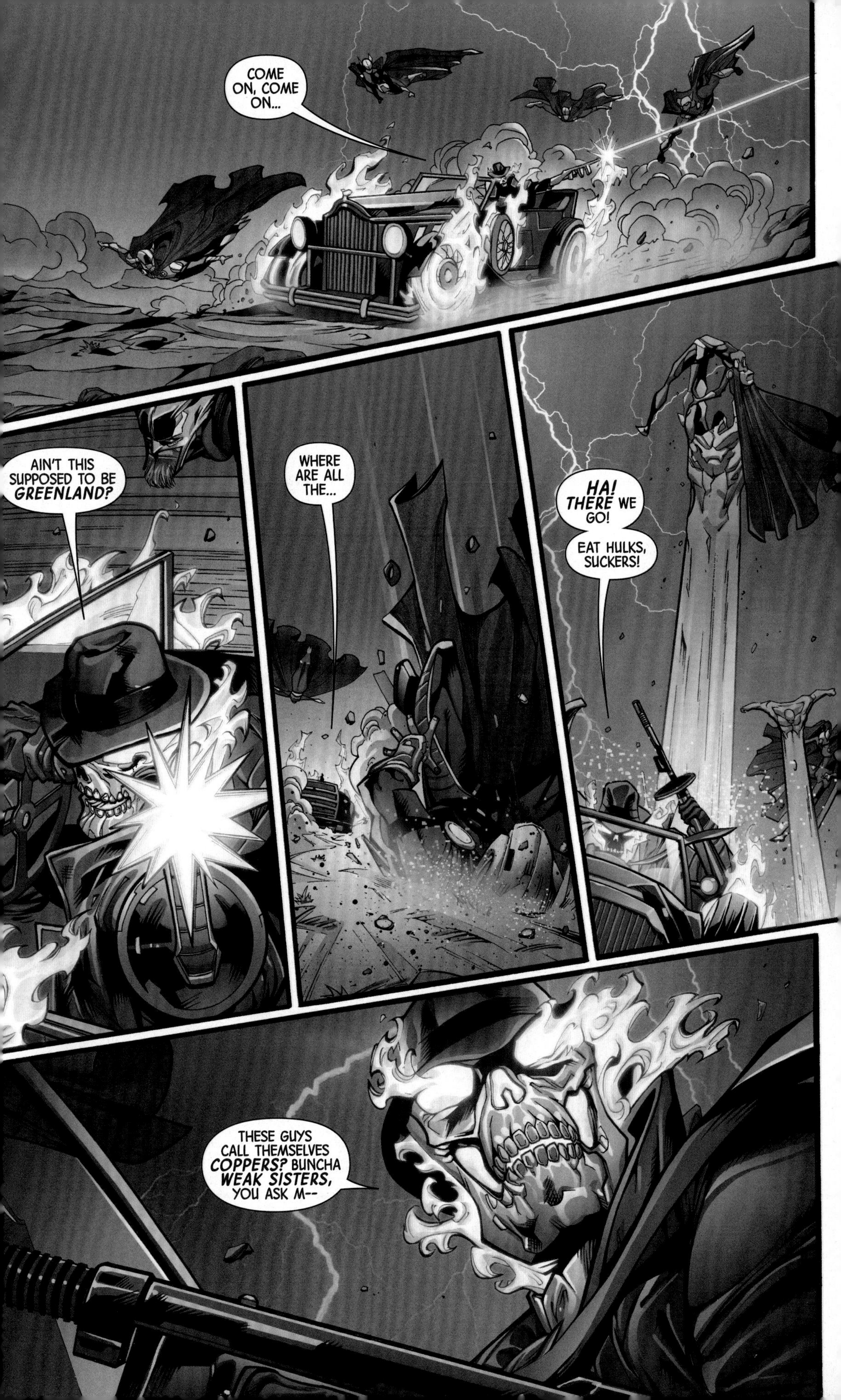
COME ON, COME ON...
AIN'T THIS SUPPOSED TO BE GREENLAND?
WHERE ARE ALL THE...
HA! THERE WE GO!
EAT HULKS, SUCKERS!
THESE GUYS CALL THEMSELVES COPPERS? BUNCHA WEAK SISTERS, YOU ASK M--

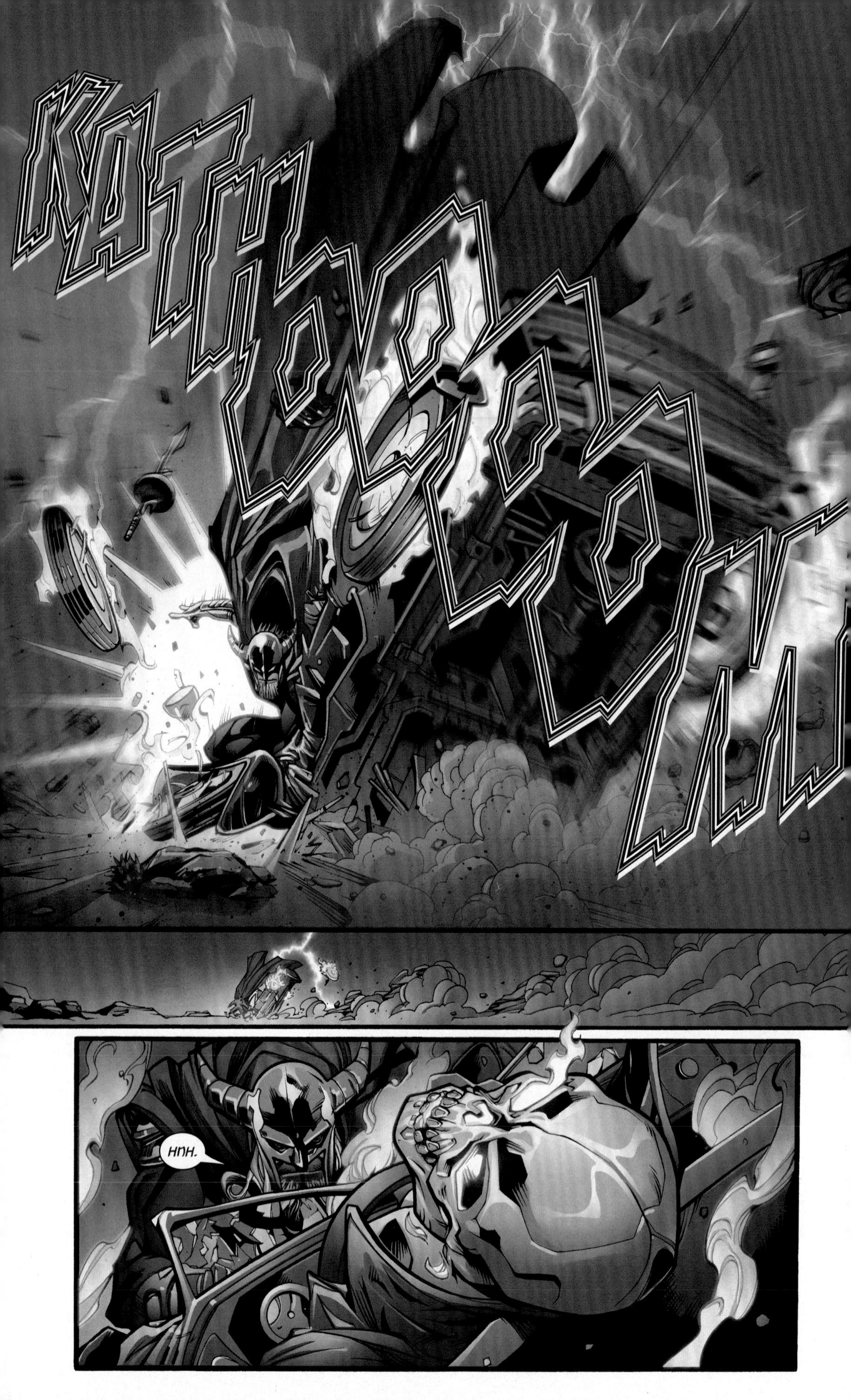
HNH.

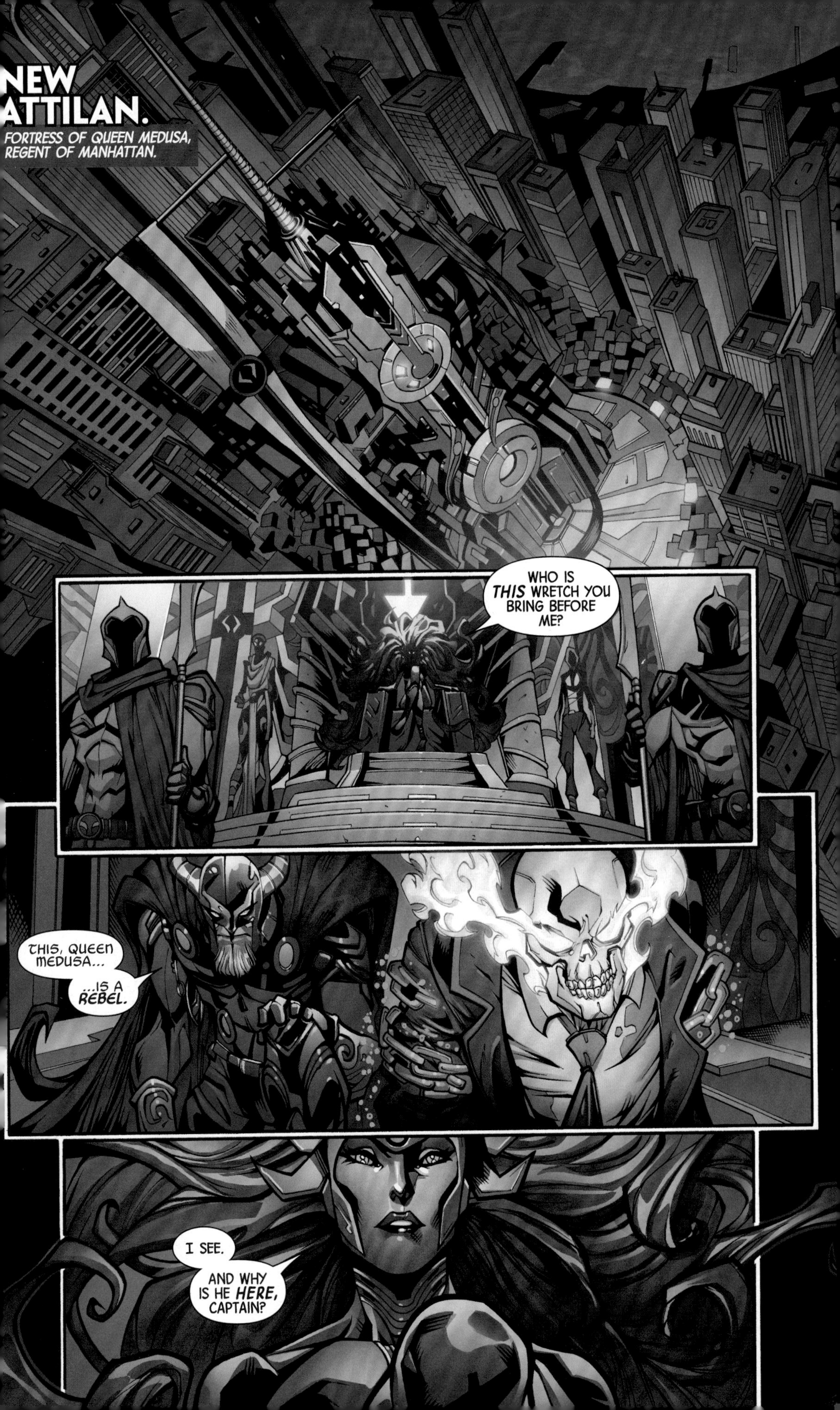
NEW ATTILAN.
FORTRESS OF QUEEN MEDUSA, REGENT OF MANHATTAN.
WHO IS THIS WRETCH YOU BRING BEFORE ME?
THIS, QUEEN MEDUSA...
...IS A REBEL.
I SEE.
AND WHY IS HE HERE, CAPTAIN?

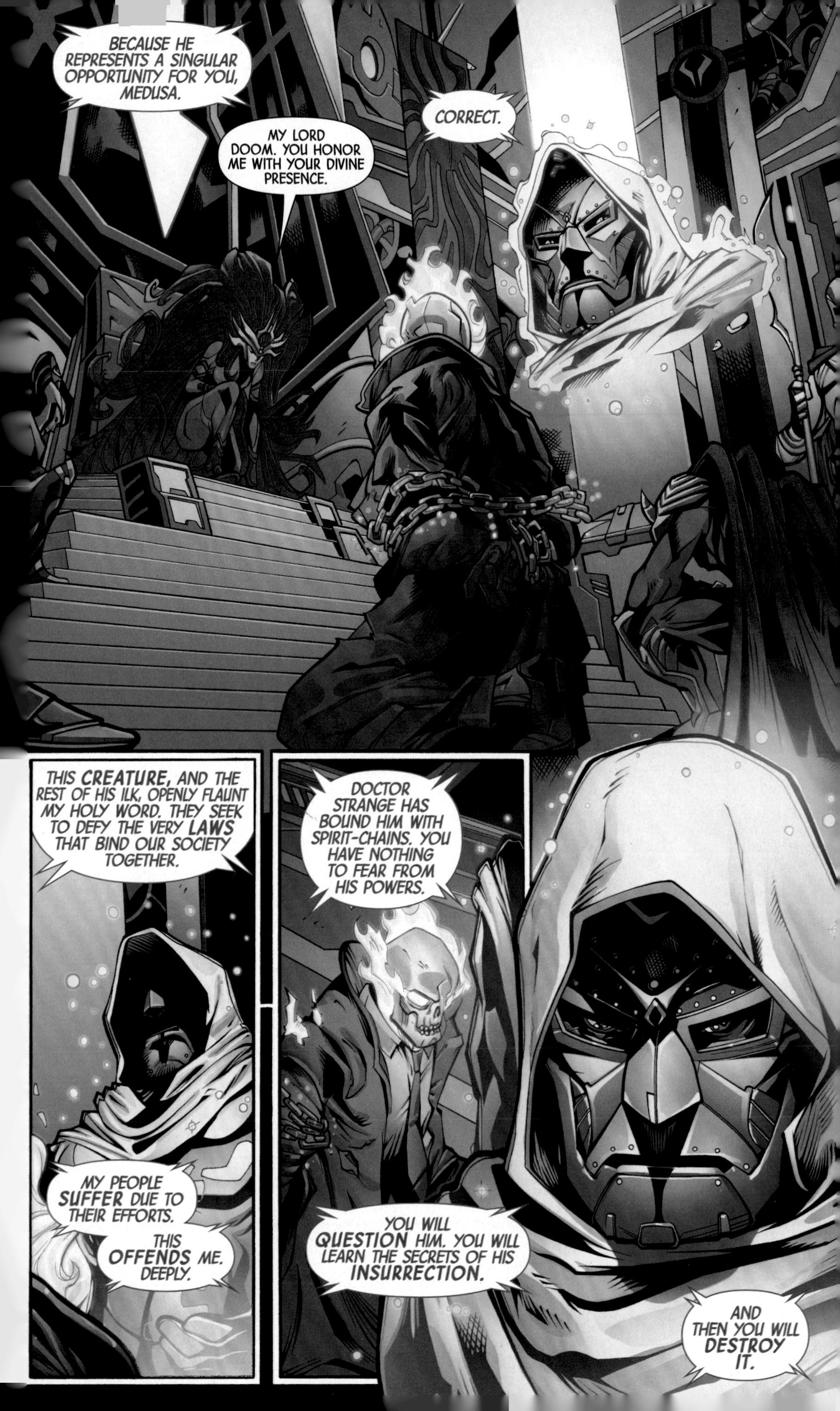
BECAUSE HE REPRESENTS A SINGULAR OPPORTUNITY FOR YOU, MEDUSA.
MY LORD DOOM. YOU HONOR ME WITH YOUR DIVINE PRESENCE.
CORRECT.
THIS CREATURE, AND THE REST OF HIS ILK, OPENLY FLAUNT MY HOLY WORD. THEY SEEK TO DEFY THE VERY LAWS THAT BIND OUR SOCIETY TOGETHER.
MY PEOPLE SUFFER DUE TO THEIR EFFORTS.
THIS OFFENDS ME. DEEPLY.
DOCTOR STRANGE HAS BOUND HIM WITH SPIRIT-CHAINS. YOU HAVE NOTHING TO FEAR FROM HIS POWERS.
YOU WILL QUESTION HIM. YOU WILL LEARN THE SECRETS OF HIS INSURRECTION.
AND THEN YOU WILL DESTROY IT.

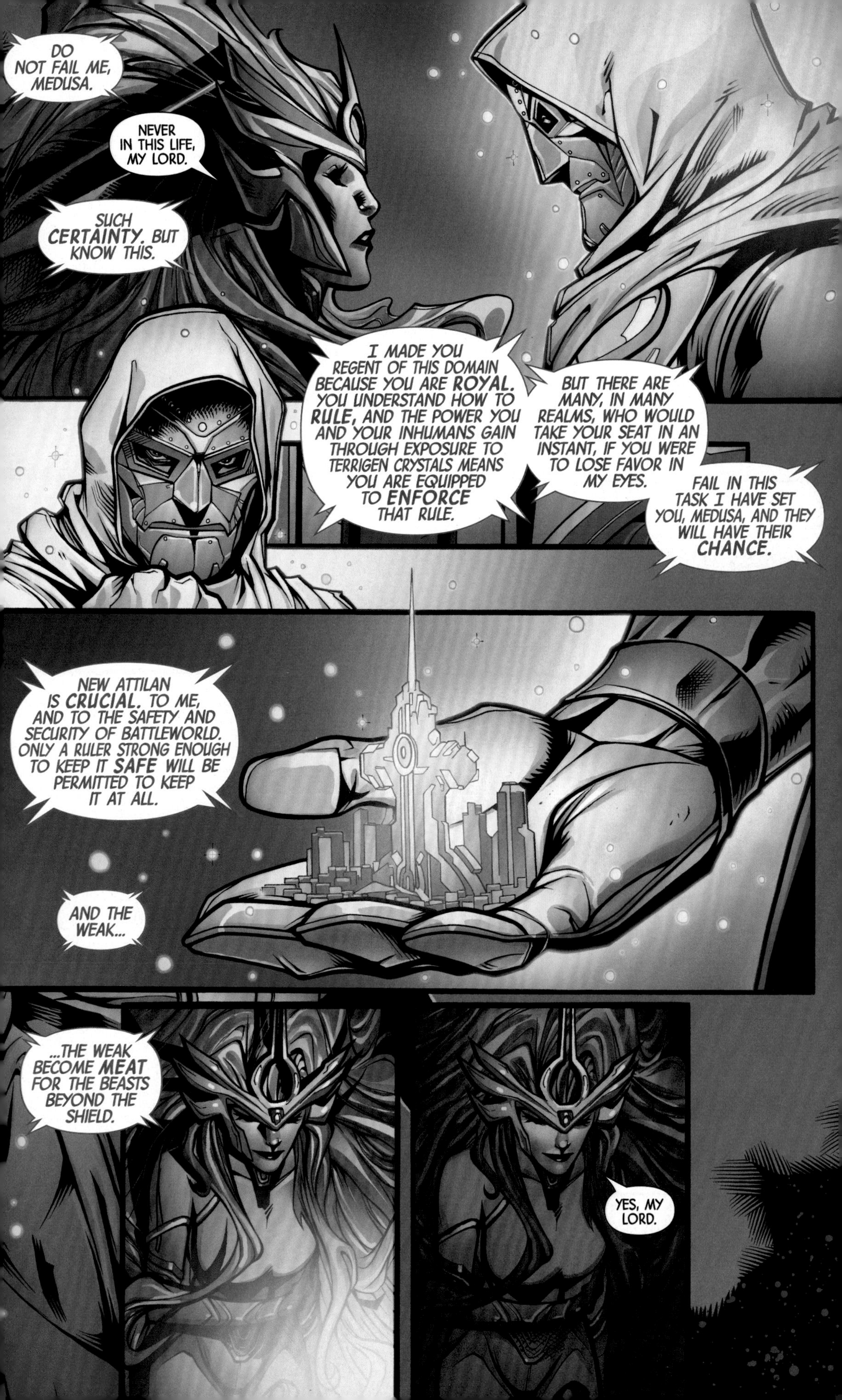
DO NOT FAIL ME, MEDUSA.
NEVER IN THIS LIFE, MY LORD.
SUCH CERTAINTY. BUT KNOW THIS.
I MADE YOU REGENT OF THIS DOMAIN BECAUSE YOU ARE ROYAL. YOU UNDERSTAND HOW TO RULE, AND THE POWER YOU AND YOUR INHUMANS GAIN THROUGH EXPOSURE TO TERRIGEN CRYSTALS MEANS YOU ARE EQUIPPED TO ENFORCE THAT RULE.
BUT THERE ARE MANY, IN MANY REALMS, WHO WOULD TAKE YOUR SEAT IN AN INSTANT, IF YOU WERE TO LOSE FAVOR IN MY EYES.
FAIL IN THIS TASK I HAVE SET YOU, MEDUSA, AND THEY WILL HAVE THEIR CHANCE.
NEW ATTILAN IS CRUCIAL. TO ME, AND TO THE SAFETY AND SECURITY OF BATTLEWORLD. ONLY A RULER STRONG ENOUGH TO KEEP IT SAFE WILL BE PERMITTED TO KEEP IT AT ALL.
AND THE WEAK...
...THE WEAK BECOME MEAT FOR THE BEASTS BEYOND THE SHIELD.
YES, MY LORD.

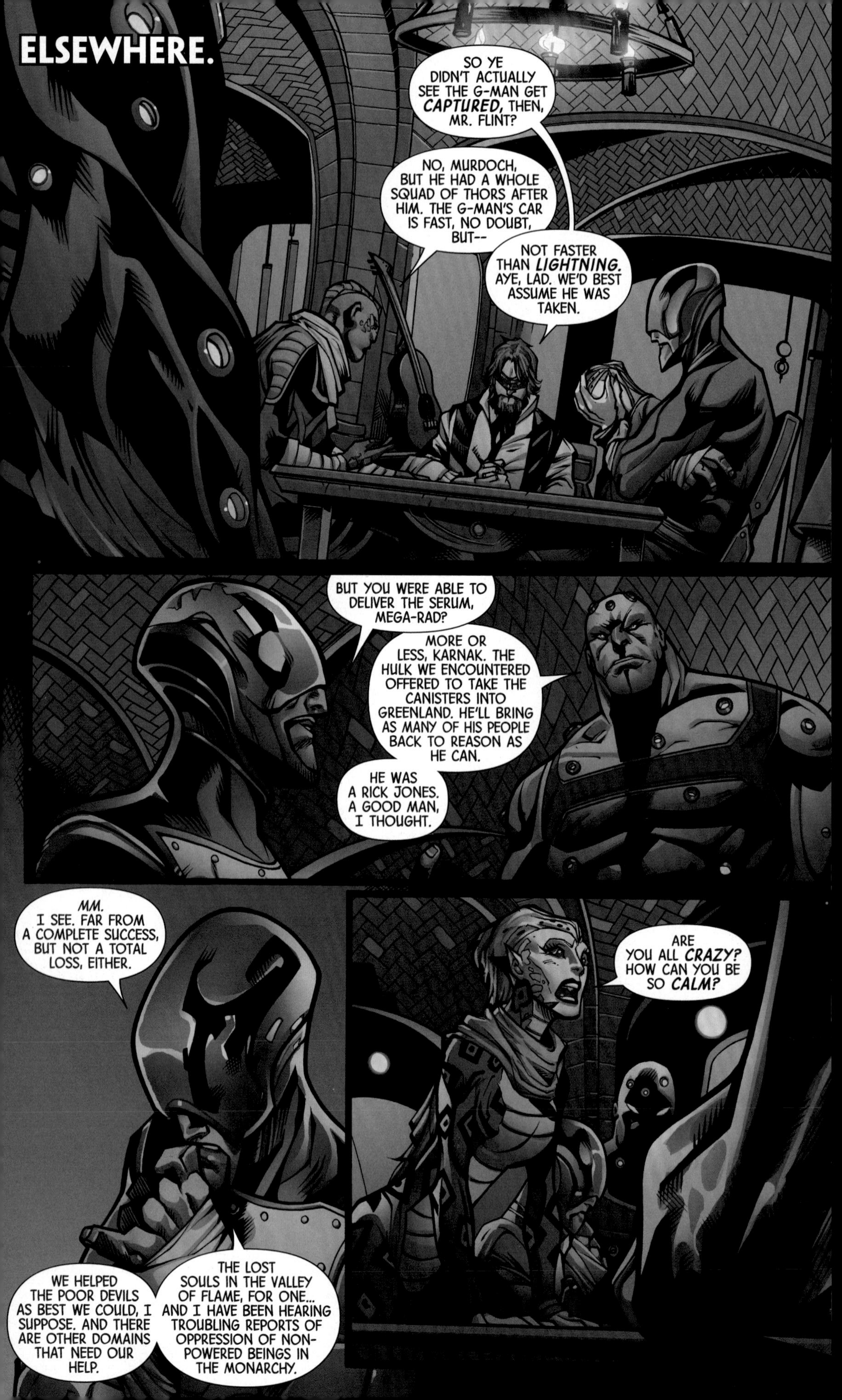

ELSEWHERE.
SO YE DIDN'T ACTUALLY SEE THE G-MAN GET CAPTURED, THEN, MR. FLINT?
NO, MURDOCH, BUT HE HAD A WHOLE SQUAD OF THORS AFTER HIM. THE G-MAN'S CAR IS FAST, NO DOUBT, BUT--
NOT FASTER THAN LIGHTNING. AYE, LAD. WE'D BEST ASSUME HE WAS TAKEN.
BUT YOU WERE ABLE TO DELIVER THE SERUM, MEGA-RAD?
MORE OR LESS, KARNAK. THE HULK WE ENCOUNTERED OFFERED TO TAKE THE CANISTERS INTO GREENLAND. HE'LL BRING AS MANY OF HIS PEOPLE BACK TO REASON AS HE CAN.
HE WAS A RICK JONES. A GOOD MAN, I THOUGHT.
MM. I SEE. FAR FROM A COMPLETE SUCCESS, BUT NOT A TOTAL LOSS, EITHER.
WE HELPED THE POOR DEVILS AS BEST WE COULD, I SUPPOSE. AND THERE ARE OTHER DOMAINS THAT NEED OUR HELP.
THE LOST SOULS IN THE VALLEY OF FLAME, FOR ONE... AND I HAVE BEEN HEARING TROUBLING REPORTS OF OPPRESSION OF NON-POWERED BEINGS IN THE MONARCHY.
ARE YOU ALL CRAZY? HOW CAN YOU BE SO CALM?

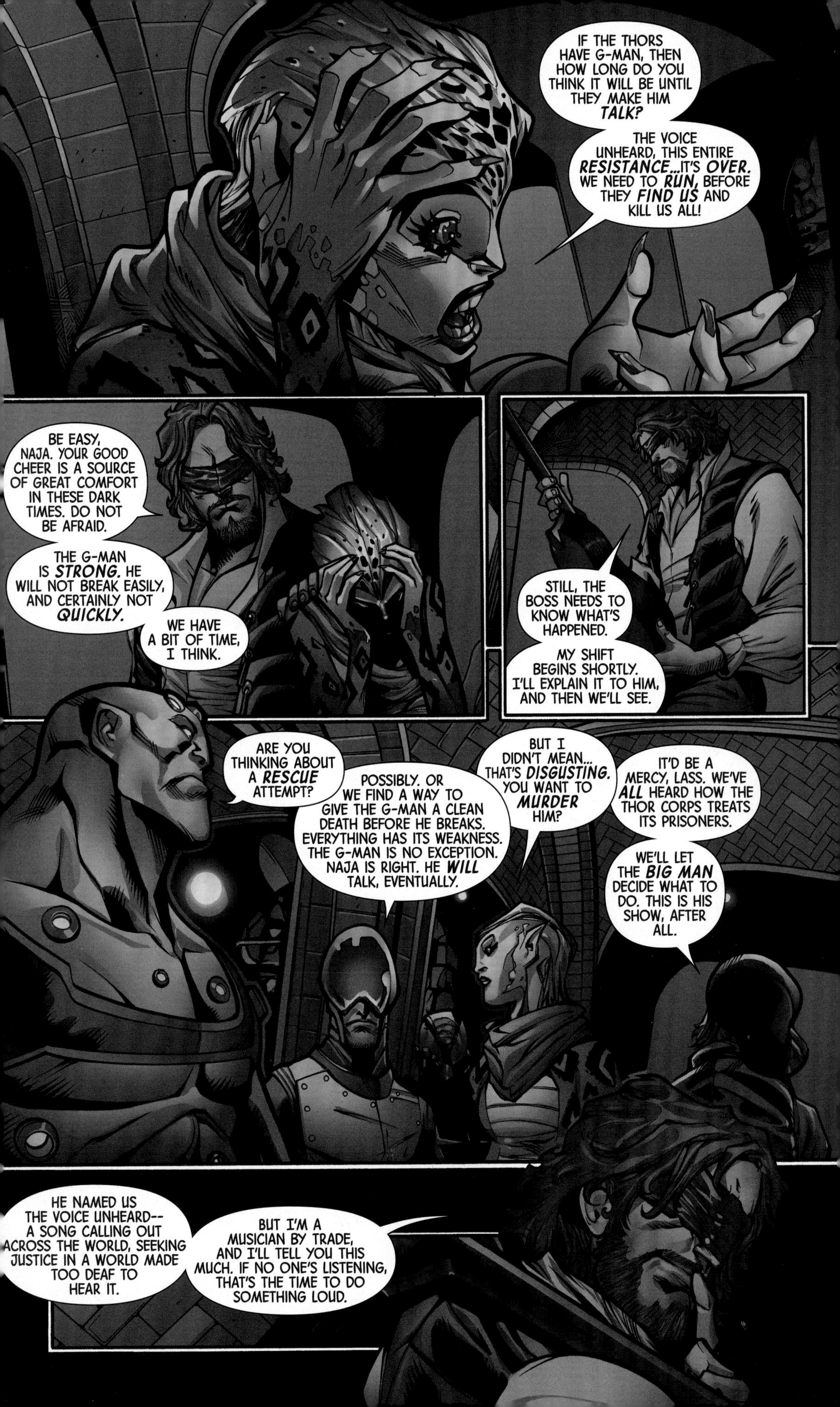
IF THE THORS HAVE G-MAN, THEN HOW LONG DO YOU THINK IT WILL BE UNTIL THEY MAKE HIM TALK?
THE VOICE UNHEARD, THIS ENTIRE RESISTANCE...IT'S OVER. WE NEED TO RUN, BEFORE THEY FIND US AND KILL US ALL!
BE EASY, NAJA. YOUR GOOD CHEER IS A SOURCE OF GREAT COMFORT IN THESE DARK TIMES. DO NOT BE AFRAID.
THE G-MAN IS STRONG. HE WILL NOT BREAK EASILY, AND CERTAINLY NOT QUICKLY.
WE HAVE A BIT OF TIME, I THINK.
STILL, THE BOSS NEEDS TO KNOW WHAT'S HAPPENED.
MY SHIFT BEGINS SHORTLY. I'LL EXPLAIN IT TO HIM, AND THEN WE'LL SEE.
ARE YOU THINKING ABOUT A RESCUE ATTEMPT?
POSSIBLY. OR WE FIND A WAY TO GIVE THE G-MAN A CLEAN DEATH BEFORE HE BREAKS. EVERYTHING HAS ITS WEAKNESS. THE G-MAN IS NO EXCEPTION. NAJA IS RIGHT. HE WILL TALK, EVENTUALLY.
BUT I DIDN'T MEAN... THAT'S DISGUSTING. YOU WANT TO MURDER HIM?
IT'D BE A MERCY, LASS. WE'VE ALL HEARD HOW THE THOR CORPS TREATS ITS PRISONERS.
WE'LL LET THE BIG MAN DECIDE WHAT TO DO. THIS IS HIS SHOW, AFTER ALL.
HE NAMED US THE VOICE UNHEARD-- A SONG CALLING OUT ACROSS THE WORLD, SEEKING JUSTICE IN A WORLD MADE TOO DEAF TO HEAR IT.
BUT I'M A MUSICIAN BY TRADE, AND I'LL TELL YOU THIS MUCH. IF NO ONE'S LISTENING, THAT'S THE TIME TO DO SOMETHING LOUD.

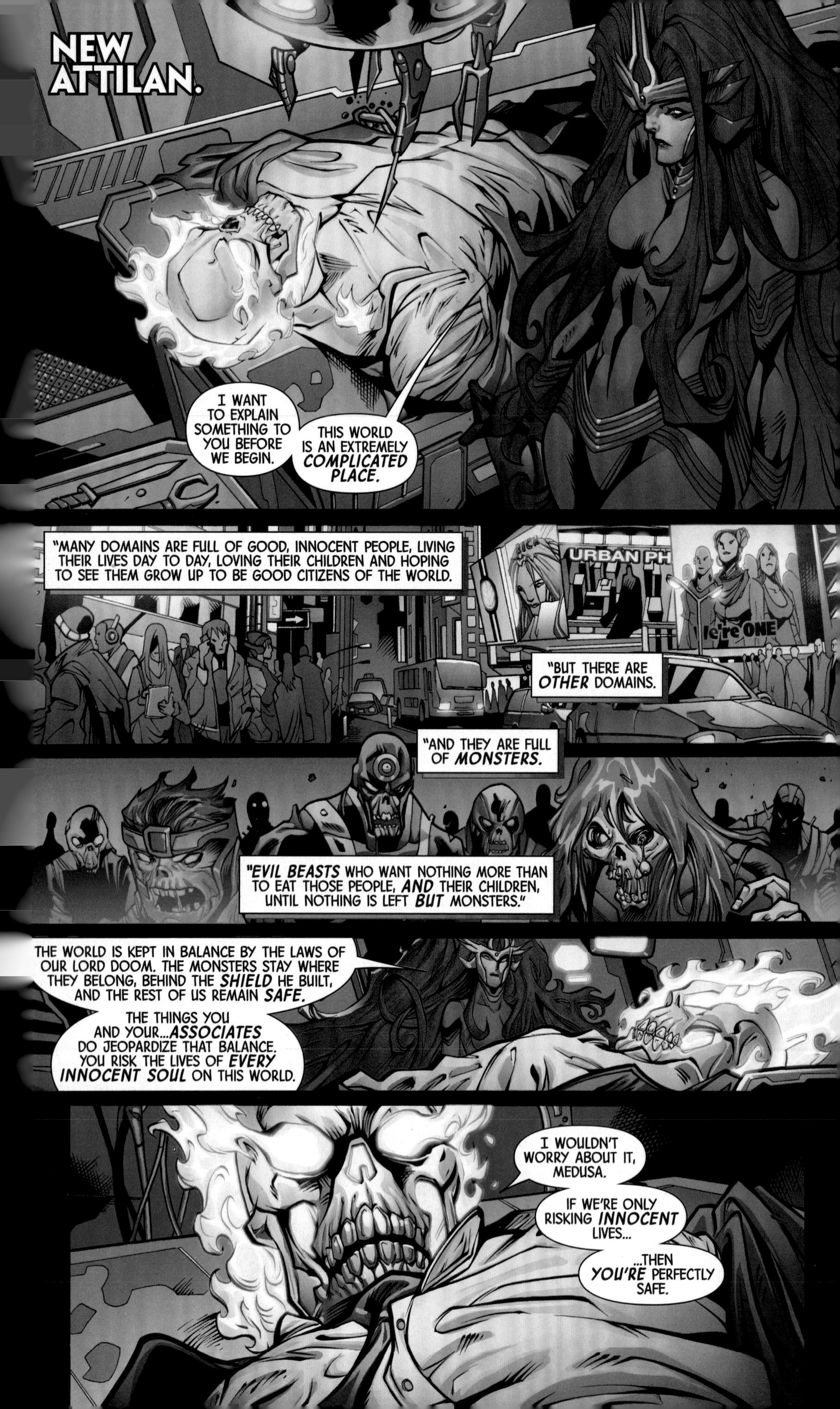
NEW ATTILAN.
I WANT TO EXPLAIN SOMETHING TO YOU BEFORE WE BEGIN.
THIS WORLD IS AN EXTREMELY COMPLICATED PLACE.
"MANY DOMAINS ARE FULL OF GOOD, INNOCENT PEOPLE, LIVING THEIR LIVES DAY TO DAY, LOVING THEIR CHILDREN AND HOPING TO SEE THEM GROW UP TO BE GOOD CITIZENS OF THE WORLD.
URBAN PH
"BUT THERE ARE OTHER DOMAINS.
"AND THEY ARE FULL OF MONSTERS.
"EVIL BEASTS WHO WANT NOTHING MORE THAN TO EAT THOSE PEOPLE, AND THEIR CHILDREN, UNTIL NOTHING IS LEFT BUT MONSTERS."
THE WORLD IS KEPT IN BALANCE BY THE LAWS OF OUR LORD DOOM. THE MONSTERS STAY WHERE THEY BELONG, BEHIND THE SHIELD HE BUILT, AND THE REST OF US REMAIN SAFE.
THE THINGS YOU AND YOUR...ASSOCIATES DO JEOPARDIZE THAT BALANCE. YOU RISK THE LIVES OF EVERY INNOCENT SOUL ON THIS WORLD.
I WOULDN'T WORRY ABOUT IT, MEDUSA.
IF WE'RE ONLY RISKING INNOCENT LIVES...
...THEN YOU'RE PERFECTLY SAFE.

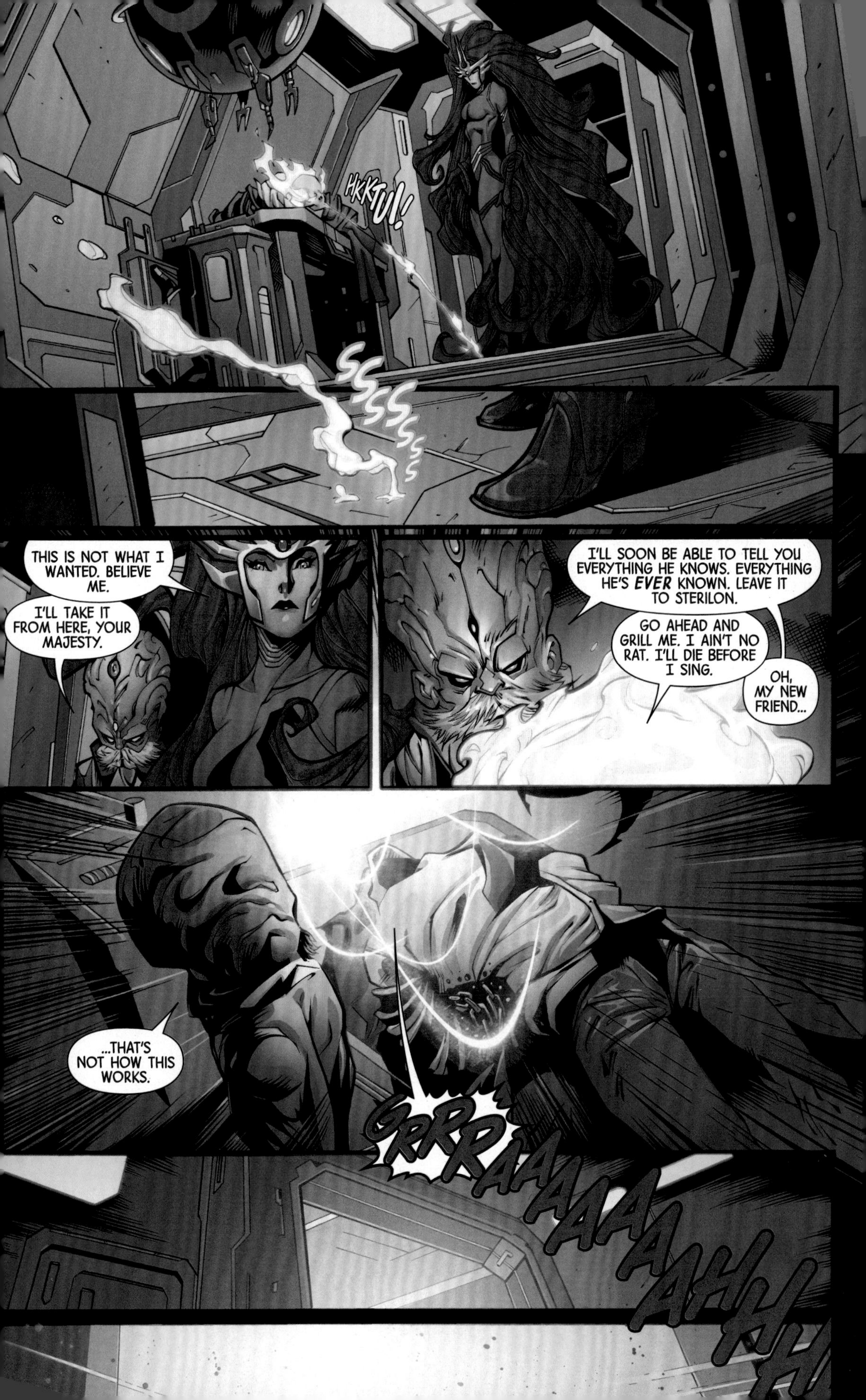
HKKTUI!
SSSSSSSS
THIS IS NOT WHAT I WANTED. BELIEVE ME.
I'LL TAKE IT FROM HERE, YOUR MAJESTY.
I'LL SOON BE ABLE TO TELL YOU EVERYTHING HE KNOWS. EVERYTHING HE'S EVER KNOWN. LEAVE IT TO STERILON.
GO AHEAD AND GRILL ME. I AIN'T NO RAT. I'LL DIE BEFORE I SING.
OH, MY NEW FRIEND...
...THAT'S NOT HOW THIS WORKS.
GRRRAAAAAAAHHH

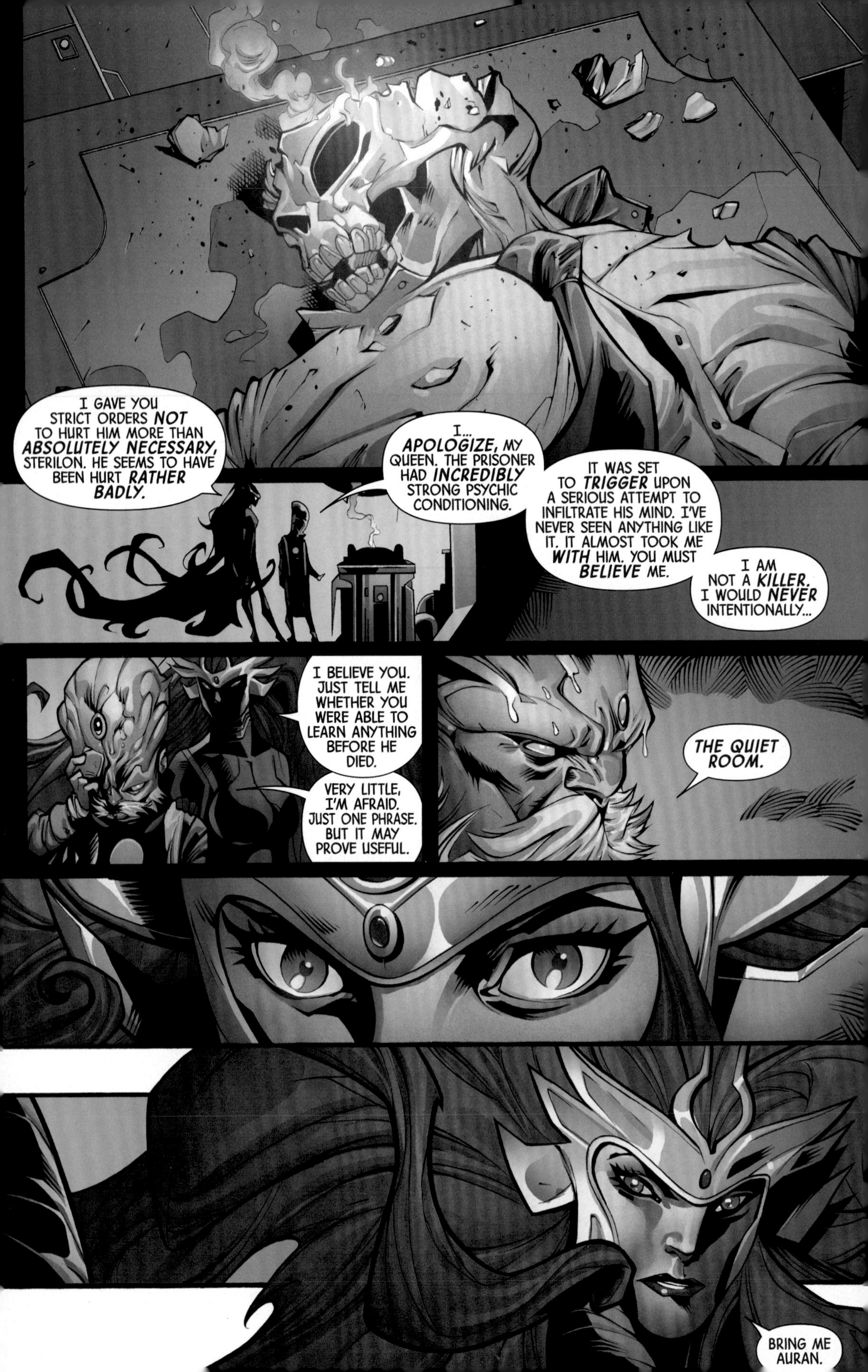
I GAVE YOU STRICT ORDERS NOT TO HURT HIM MORE THAN ABSOLUTELY NECESSARY, STERILON. HE SEEMS TO HAVE BEEN HURT RATHER BADLY.
I... APOLOGIZE, MY QUEEN. THE PRISONER HAD INCREDIBLY STRONG PSYCHIC CONDITIONING.
IT WAS SET TO TRIGGER UPON A SERIOUS ATTEMPT TO INFILTRATE HIS MIND. I'VE NEVER SEEN ANYTHING LIKE IT. IT ALMOST TOOK ME WITH HIM. YOU MUST BELIEVE ME.
I AM NOT A KILLER. I WOULD NEVER INTENTIONALLY...
I BELIEVE YOU. JUST TELL ME WHETHER YOU WERE ABLE TO LEARN ANYTHING BEFORE HE DIED.
VERY LITTLE, I'M AFRAID. JUST ONE PHRASE. BUT IT MAY PROVE USEFUL.
THE QUIET ROOM.
BRING ME AURAN.

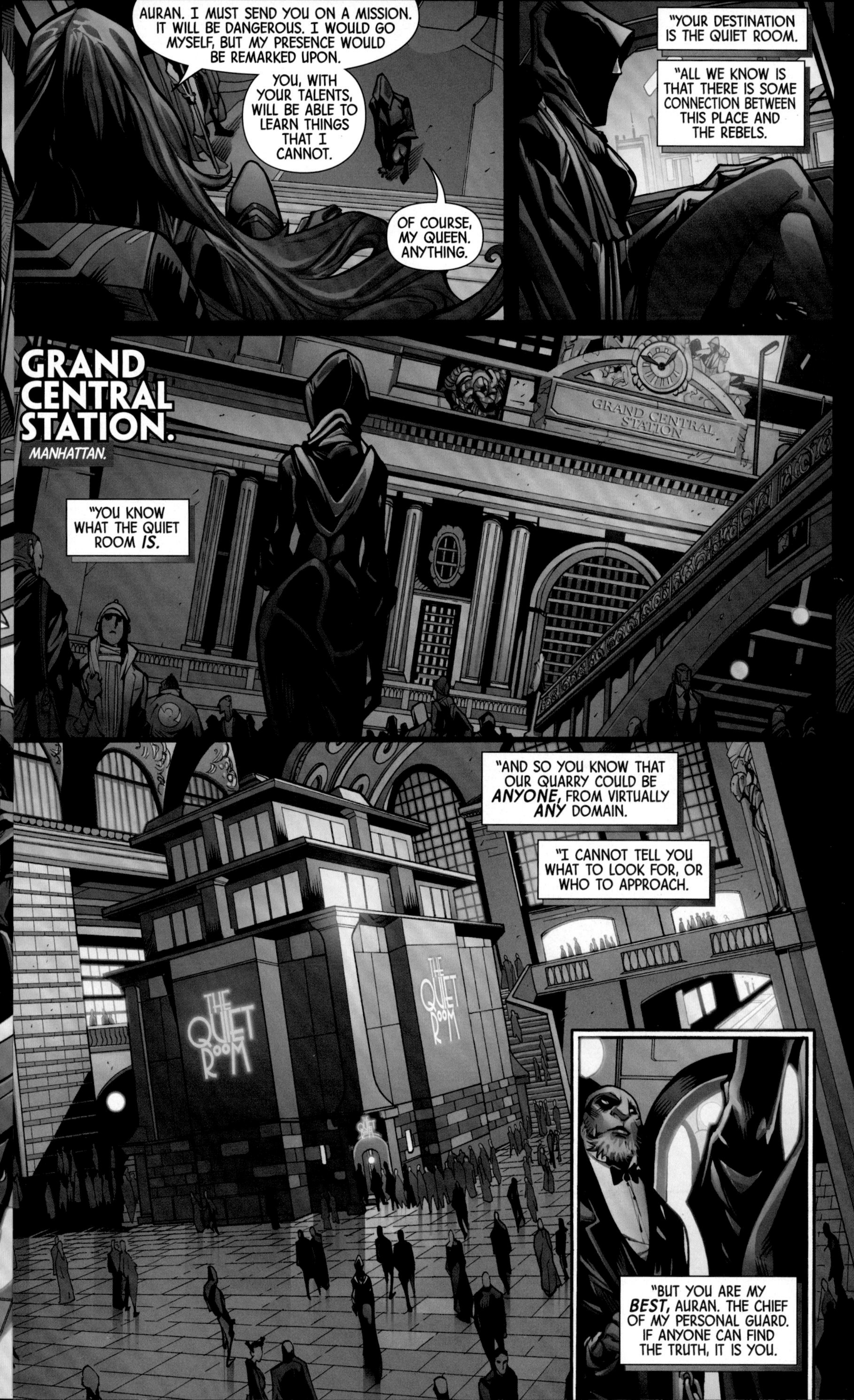
AURAN. I MUST SEND YOU ON A MISSION. IT WILL BE DANGEROUS. I WOULD GO MYSELF, BUT MY PRESENCE WOULD BE REMARKED UPON.
YOU, WITH YOUR TALENTS, WILL BE ABLE TO LEARN THINGS THAT I CANNOT.
OF COURSE, MY QUEEN. ANYTHING.
"YOUR DESTINATION IS THE QUIET ROOM.
"ALL WE KNOW IS THAT THERE IS SOME CONNECTION BETWEEN THIS PLACE AND THE REBELS.
GRAND CENTRAL STATION.
MANHATTAN.
GRAND CENTRAL STATION
"YOU KNOW WHAT THE QUIET ROOM *IS.*
"AND SO YOU KNOW THAT OUR QUARRY COULD BE *ANYONE,* FROM VIRTUALLY *ANY* DOMAIN.
"I CANNOT TELL YOU WHAT TO LOOK FOR, OR WHO TO APPROACH.
THE QUIET ROOM
THE QUIET ROOM
"BUT YOU ARE MY *BEST,* AURAN. THE CHIEF OF MY PERSONAL GUARD. IF ANYONE CAN FIND THE TRUTH, IT IS YOU.

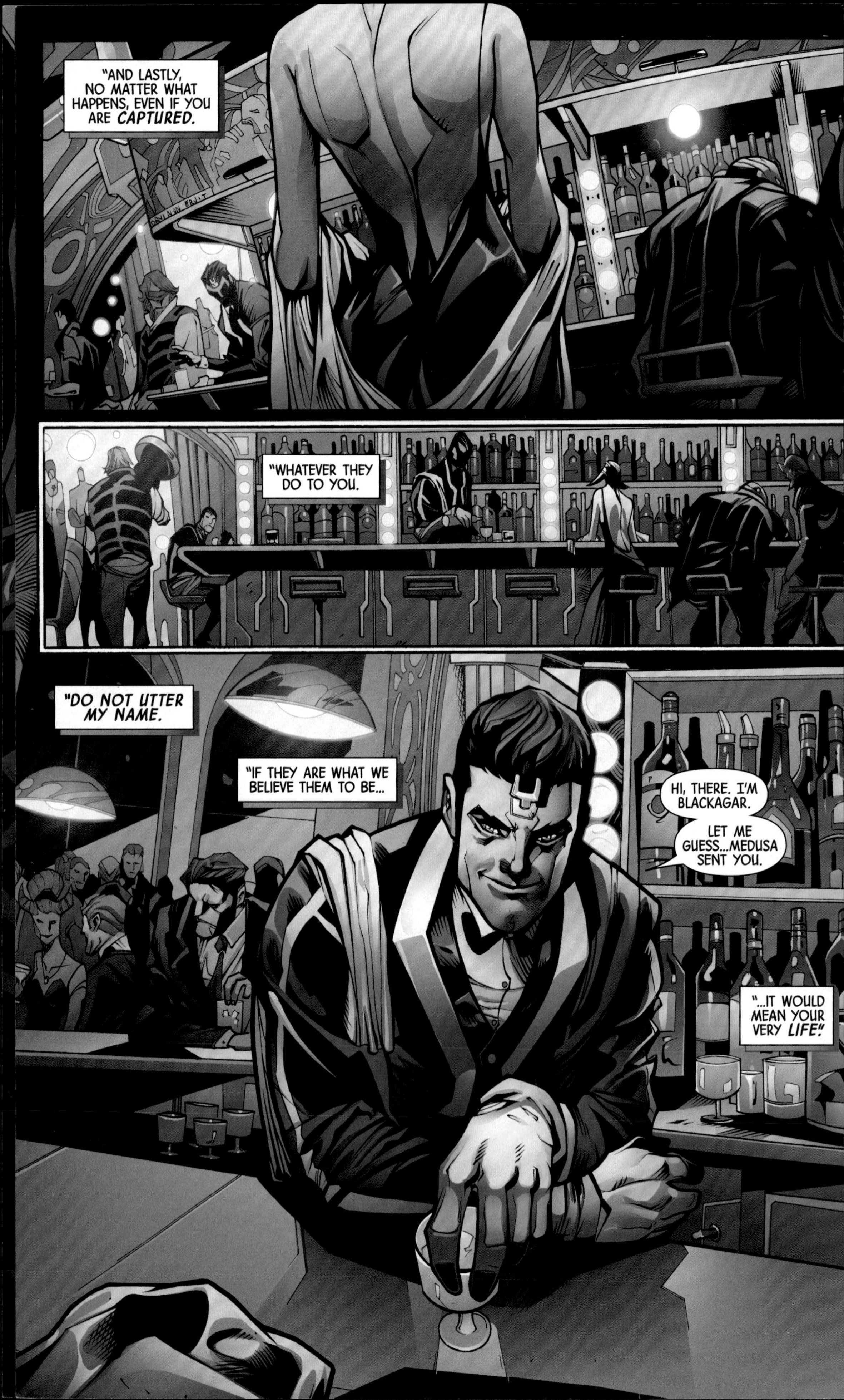
"AND LASTLY, NO MATTER WHAT HAPPENS, EVEN IF YOU ARE CAPTURED.
"WHATEVER THEY DO TO YOU.
"DO NOT UTTER MY NAME.
"IF THEY ARE WHAT WE BELIEVE THEM TO BE...
HI, THERE. I'M BLACKAGAR.
LET ME GUESS...MEDUSA SENT YOU.
"...IT WOULD MEAN YOUR VERY LIFE!"

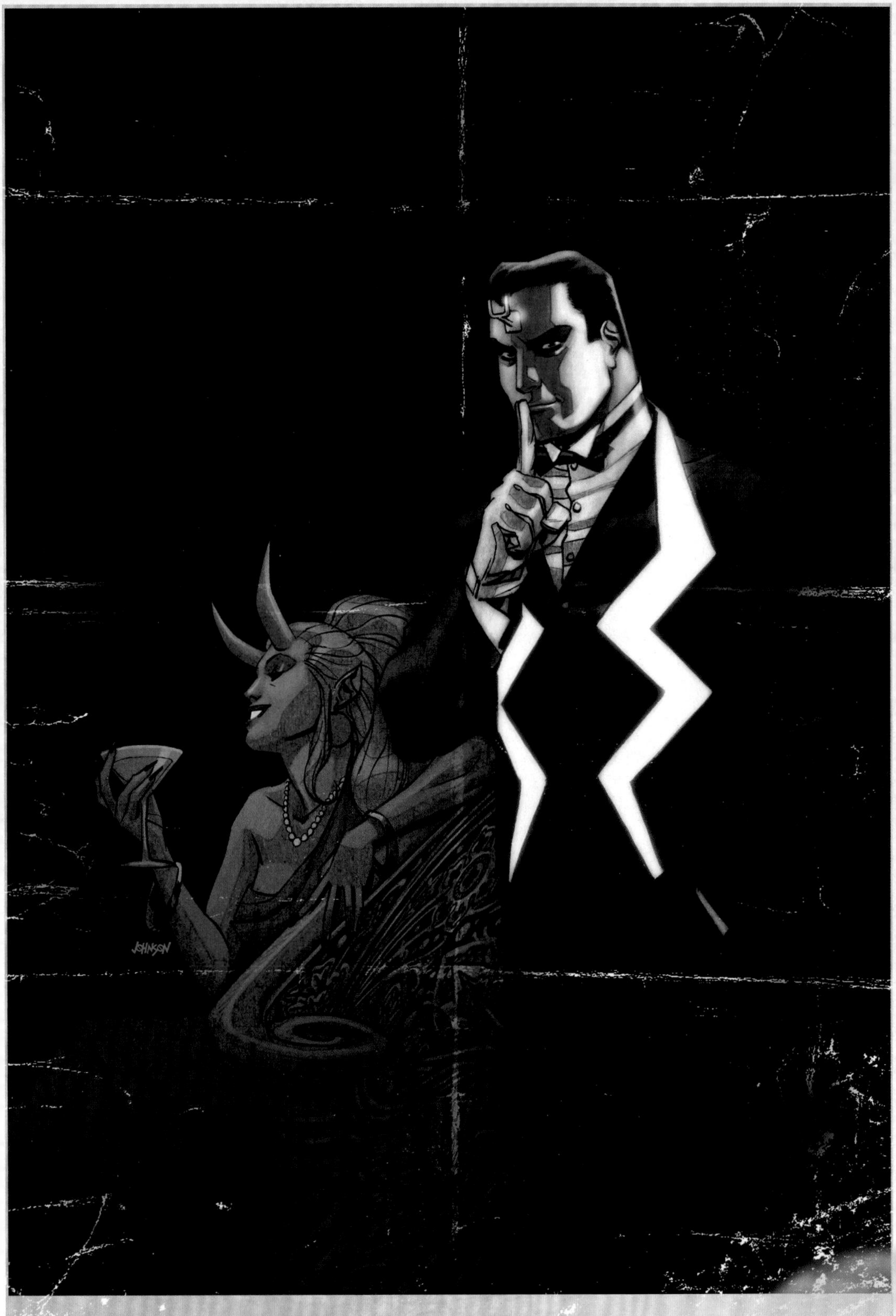
JOHNSON

PART 2: THE QUIET ROOM

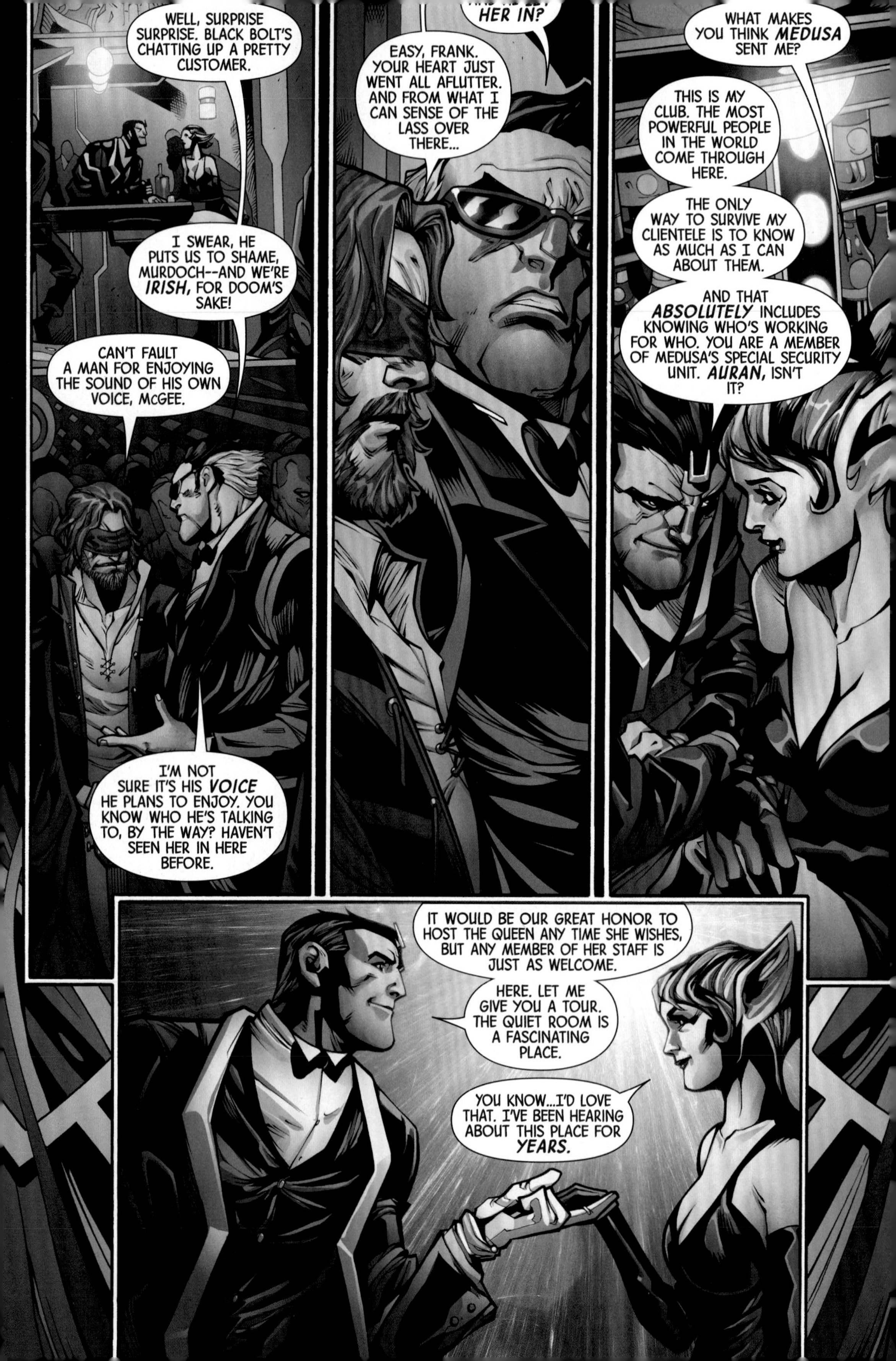
WELL, SURPRISE SURPRISE. BLACK BOLT'S CHATTING UP A PRETTY CUSTOMER.
I SWEAR, HE PUTS US TO SHAME, MURDOCH--AND WE'RE IRISH, FOR DOOM'S SAKE!
CAN'T FAULT A MAN FOR ENJOYING THE SOUND OF HIS OWN VOICE, McGEE.
I'M NOT SURE IT'S HIS VOICE HE PLANS TO ENJOY. YOU KNOW WHO HE'S TALKING TO, BY THE WAY? HAVEN'T SEEN HER IN HERE BEFORE.
HER IN?
EASY, FRANK. YOUR HEART JUST WENT ALL AFLUTTER. AND FROM WHAT I CAN SENSE OF THE LASS OVER THERE...
WHAT MAKES YOU THINK MEDUSA SENT ME?
THIS IS MY CLUB. THE MOST POWERFUL PEOPLE IN THE WORLD COME THROUGH HERE.
THE ONLY WAY TO SURVIVE MY CLIENTELE IS TO KNOW AS MUCH AS I CAN ABOUT THEM.
AND THAT ABSOLUTELY INCLUDES KNOWING WHO'S WORKING FOR WHO. YOU ARE A MEMBER OF MEDUSA'S SPECIAL SECURITY UNIT. AURAN, ISN'T IT?
IT WOULD BE OUR GREAT HONOR TO HOST THE QUEEN ANY TIME SHE WISHES, BUT ANY MEMBER OF HER STAFF IS JUST AS WELCOME.
HERE. LET ME GIVE YOU A TOUR. THE QUIET ROOM IS A FASCINATING PLACE.
YOU KNOW...I'D LOVE THAT. I'VE BEEN HEARING ABOUT THIS PLACE FOR YEARS.

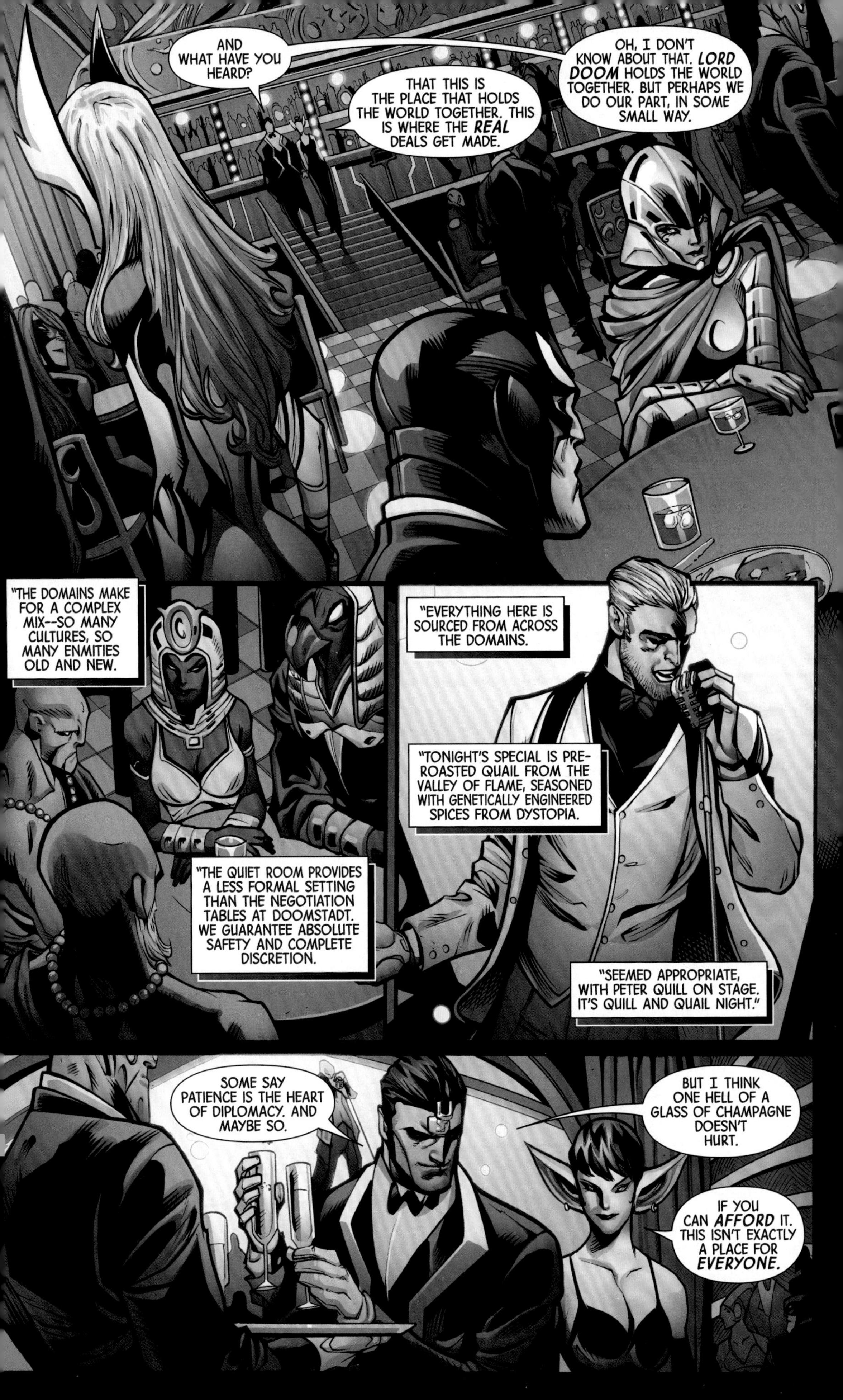
AND WHAT HAVE YOU HEARD?
THAT THIS IS THE PLACE THAT HOLDS THE WORLD TOGETHER. THIS IS WHERE THE REAL DEALS GET MADE.
OH, I DON'T KNOW ABOUT THAT. LORD DOOM HOLDS THE WORLD TOGETHER. BUT PERHAPS WE DO OUR PART, IN SOME SMALL WAY.
"THE DOMAINS MAKE FOR A COMPLEX MIX--SO MANY CULTURES, SO MANY ENMITIES OLD AND NEW.
"THE QUIET ROOM PROVIDES A LESS FORMAL SETTING THAN THE NEGOTIATION TABLES AT DOOMSTADT. WE GUARANTEE ABSOLUTE SAFETY AND COMPLETE DISCRETION.
"EVERYTHING HERE IS SOURCED FROM ACROSS THE DOMAINS.
"TONIGHT'S SPECIAL IS PRE-ROASTED QUAIL FROM THE VALLEY OF FLAME, SEASONED WITH GENETICALLY ENGINEERED SPICES FROM DYSTOPIA.
"SEEMED APPROPRIATE, WITH PETER QUILL ON STAGE. IT'S QUILL AND QUAIL NIGHT."
SOME SAY PATIENCE IS THE HEART OF DIPLOMACY. AND MAYBE SO.
BUT I THINK ONE HELL OF A GLASS OF CHAMPAGNE DOESN'T HURT.
IF YOU CAN AFFORD IT. THIS ISN'T EXACTLY A PLACE FOR EVERYONE.

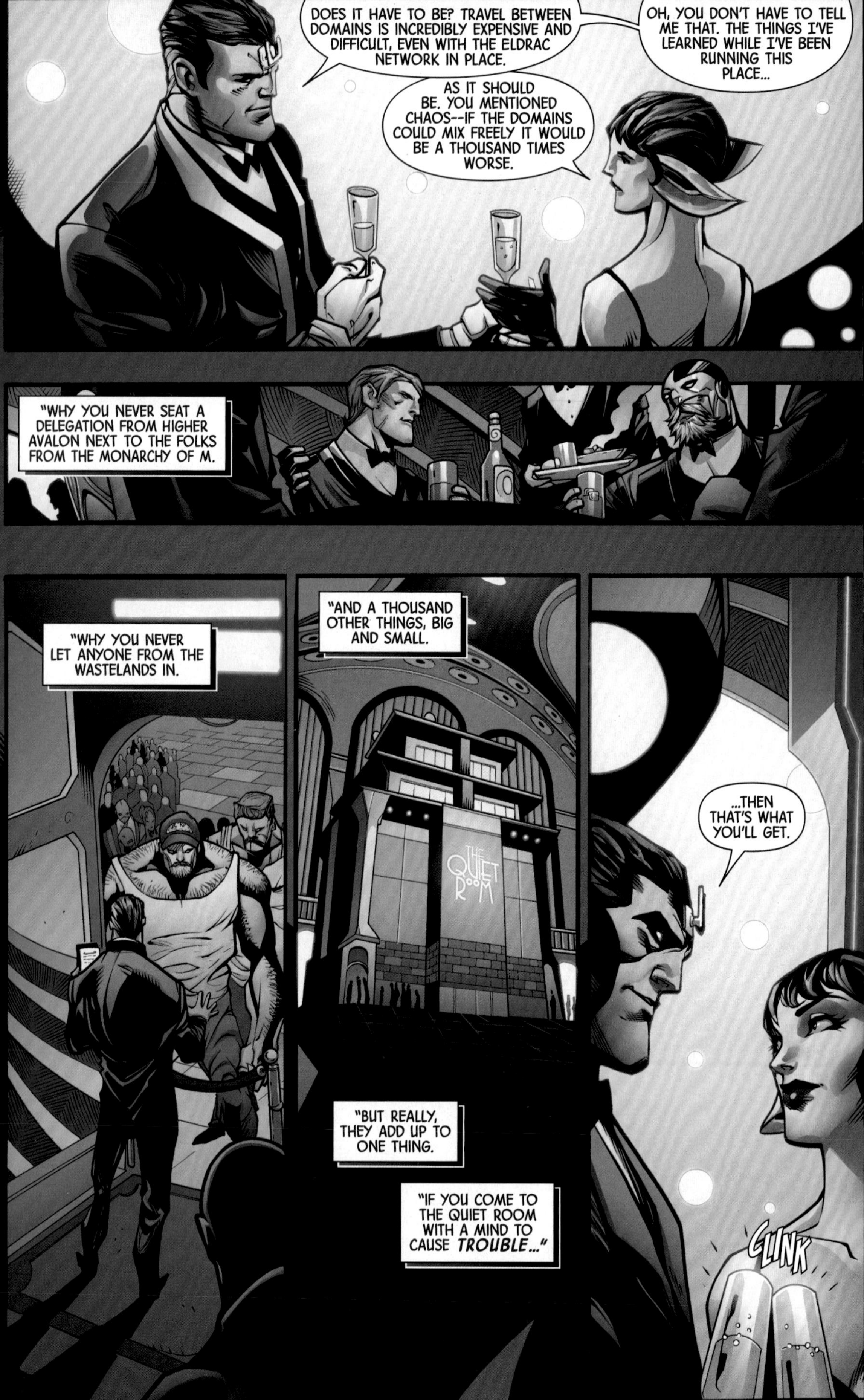
DOES IT HAVE TO BE? TRAVEL BETWEEN DOMAINS IS INCREDIBLY EXPENSIVE AND DIFFICULT, EVEN WITH THE ELDRAC NETWORK IN PLACE.
AS IT SHOULD BE. YOU MENTIONED CHAOS--IF THE DOMAINS COULD MIX FREELY IT WOULD BE A THOUSAND TIMES WORSE.
OH, YOU DON'T HAVE TO TELL ME THAT. THE THINGS I'VE LEARNED WHILE I'VE BEEN RUNNING THIS PLACE...
"WHY YOU NEVER SEAT A DELEGATION FROM HIGHER AVALON NEXT TO THE FOLKS FROM THE MONARCHY OF M.
"WHY YOU NEVER LET ANYONE FROM THE WASTELANDS IN.
"AND A THOUSAND OTHER THINGS, BIG AND SMALL.
THE QUIET ROOM
"BUT REALLY, THEY ADD UP TO ONE THING.
"IF YOU COME TO THE QUIET ROOM WITH A MIND TO CAUSE *TROUBLE*..."
...THEN THAT'S WHAT YOU'LL GET.
CLINK

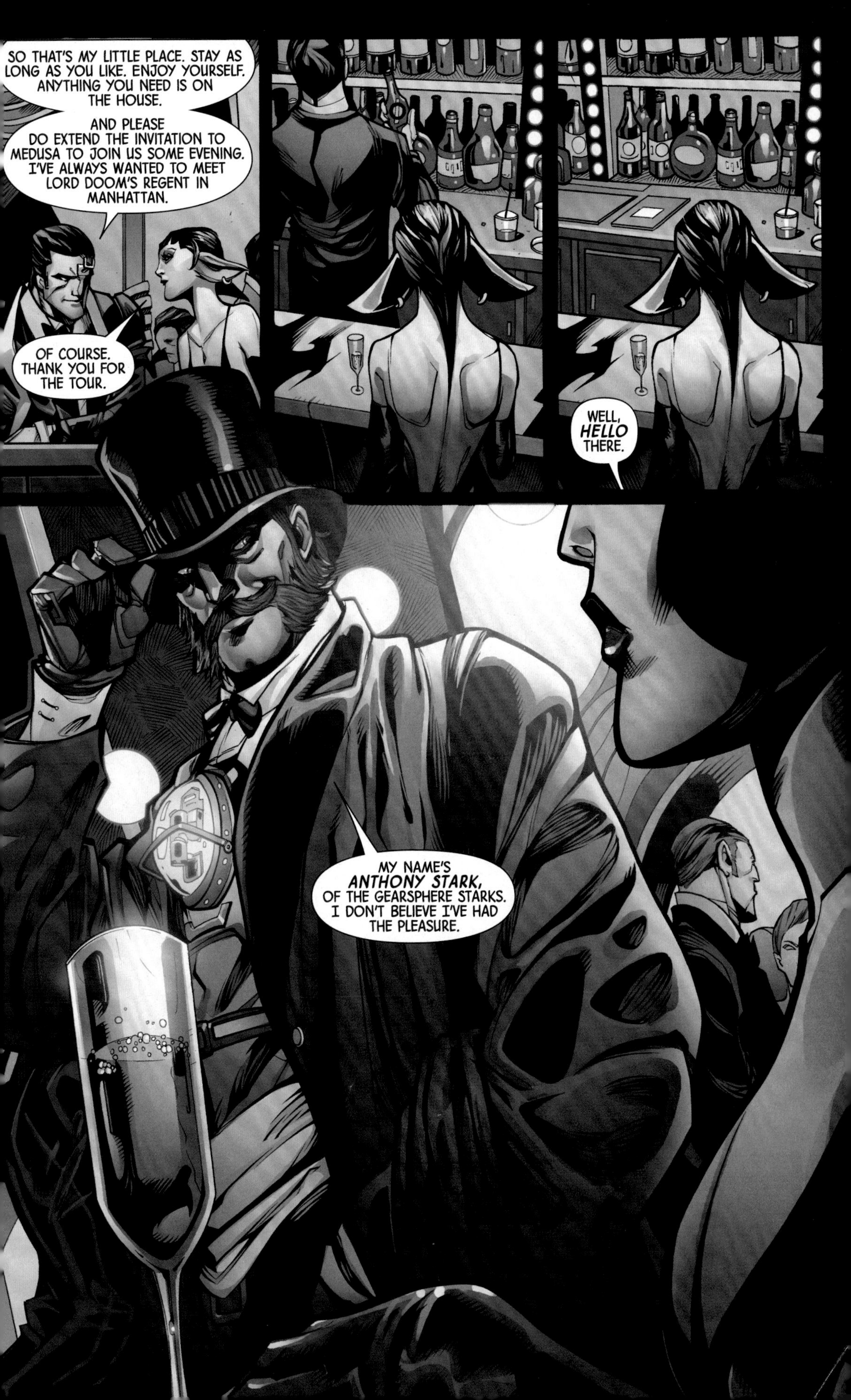
SO THAT'S MY LITTLE PLACE. STAY AS LONG AS YOU LIKE. ENJOY YOURSELF. ANYTHING YOU NEED IS ON THE HOUSE.
AND PLEASE DO EXTEND THE INVITATION TO MEDUSA TO JOIN US SOME EVENING. I'VE ALWAYS WANTED TO MEET LORD DOOM'S REGENT IN MANHATTAN.
OF COURSE. THANK YOU FOR THE TOUR.
WELL, *HELLO* THERE.
MY NAME'S *ANTHONY STARK,* OF THE GEARSPHERE STARKS. I DON'T BELIEVE I'VE HAD THE PLEASURE.

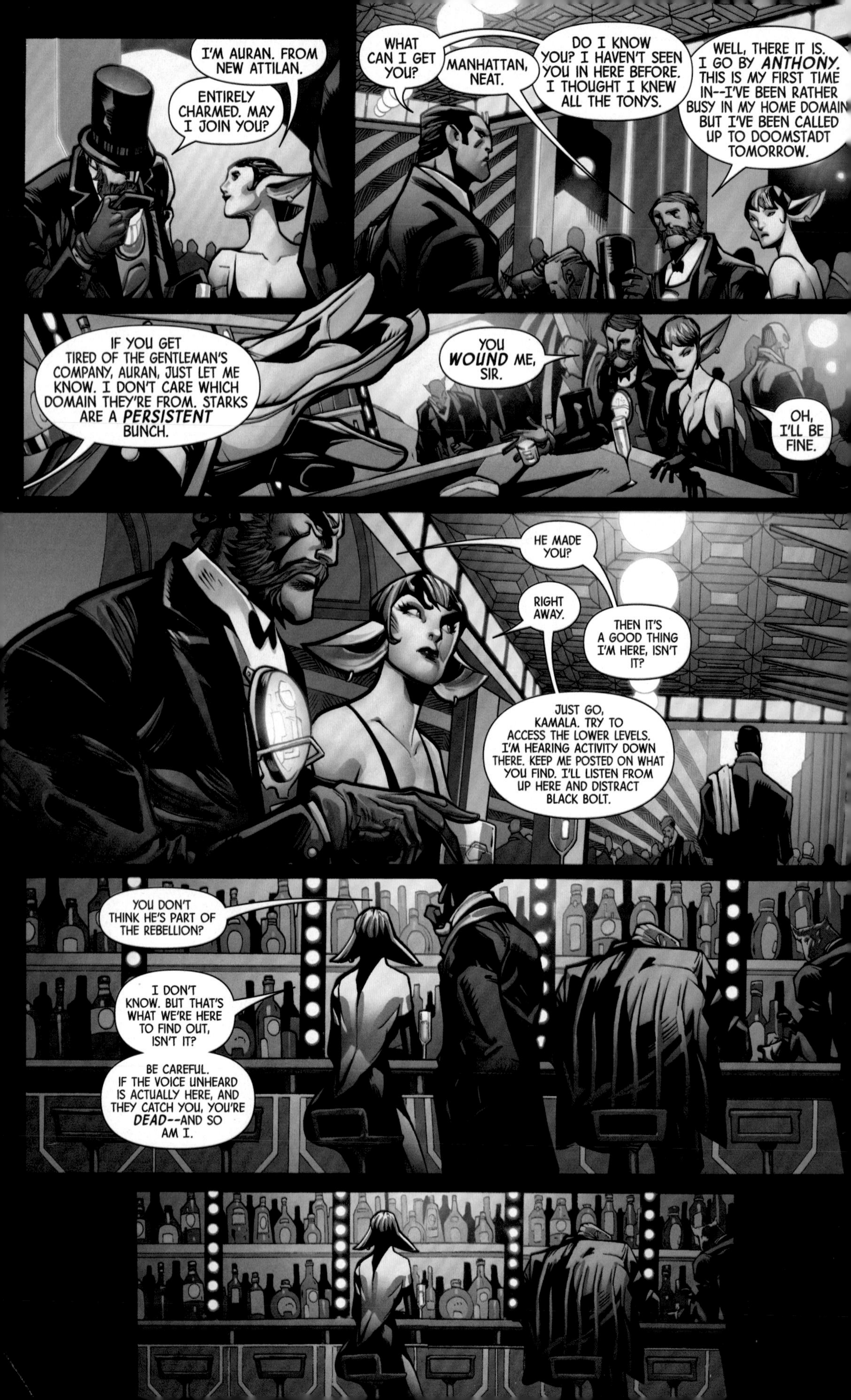

I'M AURAN. FROM NEW ATTILAN.
ENTIRELY CHARMED. MAY I JOIN YOU?
WHAT CAN I GET YOU?
MANHATTAN, NEAT.
DO I KNOW YOU? I HAVEN'T SEEN YOU IN HERE BEFORE. I THOUGHT I KNEW ALL THE TONYS.
WELL, THERE IT IS. I GO BY ANTHONY. THIS IS MY FIRST TIME IN--I'VE BEEN RATHER BUSY IN MY HOME DOMAIN BUT I'VE BEEN CALLED UP TO DOOMSTADT TOMORROW.
IF YOU GET TIRED OF THE GENTLEMAN'S COMPANY, AURAN, JUST LET ME KNOW. I DON'T CARE WHICH DOMAIN THEY'RE FROM. STARKS ARE A PERSISTENT BUNCH.
YOU WOUND ME, SIR.
OH, I'LL BE FINE.
HE MADE YOU?
RIGHT AWAY.
THEN IT'S A GOOD THING I'M HERE, ISN'T IT?
JUST GO, KAMALA. TRY TO ACCESS THE LOWER LEVELS. I'M HEARING ACTIVITY DOWN THERE. KEEP ME POSTED ON WHAT YOU FIND. I'LL LISTEN FROM UP HERE AND DISTRACT BLACK BOLT.
YOU DON'T THINK HE'S PART OF THE REBELLION?
I DON'T KNOW. BUT THAT'S WHAT WE'RE HERE TO FIND OUT, ISN'T IT?
BE CAREFUL. IF THE VOICE UNHEARD IS ACTUALLY HERE, AND THEY CATCH YOU, YOU'RE DEAD--AND SO AM I.

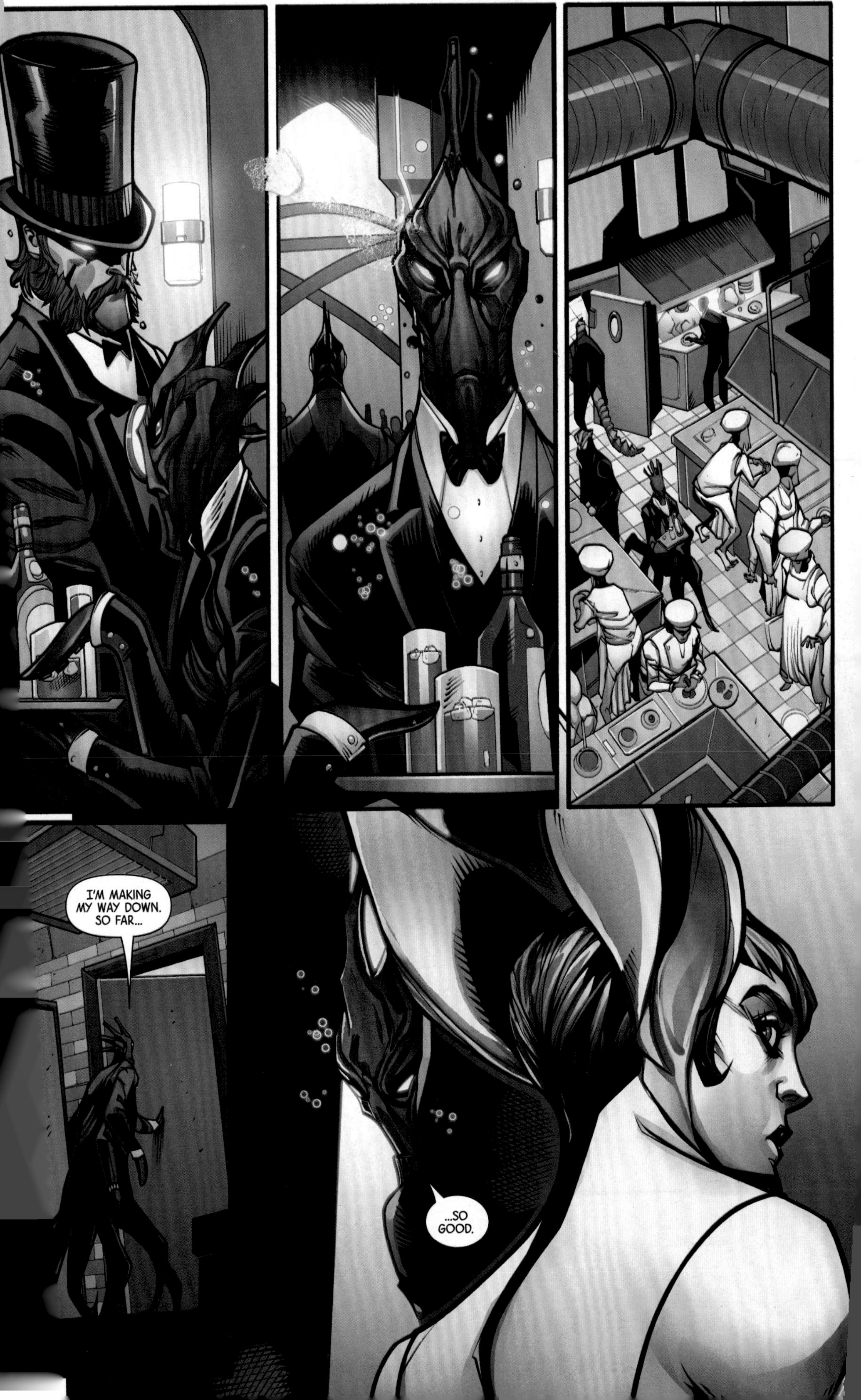
I'M MAKING MY WAY DOWN. SO FAR...
...SO GOOD.

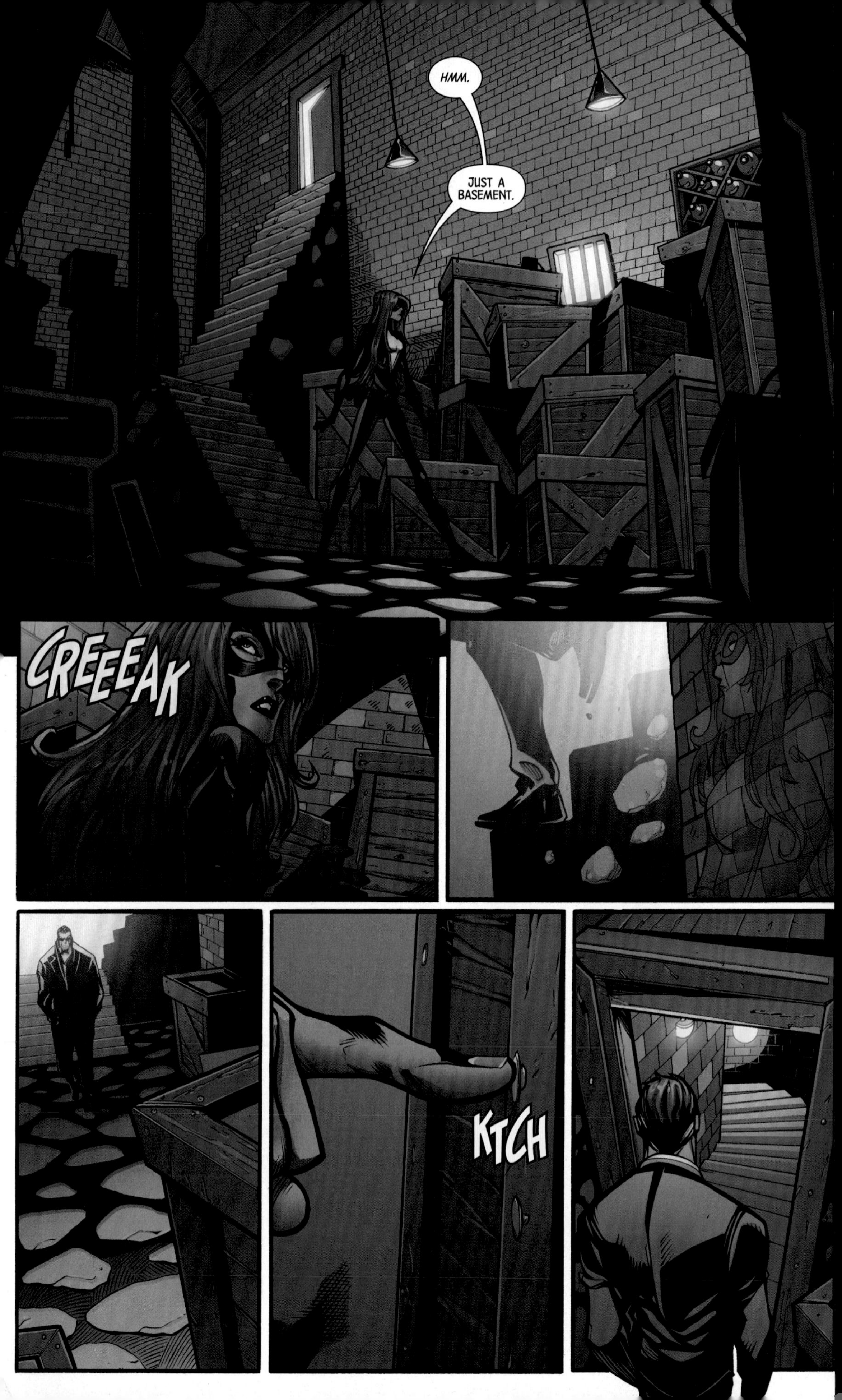
HMM.
JUST A BASEMENT.
CREEEAK
KTCH

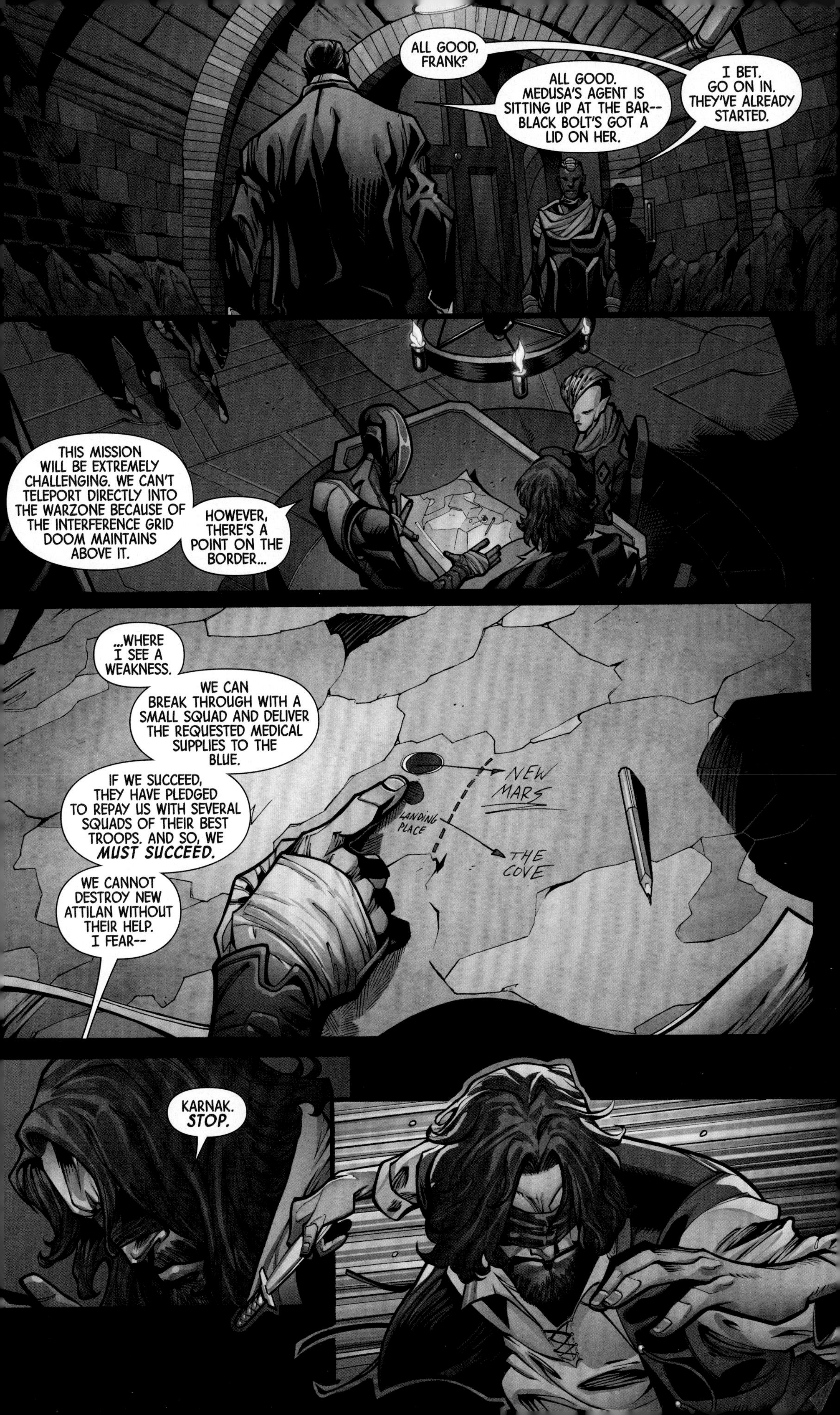
ALL GOOD, FRANK?
ALL GOOD. MEDUSA'S AGENT IS SITTING UP AT THE BAR-- BLACK BOLT'S GOT A LID ON HER.
I BET. GO ON IN. THEY'VE ALREADY STARTED.
THIS MISSION WILL BE EXTREMELY CHALLENGING. WE CAN'T TELEPORT DIRECTLY INTO THE WARZONE BECAUSE OF THE INTERFERENCE GRID DOOM MAINTAINS ABOVE IT.
HOWEVER, THERE'S A POINT ON THE BORDER...
...WHERE I SEE A WEAKNESS.
WE CAN BREAK THROUGH WITH A SMALL SQUAD AND DELIVER THE REQUESTED MEDICAL SUPPLIES TO THE BLUE.
NEW MARS
LANDING PLACE
THE COVE
IF WE SUCCEED, THEY HAVE PLEDGED TO REPAY US WITH SEVERAL SQUADS OF THEIR BEST TROOPS. AND SO, WE MUST SUCCEED.
WE CANNOT DESTROY NEW ATTILAN WITHOUT THEIR HELP. I FEAR--
KARNAK. STOP.

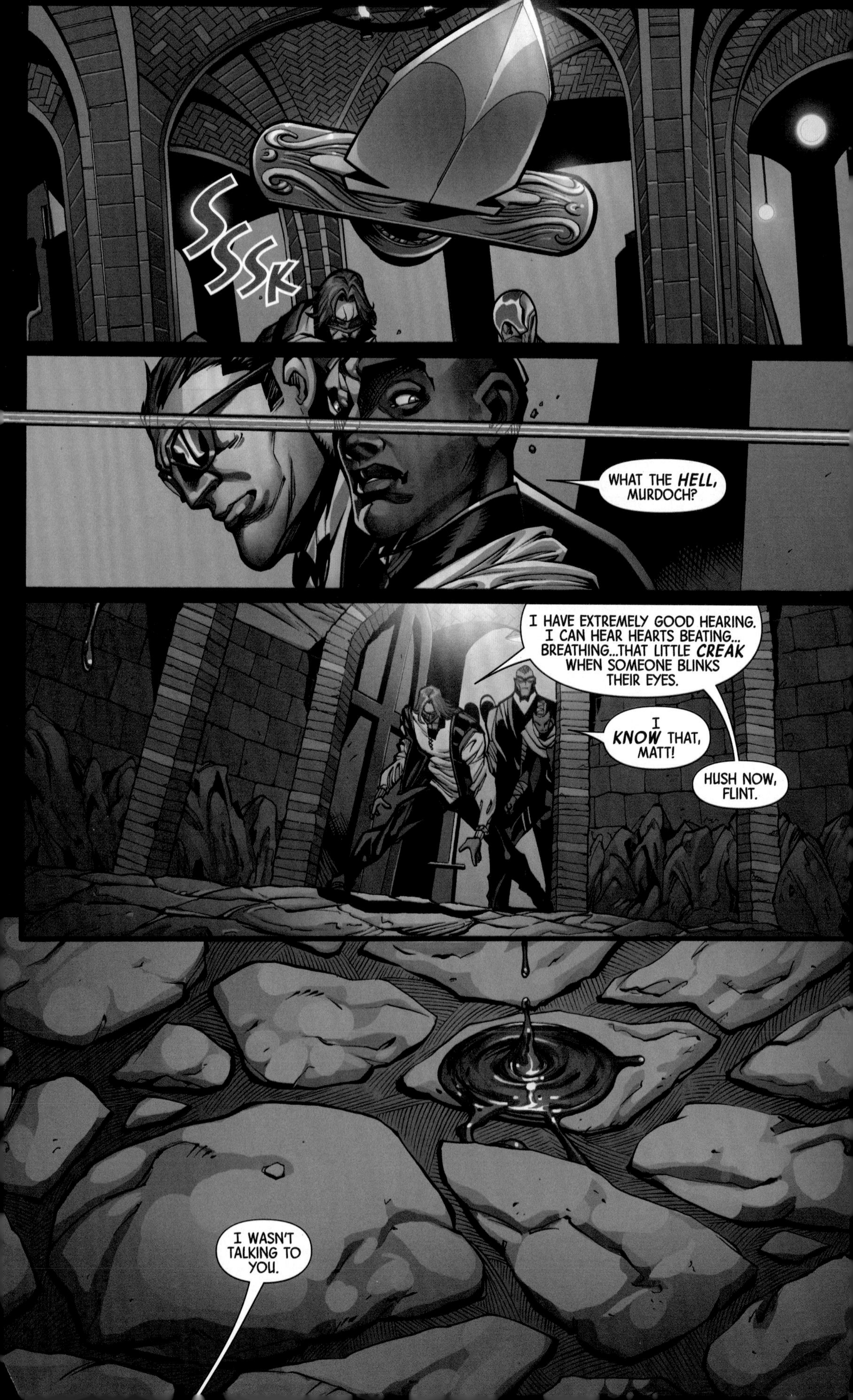
SSSK
WHAT THE HELL, MURDOCH?
I HAVE EXTREMELY GOOD HEARING. I CAN HEAR HEARTS BEATING... BREATHING...THAT LITTLE CREAK WHEN SOMEONE BLINKS THEIR EYES.
I KNOW THAT, MATT!
HUSH NOW, FLINT.
I WASN'T TALKING TO YOU.

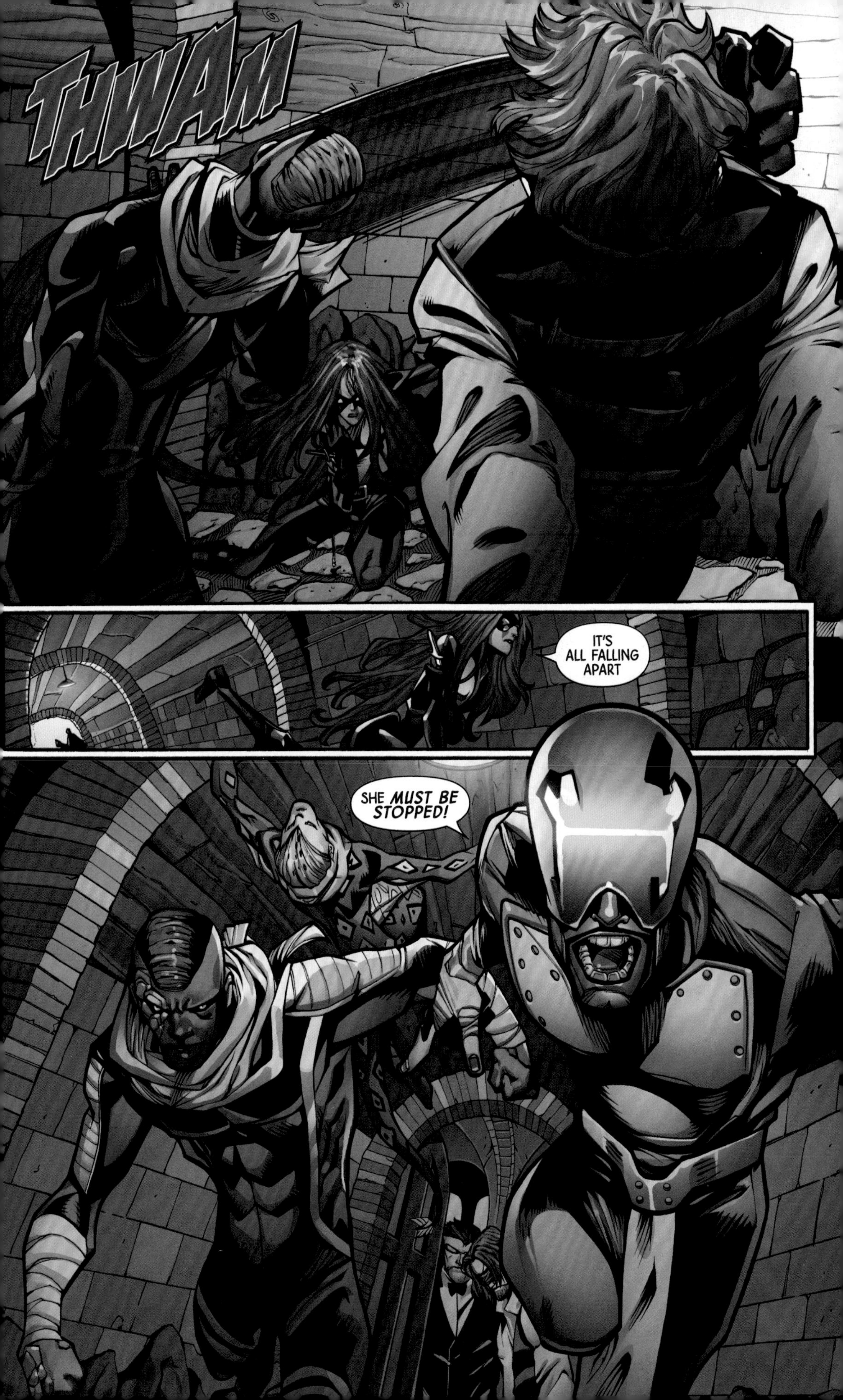
THWAM
IT'S ALL FALLING APART
SHE MUST BE STOPPED!

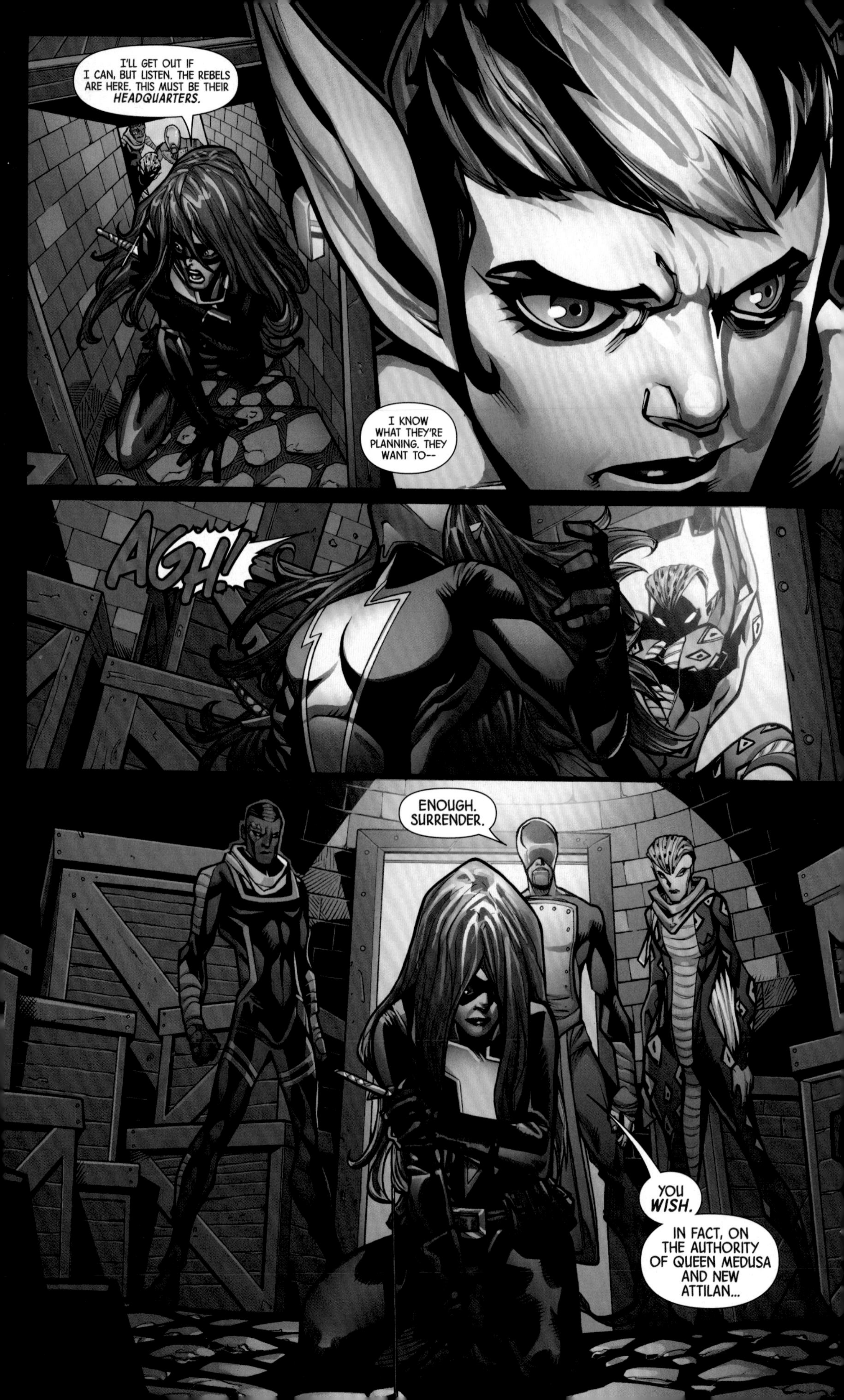
I'LL GET OUT IF I CAN, BUT LISTEN. THE REBELS ARE HERE. THIS MUST BE THEIR *HEADQUARTERS*.
I KNOW WHAT THEY'RE PLANNING. THEY WANT TO--
AGH!
ENOUGH. SURRENDER.
YOU *WISH*.
IN FACT, ON THE AUTHORITY OF QUEEN MEDUSA AND NEW ATTILAN...

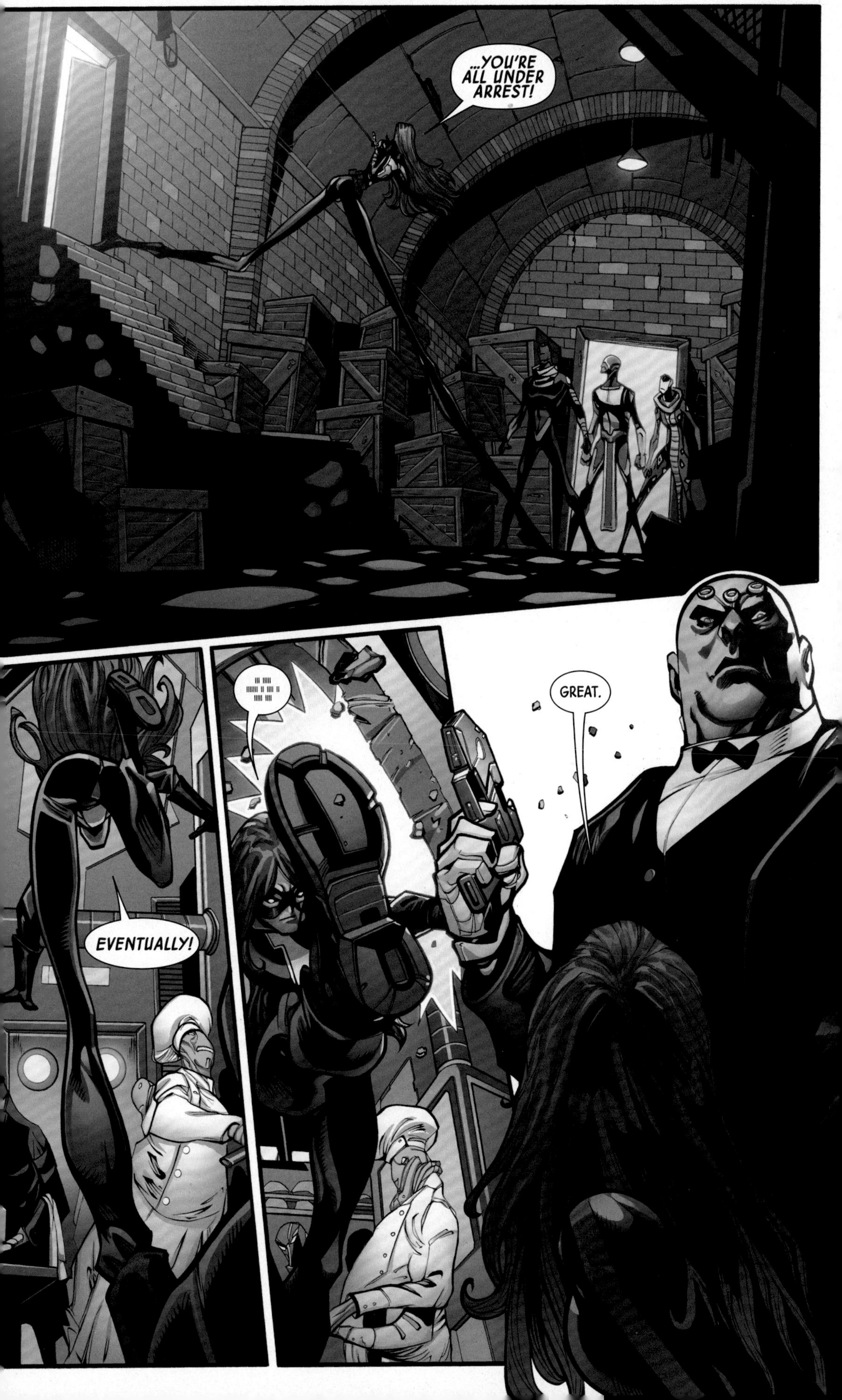
...YOU'RE ALL UNDER ARREST!
EVENTUALLY!
GREAT.

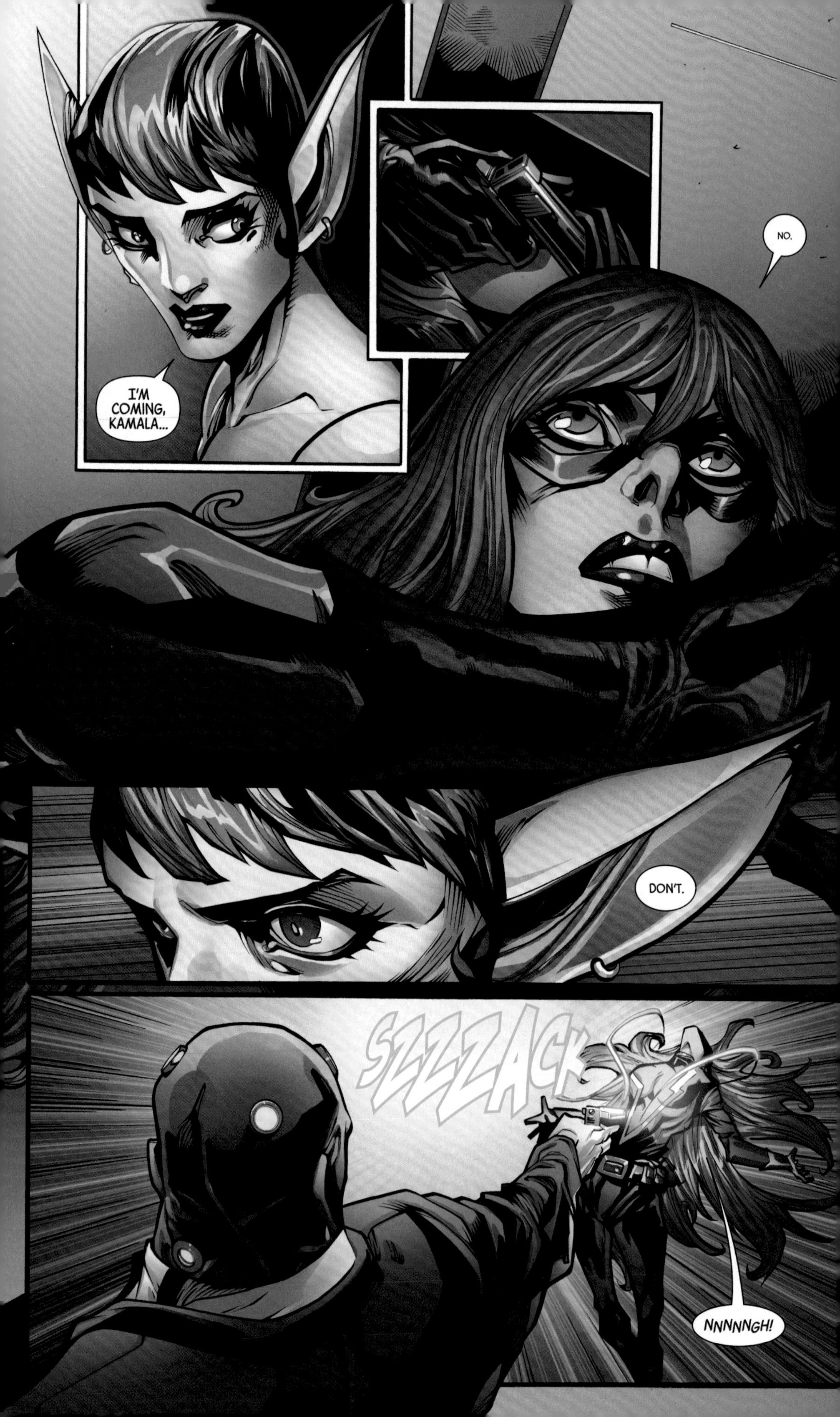
I'M COMING, KAMALA...
NO.
DON'T.
SZZZACK
NNNNNGH!

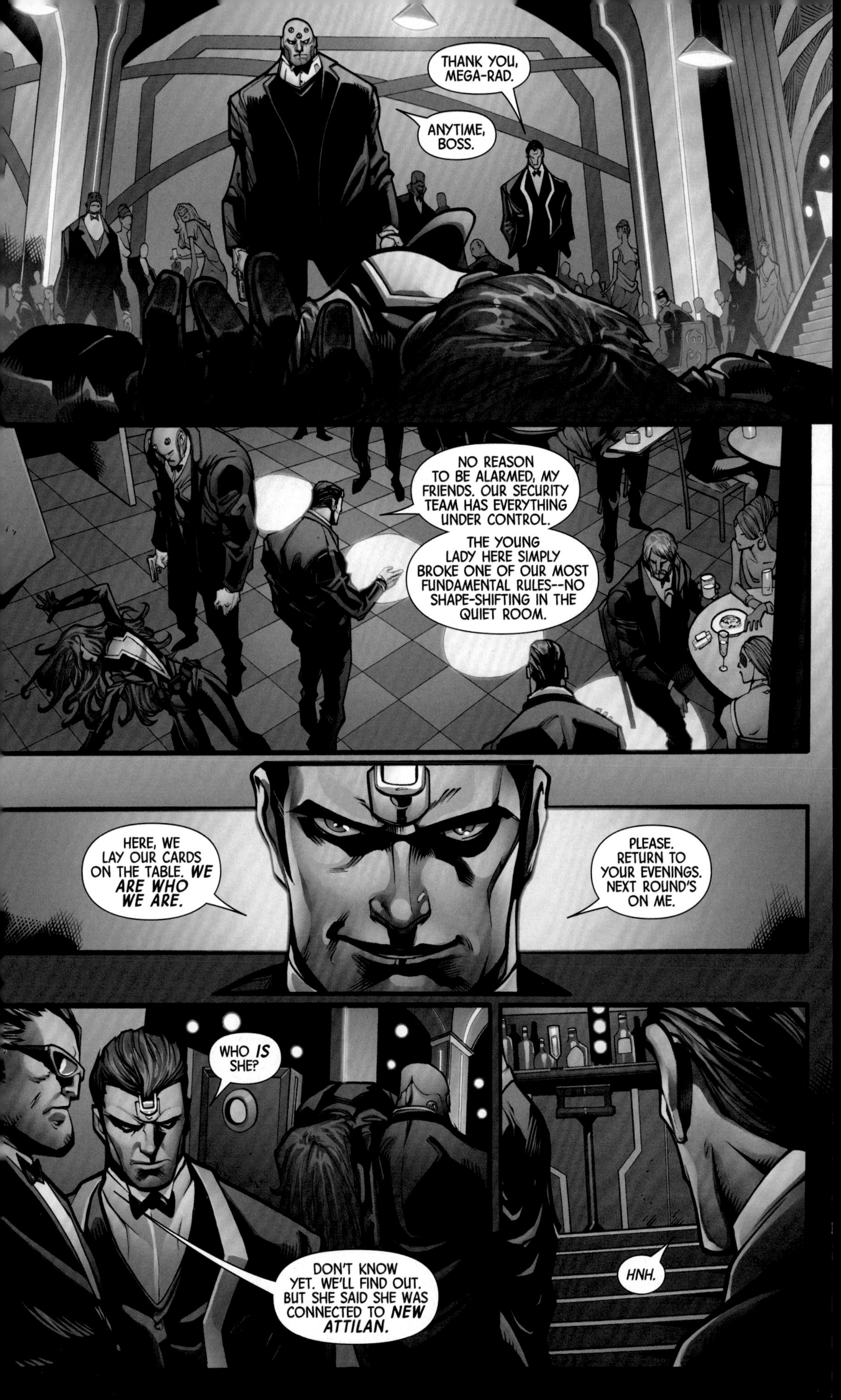
THANK YOU, MEGA-RAD.
ANYTIME, BOSS.
NO REASON TO BE ALARMED, MY FRIENDS. OUR SECURITY TEAM HAS EVERYTHING UNDER CONTROL.
THE YOUNG LADY HERE SIMPLY BROKE ONE OF OUR MOST FUNDAMENTAL RULES--NO SHAPE-SHIFTING IN THE QUIET ROOM.
HERE, WE LAY OUR CARDS ON THE TABLE. WE ARE WHO WE ARE.
PLEASE. RETURN TO YOUR EVENINGS. NEXT ROUND'S ON ME.
WHO IS SHE?
DON'T KNOW YET. WE'LL FIND OUT. BUT SHE SAID SHE WAS CONNECTED TO NEW ATTILAN.
HNH.

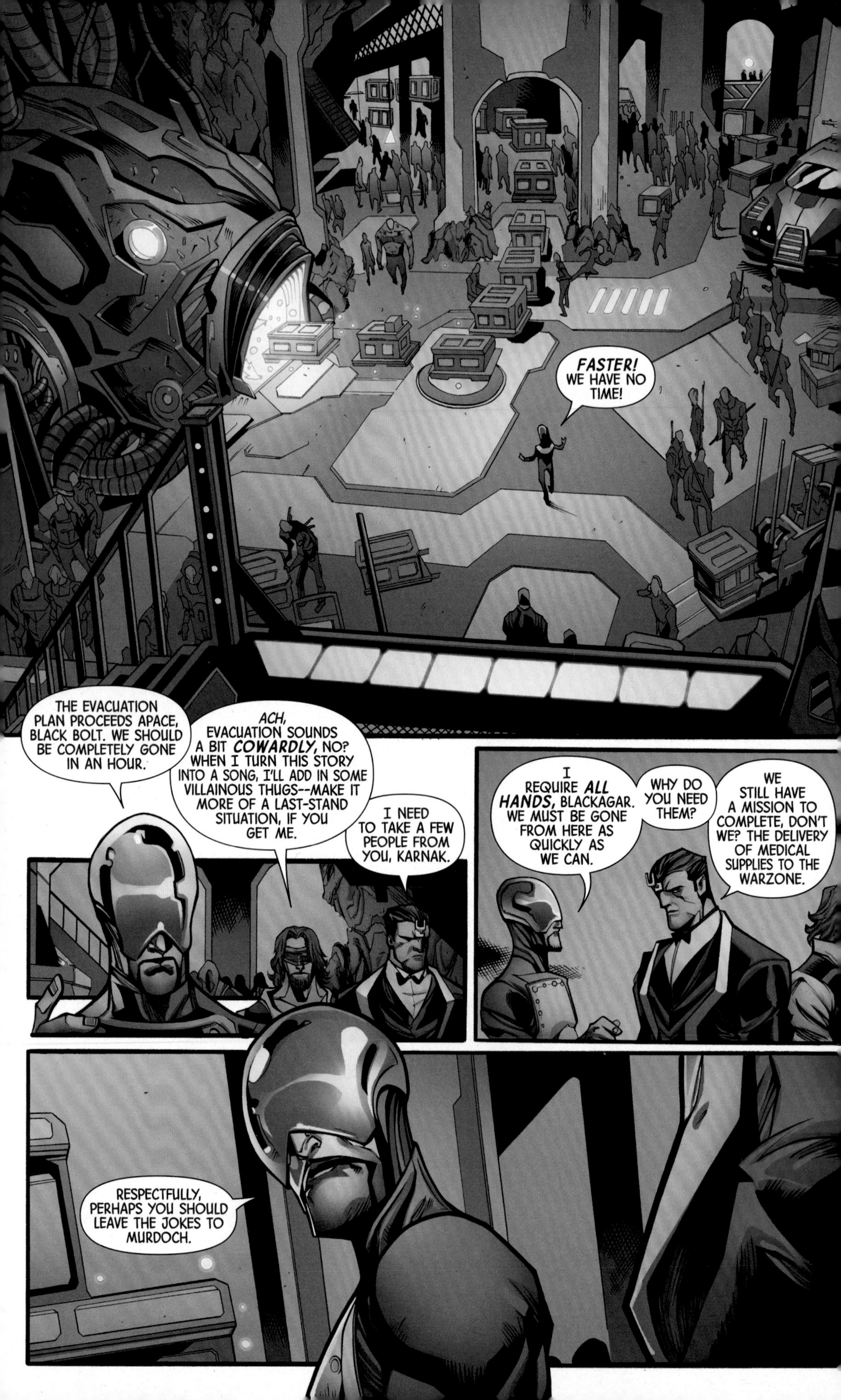

FASTER! WE HAVE NO TIME!
THE EVACUATION PLAN PROCEEDS APACE, BLACK BOLT. WE SHOULD BE COMPLETELY GONE IN AN HOUR.
ACH, EVACUATION SOUNDS A BIT COWARDLY, NO? WHEN I TURN THIS STORY INTO A SONG, I'LL ADD IN SOME VILLAINOUS THUGS--MAKE IT MORE OF A LAST-STAND SITUATION, IF YOU GET ME.
I NEED TO TAKE A FEW PEOPLE FROM YOU, KARNAK.
I REQUIRE ALL HANDS, BLACKAGAR. WE MUST BE GONE FROM HERE AS QUICKLY AS WE CAN.
WHY DO YOU NEED THEM?
WE STILL HAVE A MISSION TO COMPLETE, DON'T WE? THE DELIVERY OF MEDICAL SUPPLIES TO THE WARZONE.
RESPECTFULLY, PERHAPS YOU SHOULD LEAVE THE JOKES TO MURDOCH.

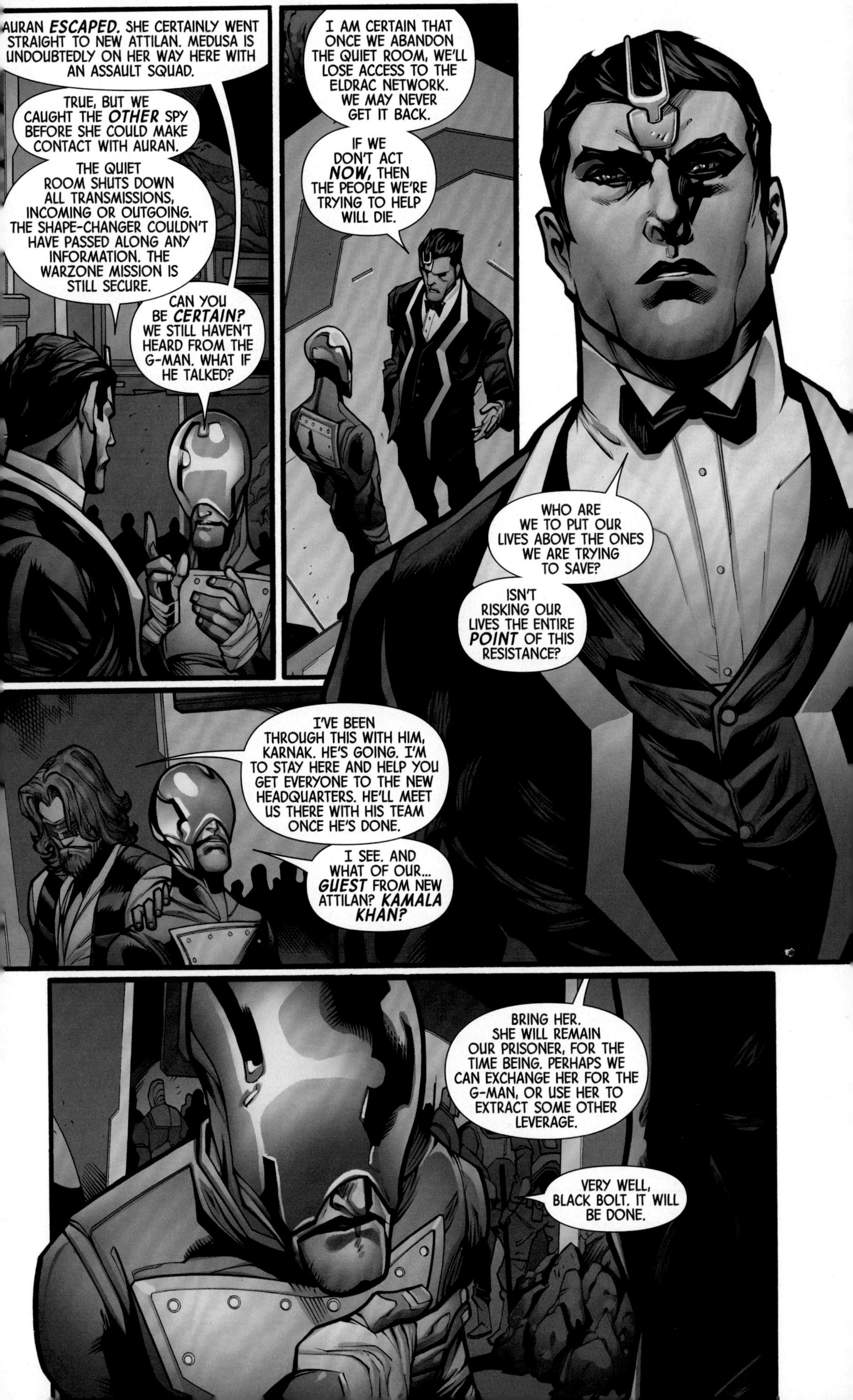
AURAN ESCAPED. SHE CERTAINLY WENT STRAIGHT TO NEW ATTILAN. MEDUSA IS UNDOUBTEDLY ON HER WAY HERE WITH AN ASSAULT SQUAD.
TRUE, BUT WE CAUGHT THE OTHER SPY BEFORE SHE COULD MAKE CONTACT WITH AURAN.
THE QUIET ROOM SHUTS DOWN ALL TRANSMISSIONS, INCOMING OR OUTGOING. THE SHAPE-CHANGER COULDN'T HAVE PASSED ALONG ANY INFORMATION. THE WARZONE MISSION IS STILL SECURE.
CAN YOU BE CERTAIN? WE STILL HAVEN'T HEARD FROM THE G-MAN. WHAT IF HE TALKED?
I AM CERTAIN THAT ONCE WE ABANDON THE QUIET ROOM, WE'LL LOSE ACCESS TO THE ELDRAC NETWORK. WE MAY NEVER GET IT BACK.
IF WE DON'T ACT NOW, THEN THE PEOPLE WE'RE TRYING TO HELP WILL DIE.
WHO ARE WE TO PUT OUR LIVES ABOVE THE ONES WE ARE TRYING TO SAVE?
ISN'T RISKING OUR LIVES THE ENTIRE POINT OF THIS RESISTANCE?
I'VE BEEN THROUGH THIS WITH HIM, KARNAK. HE'S GOING. I'M TO STAY HERE AND HELP YOU GET EVERYONE TO THE NEW HEADQUARTERS. HE'LL MEET US THERE WITH HIS TEAM ONCE HE'S DONE.
I SEE. AND WHAT OF OUR... GUEST FROM NEW ATTILAN? KAMALA KHAN?
BRING HER. SHE WILL REMAIN OUR PRISONER, FOR THE TIME BEING. PERHAPS WE CAN EXCHANGE HER FOR THE G-MAN, OR USE HER TO EXTRACT SOME OTHER LEVERAGE.
VERY WELL, BLACK BOLT. IT WILL BE DONE.

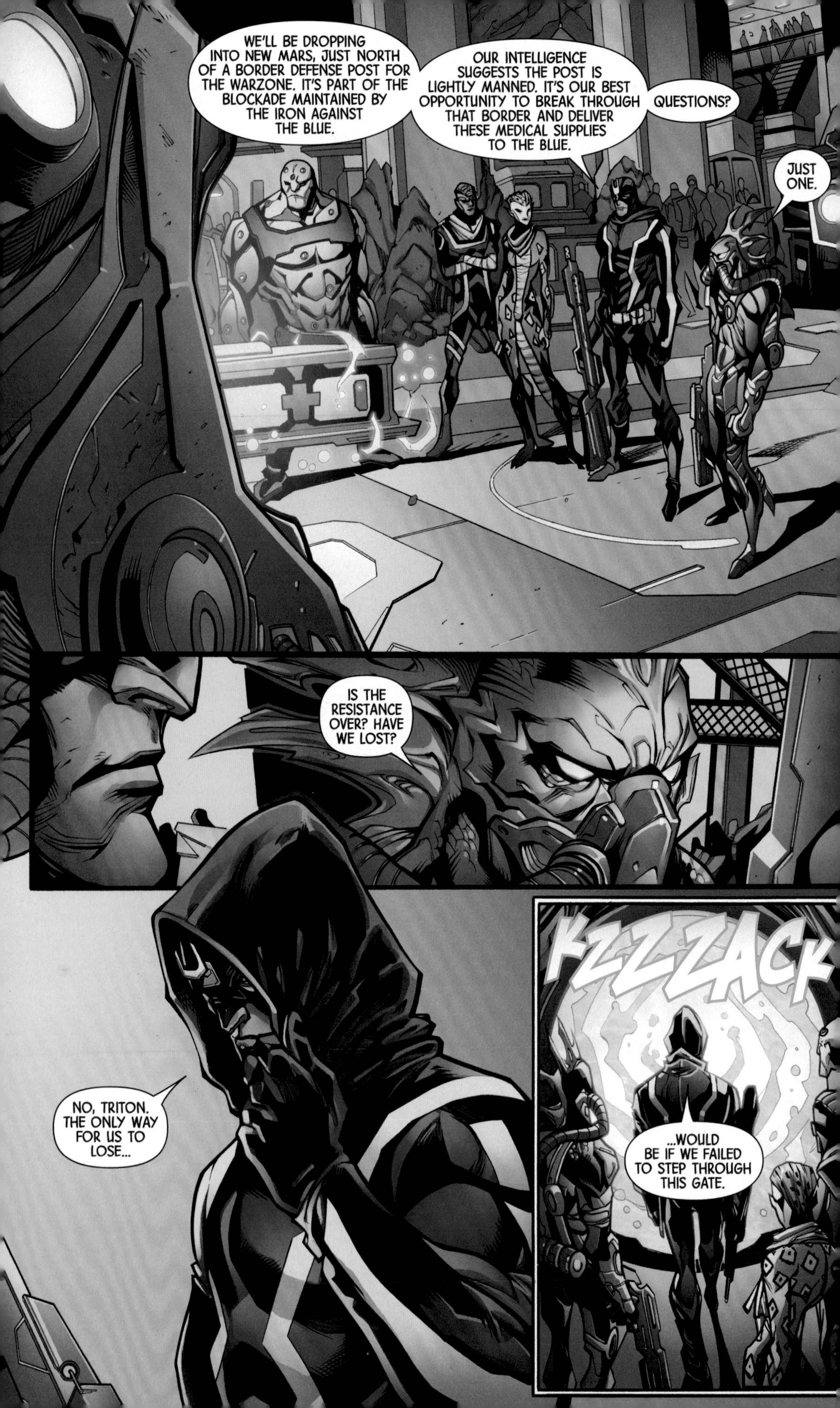
WE'LL BE DROPPING INTO NEW MARS, JUST NORTH OF A BORDER DEFENSE POST FOR THE WARZONE. IT'S PART OF THE BLOCKADE MAINTAINED BY THE IRON AGAINST THE BLUE.
OUR INTELLIGENCE SUGGESTS THE POST IS LIGHTLY MANNED. IT'S OUR BEST OPPORTUNITY TO BREAK THROUGH THAT BORDER AND DELIVER THESE MEDICAL SUPPLIES TO THE BLUE.
QUESTIONS?
JUST ONE.
IS THE RESISTANCE OVER? HAVE WE LOST?
NO, TRITON. THE ONLY WAY FOR US TO LOSE...
KZZZACK
...WOULD BE IF WE FAILED TO STEP THROUGH THIS GATE.

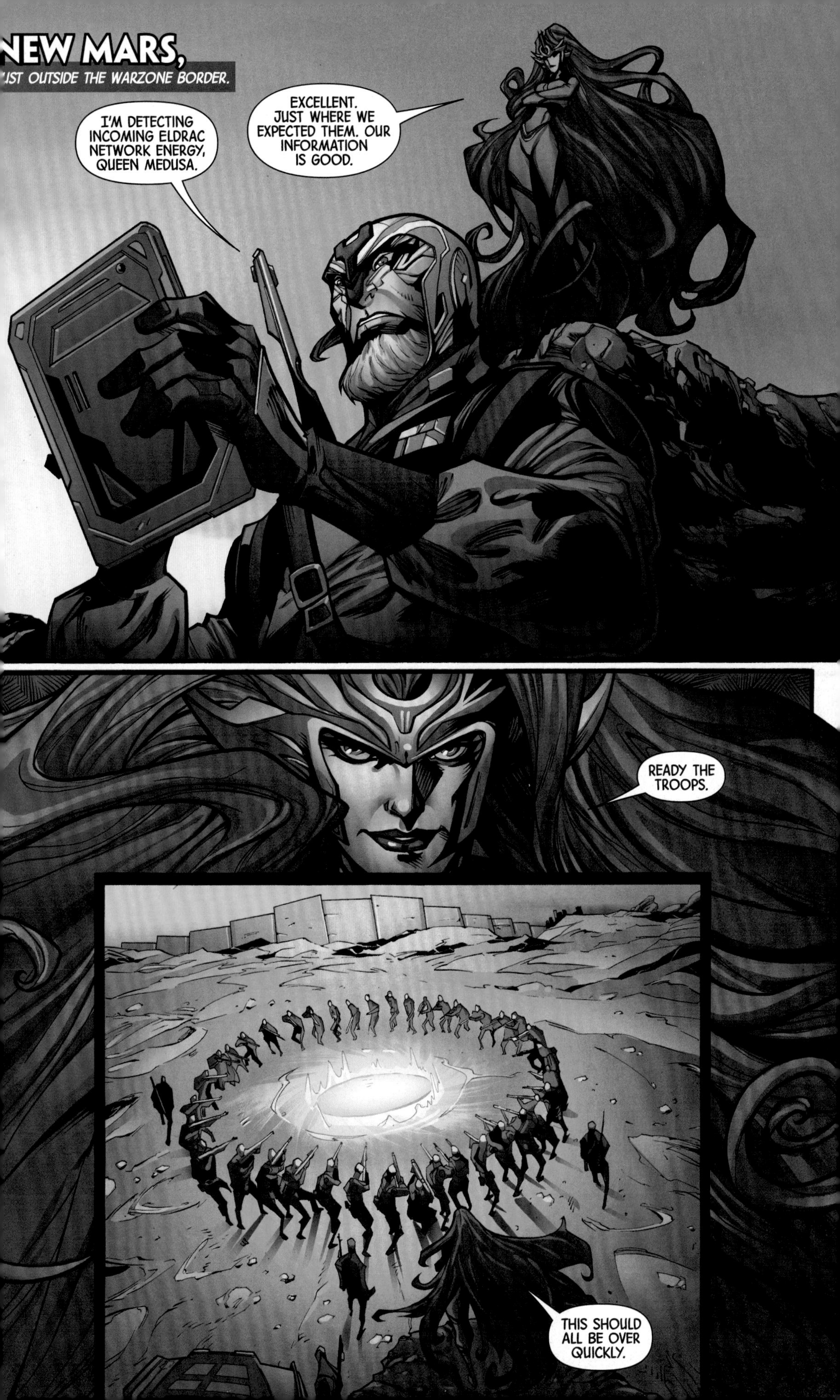
NEW MARS,
JUST OUTSIDE THE WARZONE BORDER.
I'M DETECTING INCOMING ELDRAC NETWORK ENERGY, QUEEN MEDUSA.
EXCELLENT. JUST WHERE WE EXPECTED THEM. OUR INFORMATION IS GOOD.
READY THE TROOPS.
THIS SHOULD ALL BE OVER QUICKLY.

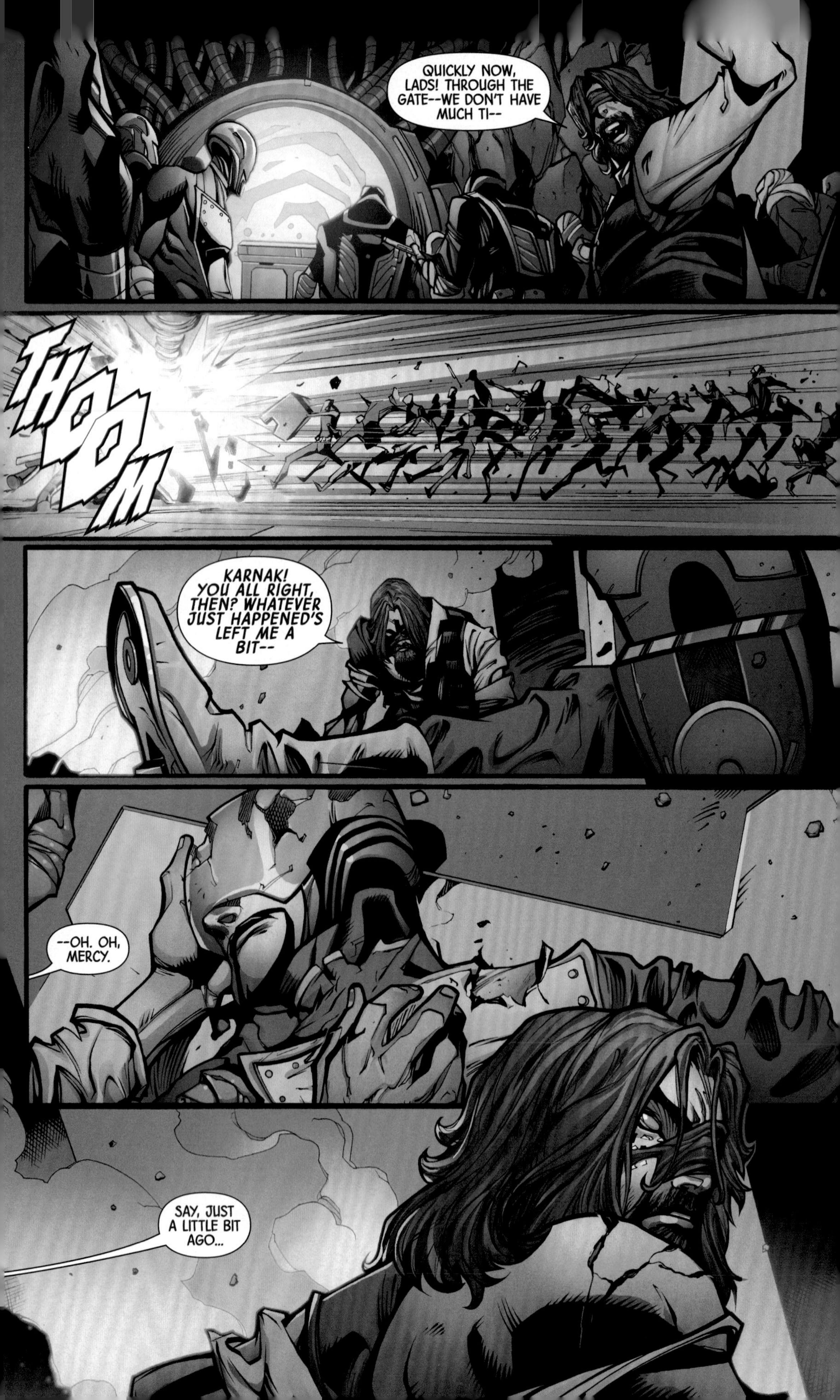
QUICKLY NOW, LADS! THROUGH THE GATE--WE DON'T HAVE MUCH TI--
THOOM
KARNAK! YOU ALL RIGHT, THEN? WHATEVER JUST HAPPENED'S LEFT ME A BIT--
--OH. OH, MERCY.
SAY, JUST A LITTLE BIT AGO...

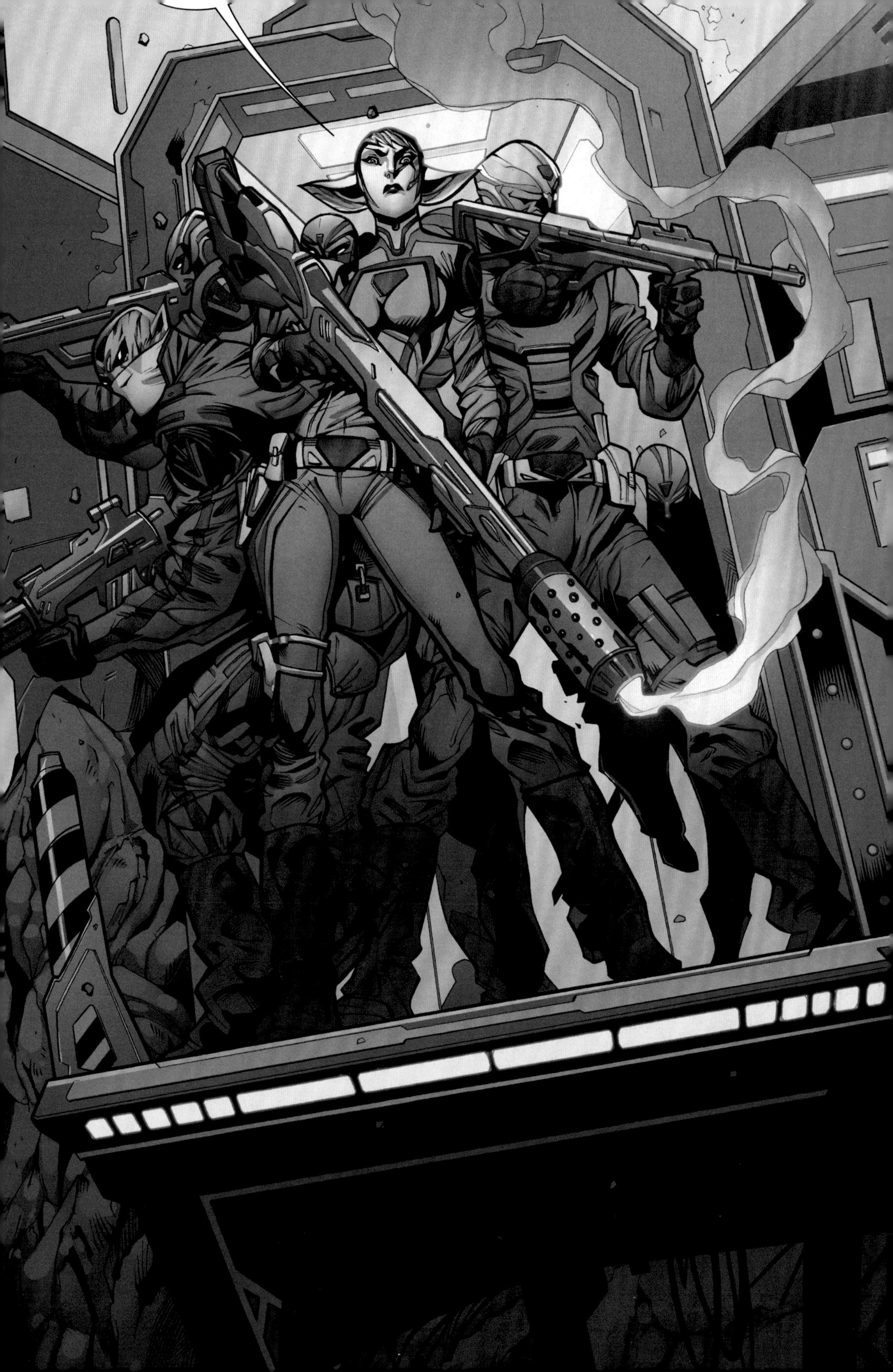

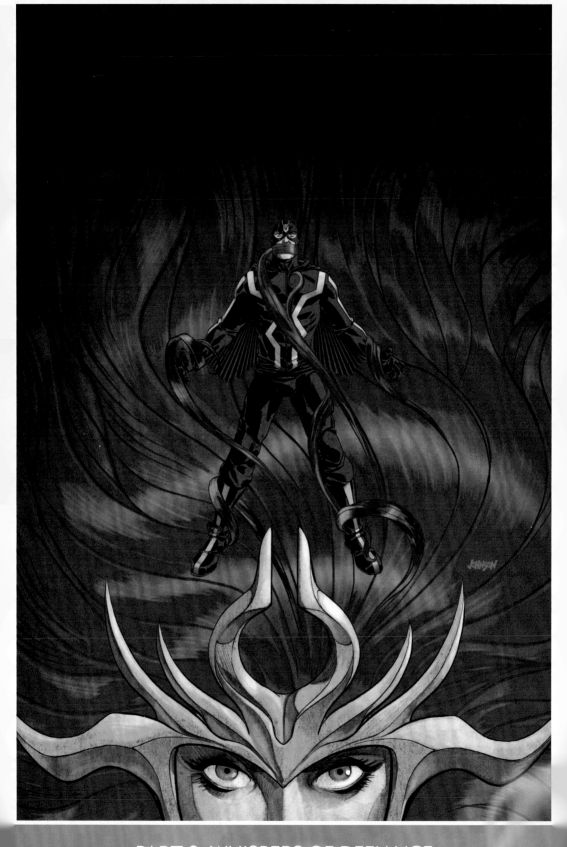

PART 3: WHISPERS OF DEFIANCE

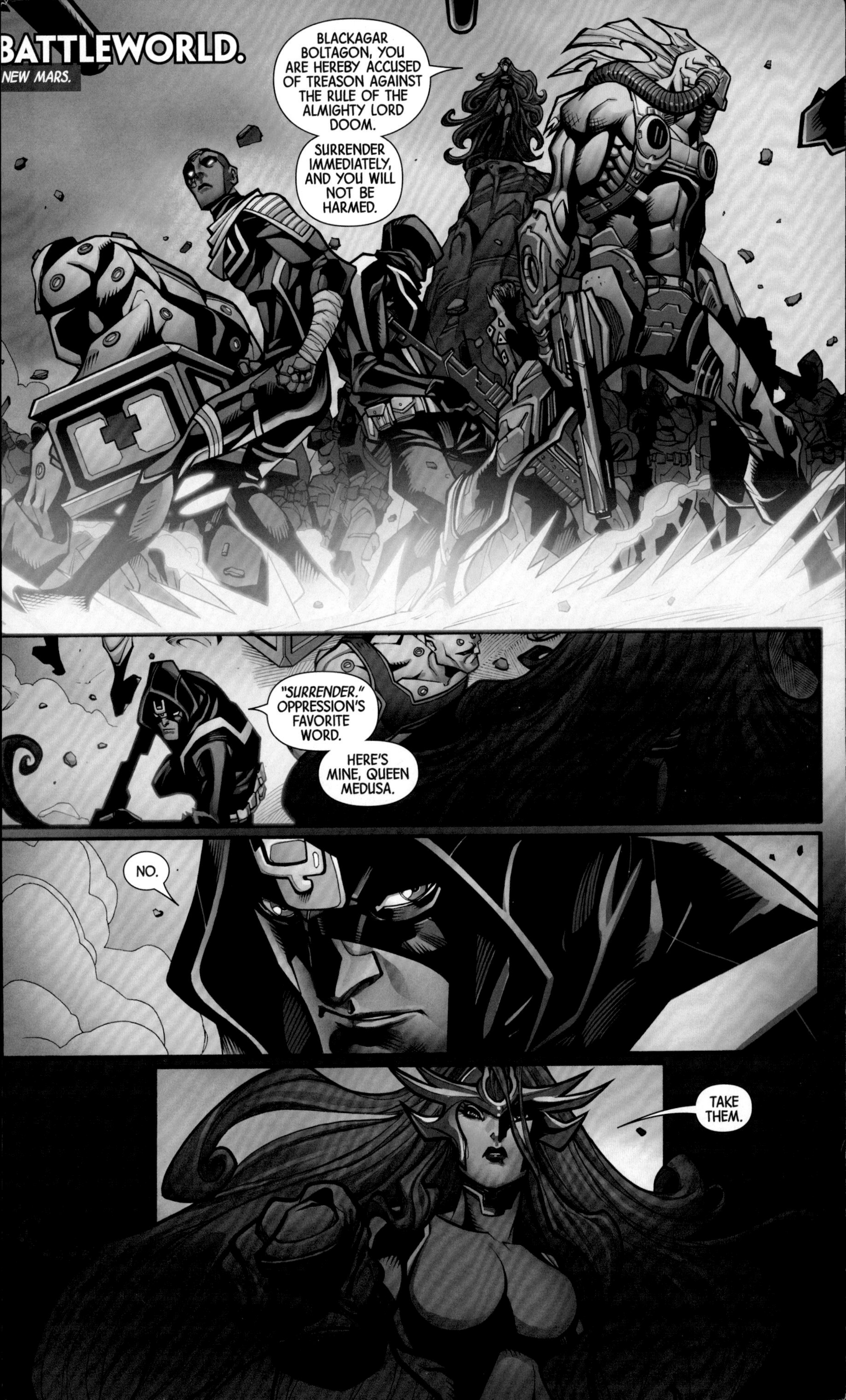
BATTLEWORLD.
NEW MARS.
BLACKAGAR BOLTAGON, YOU ARE HEREBY ACCUSED OF TREASON AGAINST THE RULE OF THE ALMIGHTY LORD DOOM.
SURRENDER IMMEDIATELY, AND YOU WILL NOT BE HARMED.
"SURRENDER." OPPRESSION'S FAVORITE WORD.
HERE'S MINE, QUEEN MEDUSA.
NO.
TAKE THEM.

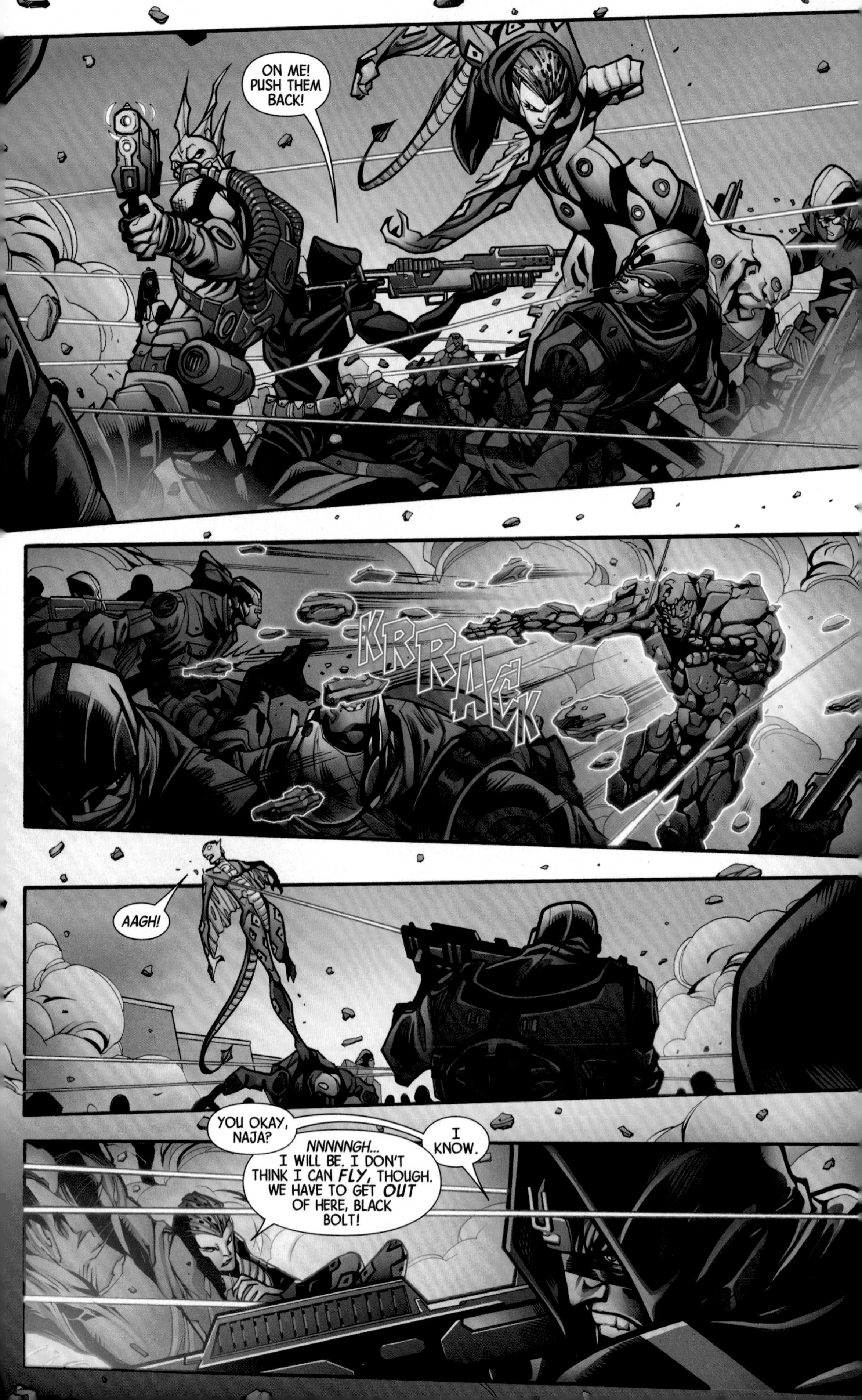
ON ME! PUSH THEM BACK!
KRRACK
AAGH!
YOU OKAY, NAJA?
NNNNNGH... I WILL BE. I DON'T THINK I CAN FLY, THOUGH. WE HAVE TO GET OUT OF HERE, BLACK BOLT!
I KNOW.

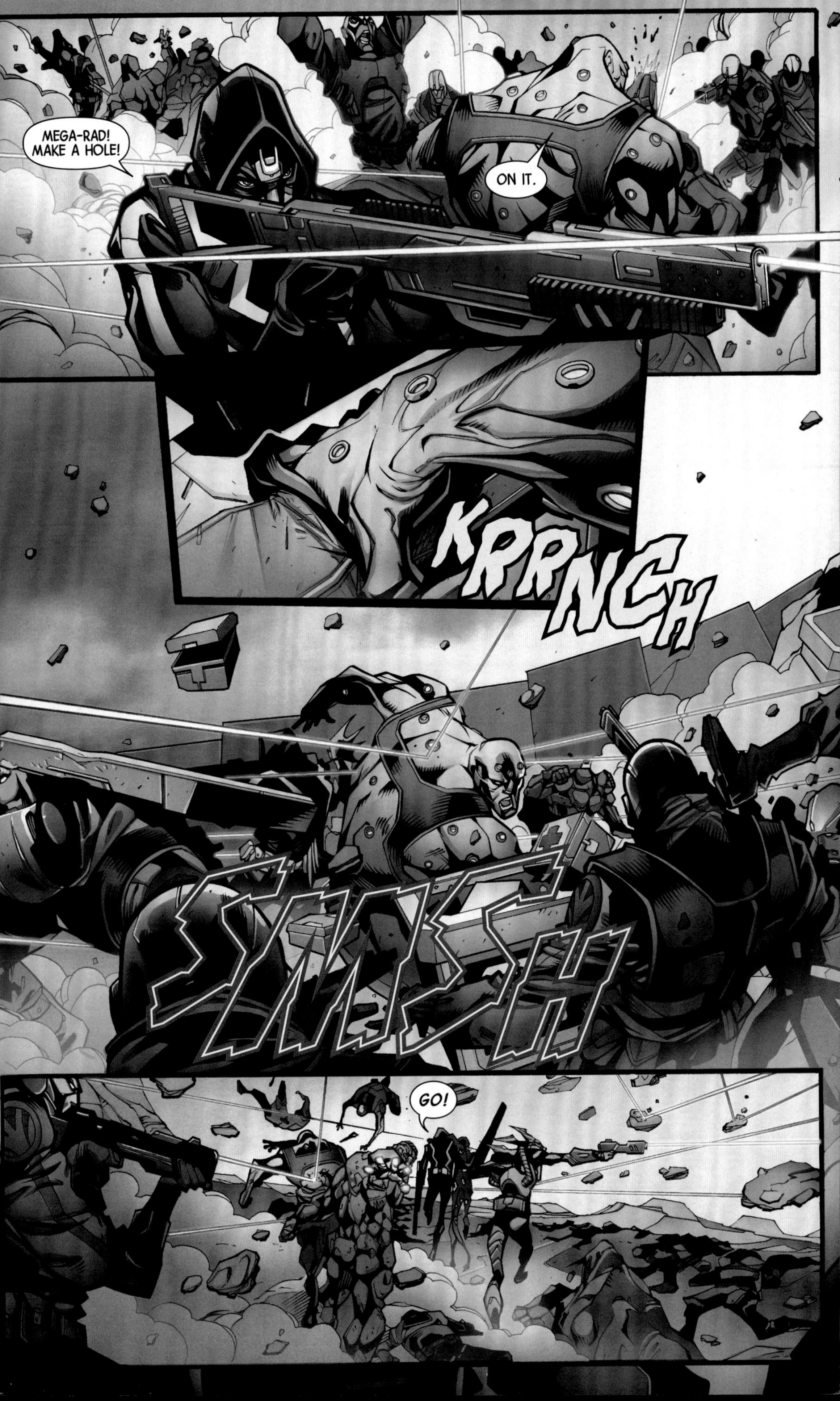
MEGA-RAD! MAKE A HOLE!
ON IT.
KRRNCH
SMASH
GO!

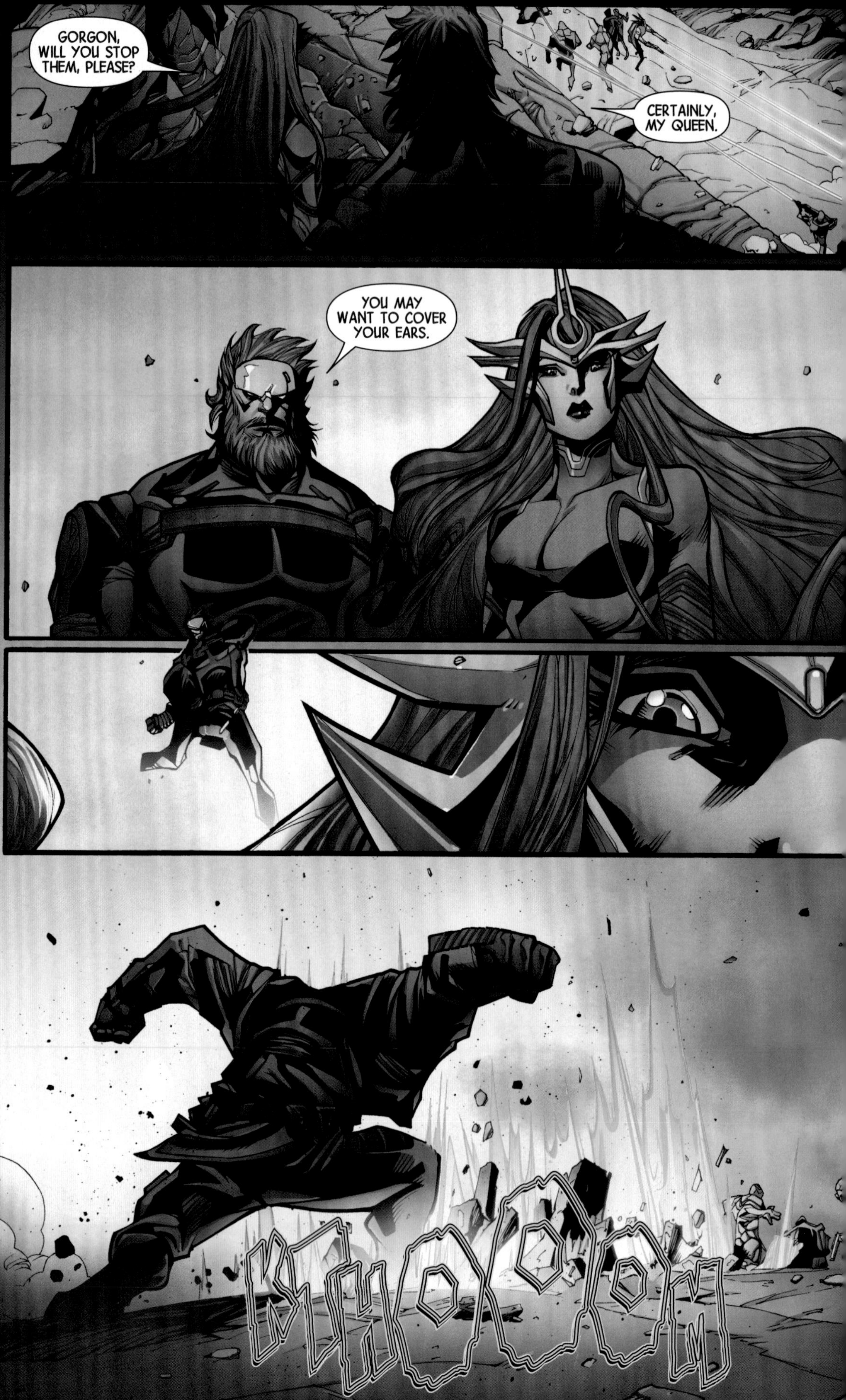
GORGON, WILL YOU STOP THEM, PLEASE?
CERTAINLY, MY QUEEN.
YOU MAY WANT TO COVER YOUR EARS.
KTHOOOOM

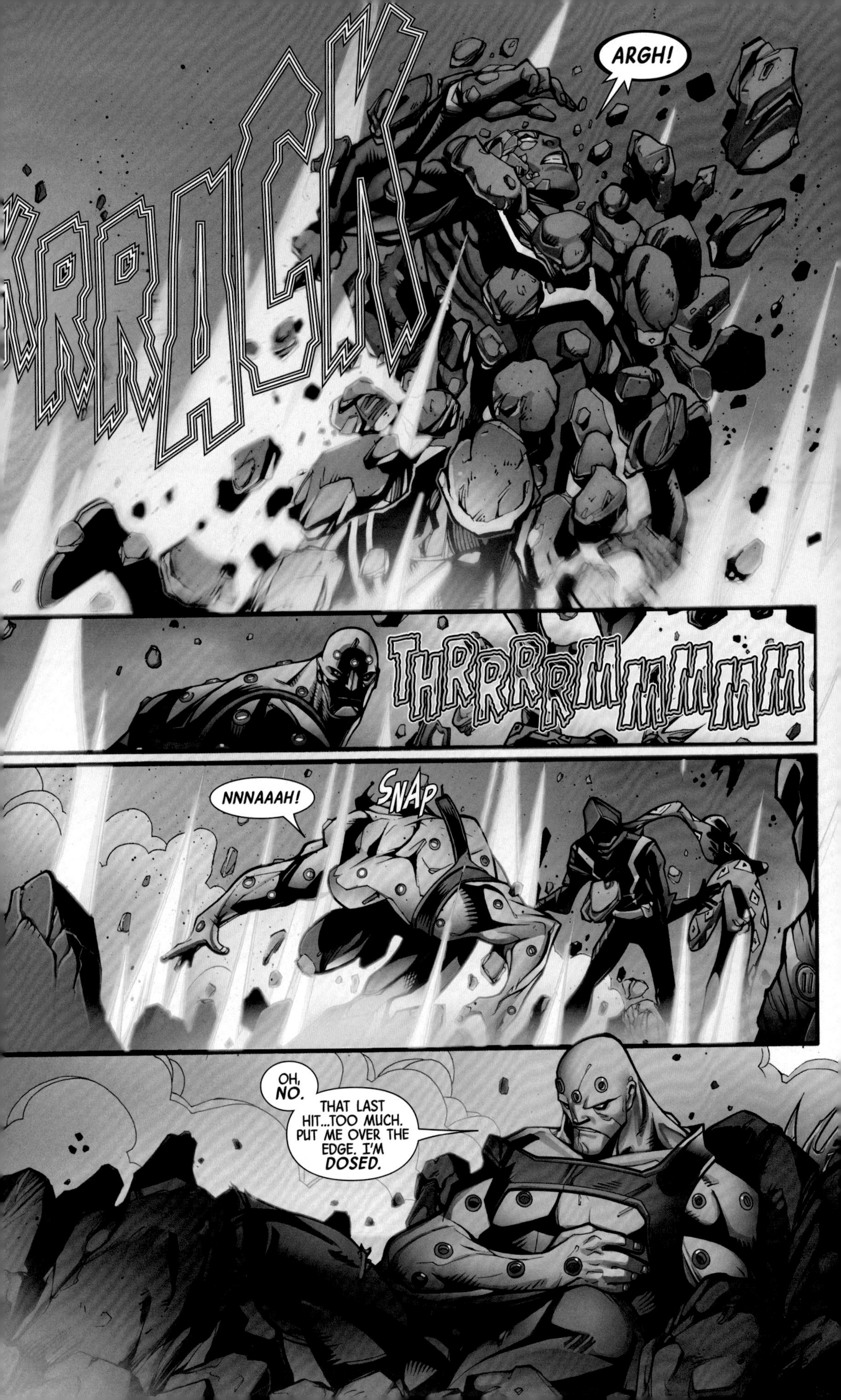
KRRACK
ARGH!
THRRRRMMMMMM
NNNAAAH!
SNAP
OH, NO.
THAT LAST HIT...TOO MUCH. PUT ME OVER THE EDGE. I'M DOSED.

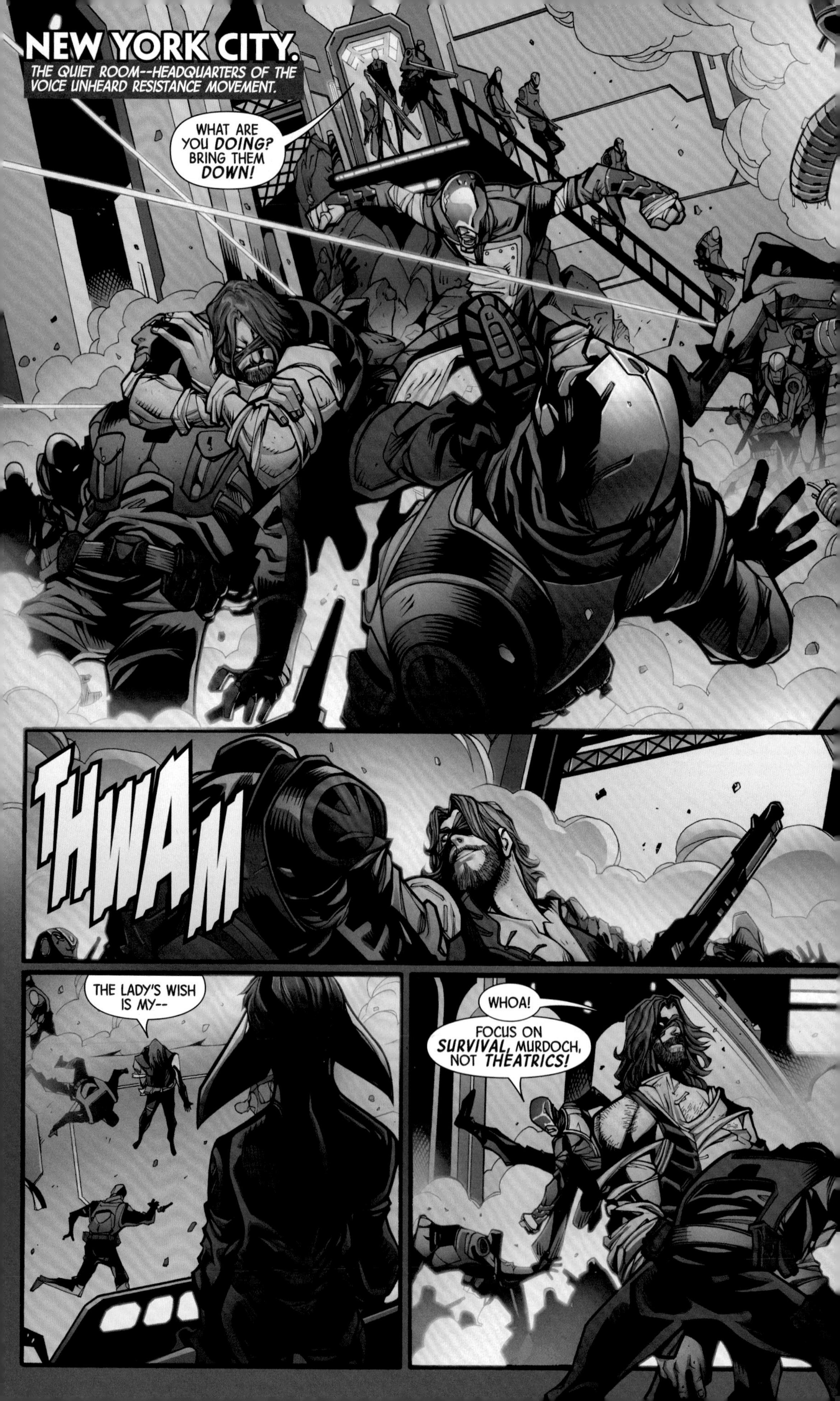
NEW YORK CITY.
THE QUIET ROOM--HEADQUARTERS OF THE VOICE UNHEARD RESISTANCE MOVEMENT.
WHAT ARE YOU DOING? BRING THEM DOWN!
THWAM
THE LADY'S WISH IS MY--
WHOA!
FOCUS ON SURVIVAL, MURDOCH, NOT THEATRICS!

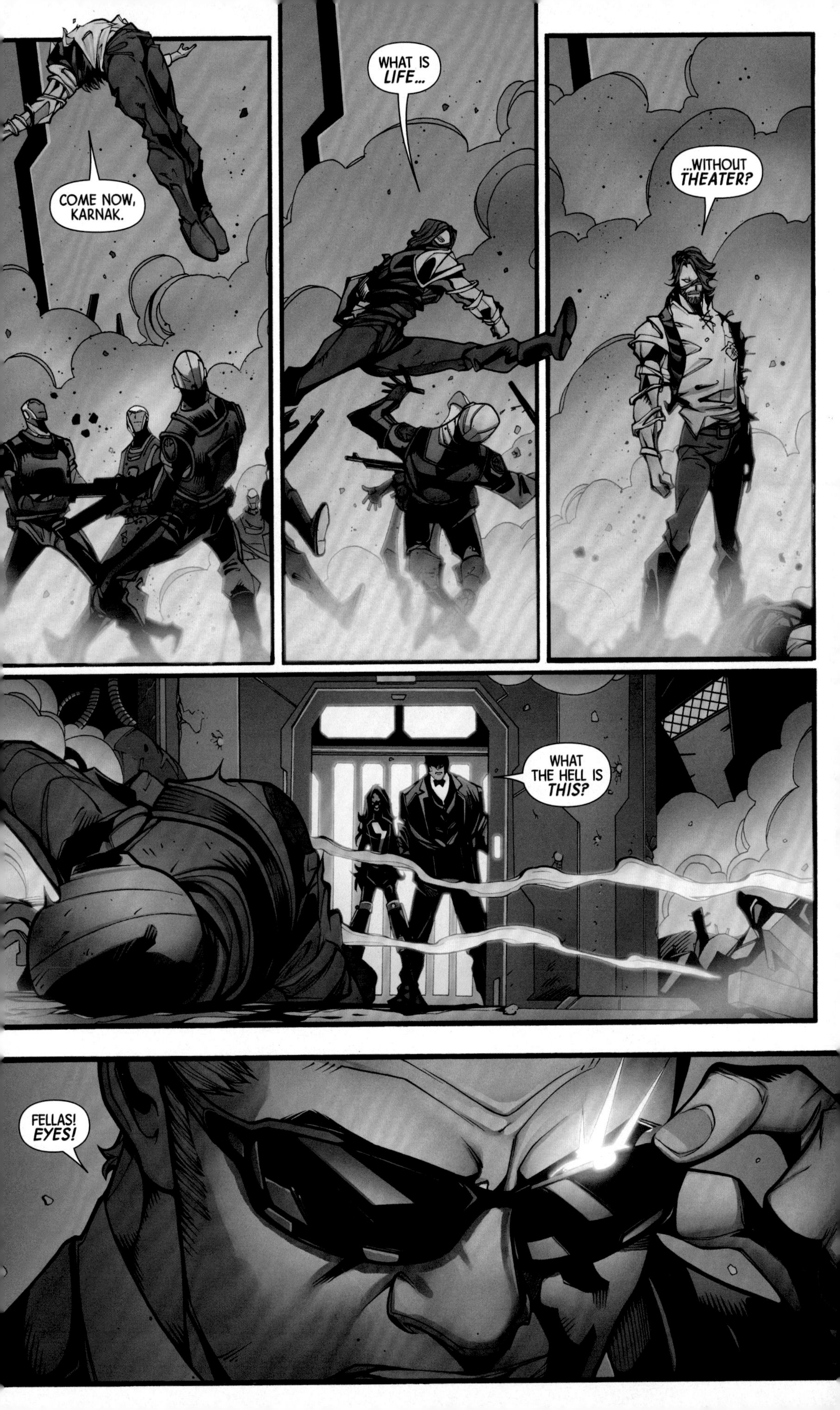
COME NOW, KARNAK.
WHAT IS LIFE...
...WITHOUT THEATER?
WHAT THE HELL IS THIS?
FELLAS! EYES!

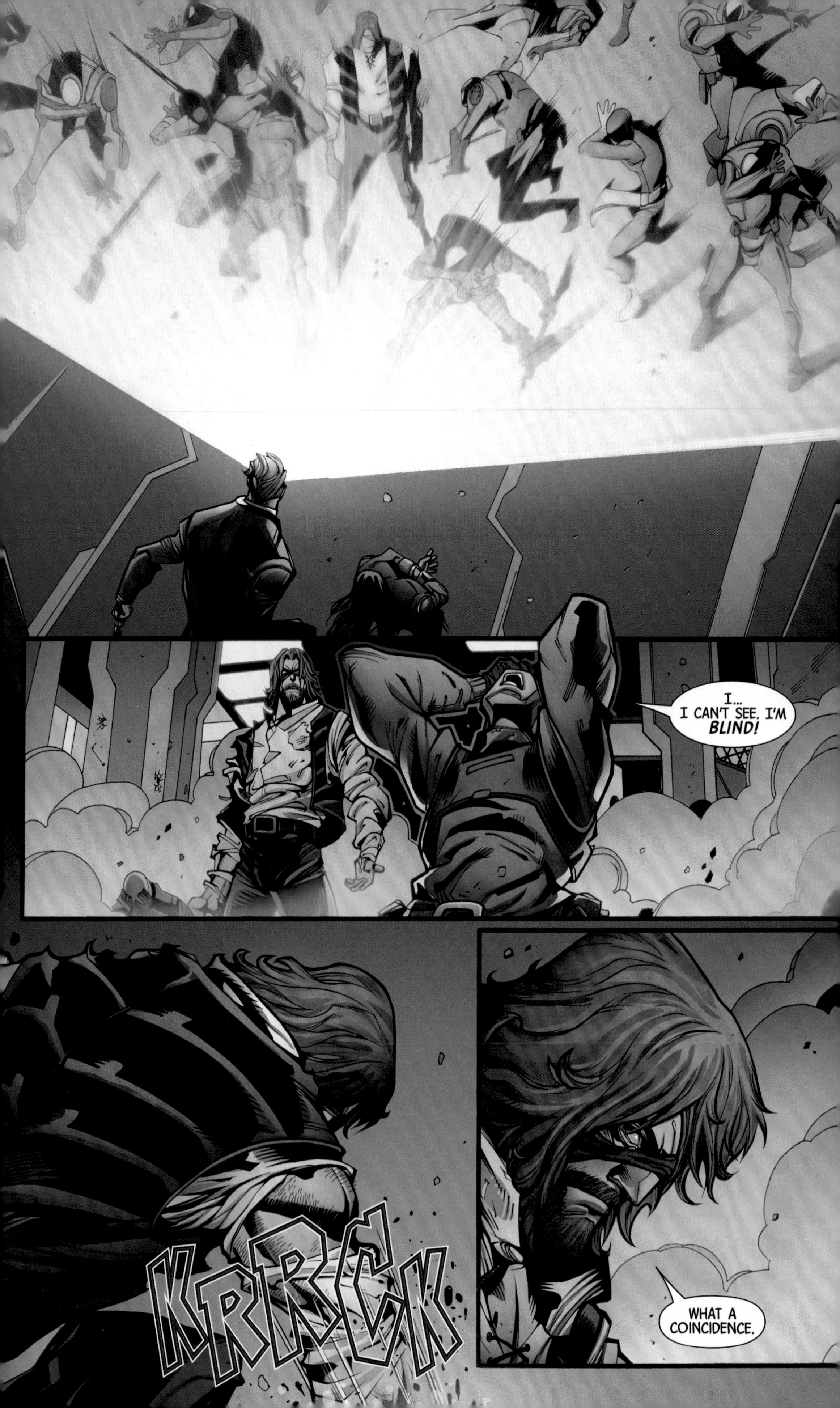

I... I CAN'T SEE. I'M *BLIND!*
KRRCK
WHAT A COINCIDENCE.

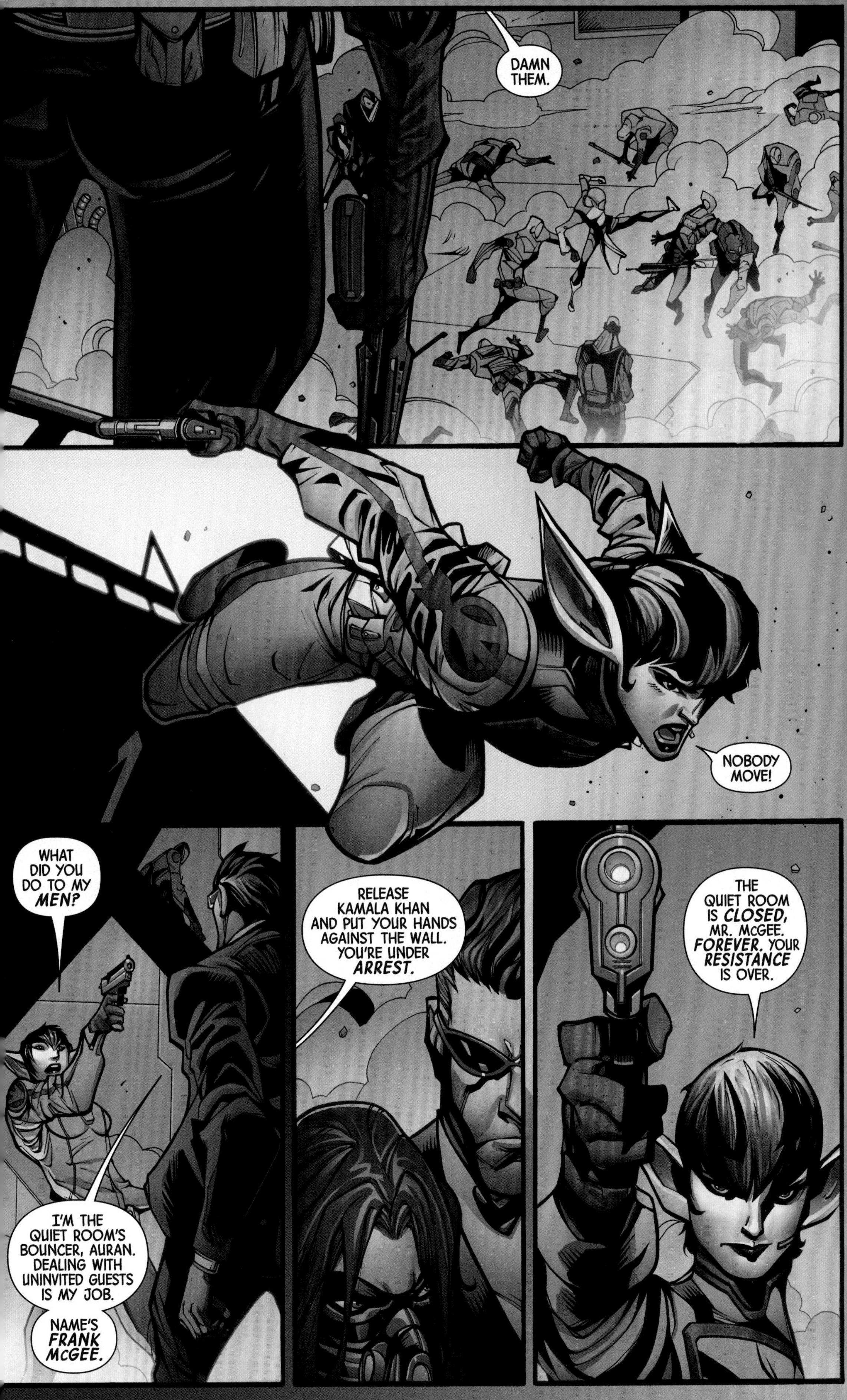
DAMN THEM.
NOBODY MOVE!
WHAT DID YOU DO TO MY MEN?
I'M THE QUIET ROOM'S BOUNCER, AURAN. DEALING WITH UNINVITED GUESTS IS MY JOB.
NAME'S FRANK McGEE.
RELEASE KAMALA KHAN AND PUT YOUR HANDS AGAINST THE WALL. YOU'RE UNDER ARREST.
THE QUIET ROOM IS CLOSED, MR. McGEE. FOREVER. YOUR RESISTANCE IS OVER.

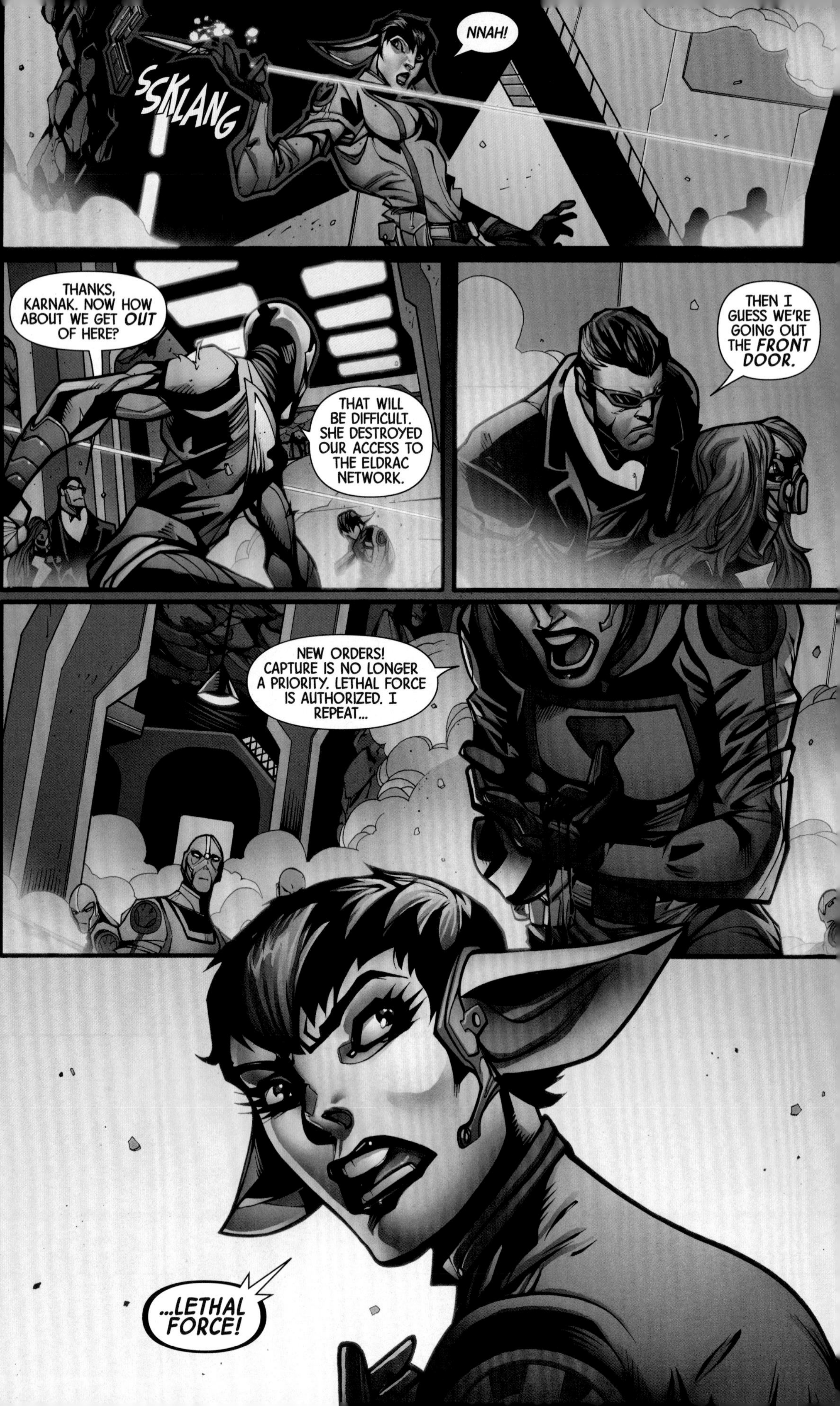
SSKLANG
NNAH!
THANKS, KARNAK. NOW HOW ABOUT WE GET OUT OF HERE?
THAT WILL BE DIFFICULT. SHE DESTROYED OUR ACCESS TO THE ELDRAC NETWORK.
THEN I GUESS WE'RE GOING OUT THE FRONT DOOR.
NEW ORDERS! CAPTURE IS NO LONGER A PRIORITY. LETHAL FORCE IS AUTHORIZED. I REPEAT...
...LETHAL FORCE!

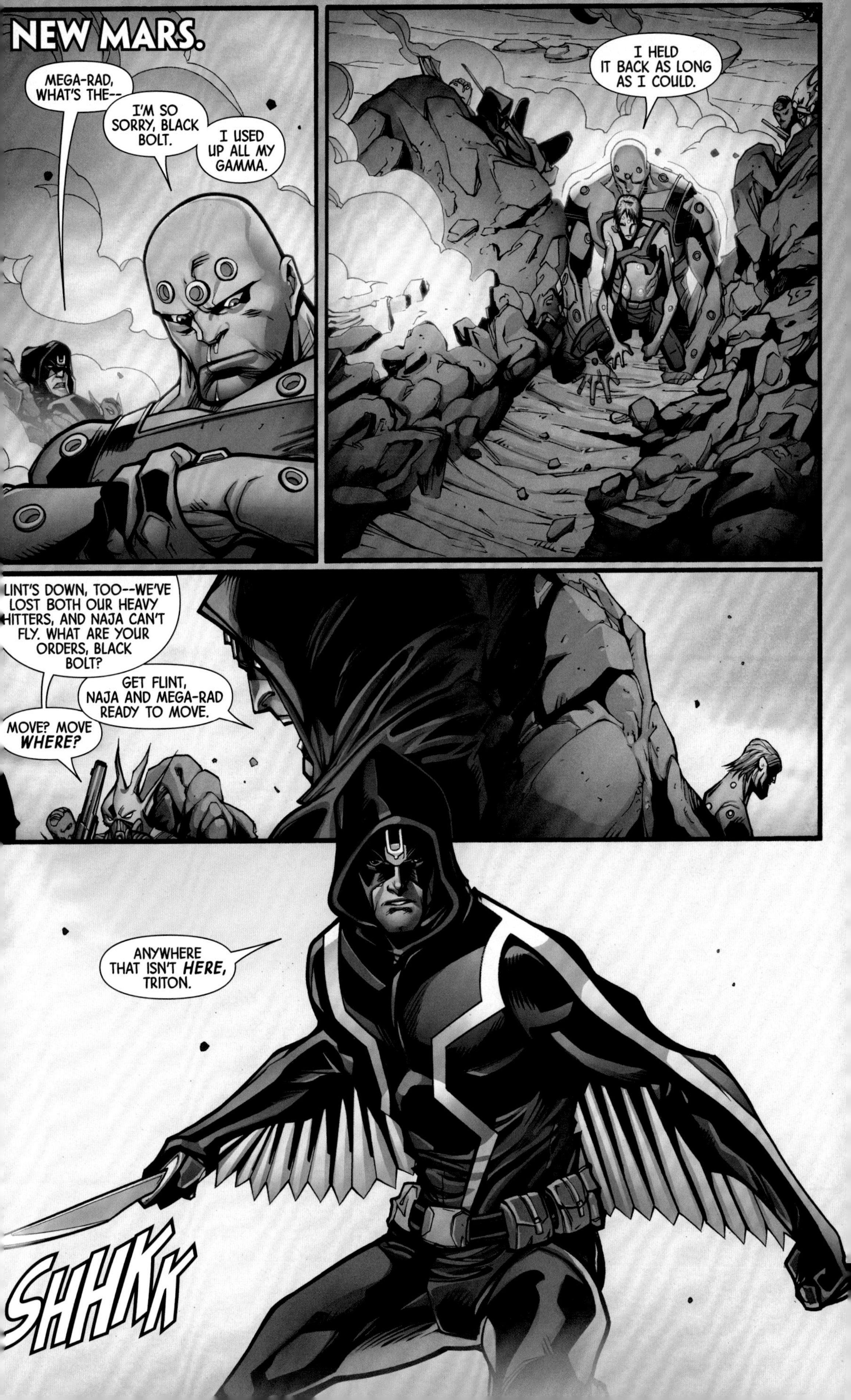
NEW MARS.
MEGA-RAD, WHAT'S THE--
I'M SO SORRY, BLACK BOLT.
I USED UP ALL MY GAMMA.
I HELD IT BACK AS LONG AS I COULD.
LINT'S DOWN, TOO--WE'VE LOST BOTH OUR HEAVY HITTERS, AND NAJA CAN'T FLY. WHAT ARE YOUR ORDERS, BLACK BOLT?
GET FLINT, NAJA AND MEGA-RAD READY TO MOVE.
MOVE? MOVE *WHERE?*
ANYWHERE THAT ISN'T *HERE,* TRITON.
SHHKK

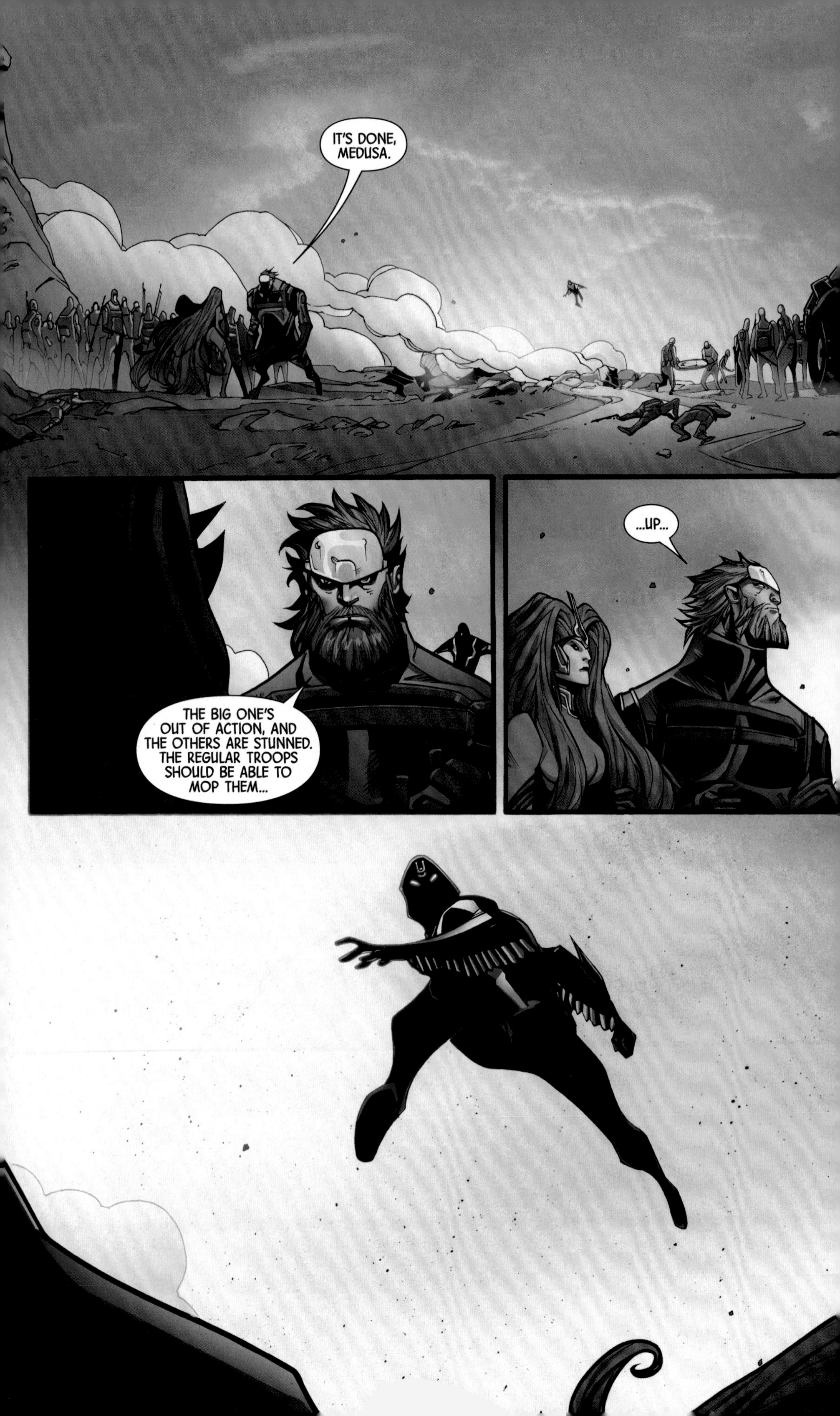
IT'S DONE, MEDUSA.
THE BIG ONE'S OUT OF ACTION, AND THE OTHERS ARE STUNNED. THE REGULAR TROOPS SHOULD BE ABLE TO MOP THEM...
...UP...

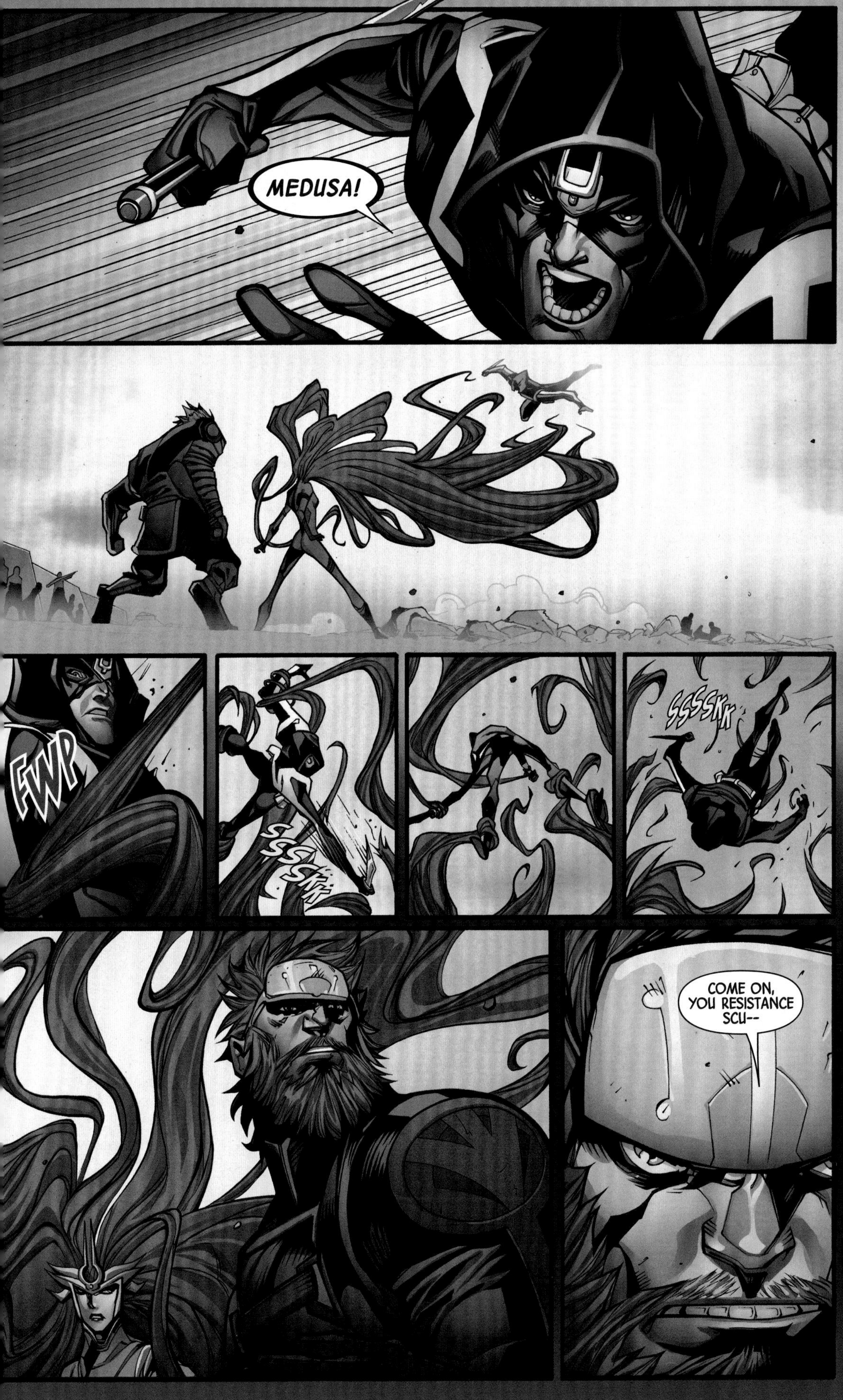
MEDUSA!
FWP
SSSSKK
SSSSKK
COME ON, YOU RESISTANCE SCU--

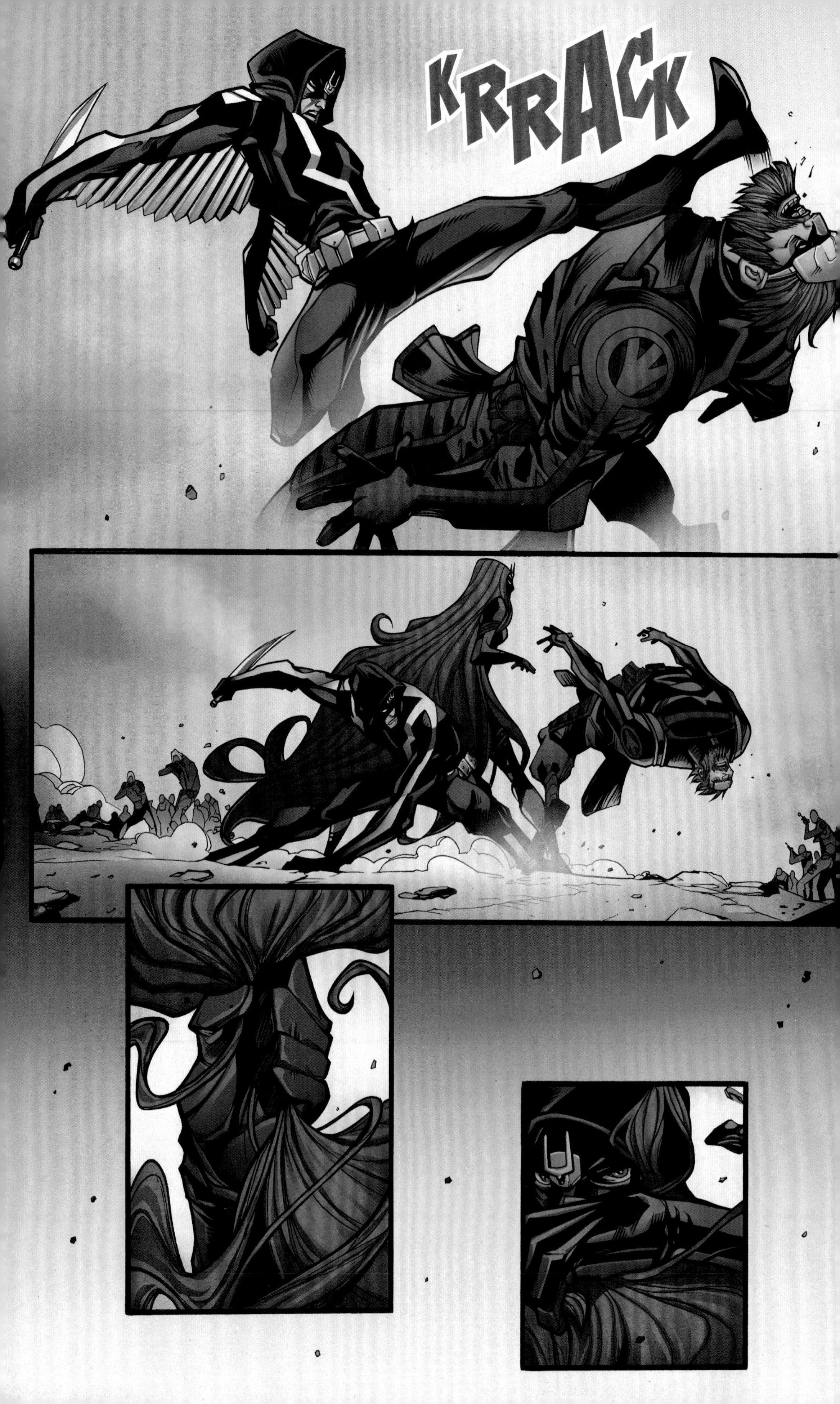
KRRACK

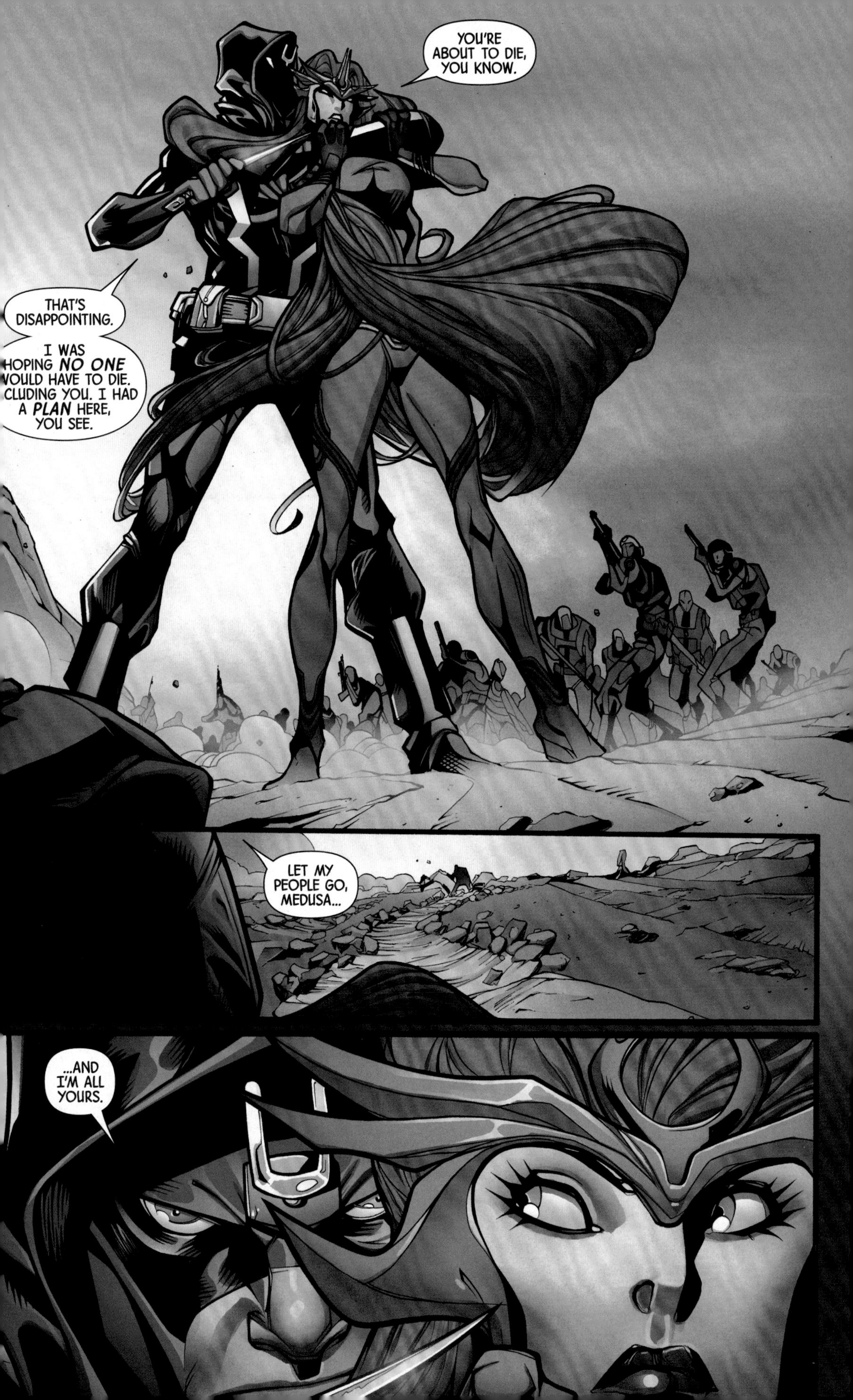
YOU'RE ABOUT TO DIE, YOU KNOW.
THAT'S DISAPPOINTING.
I WAS HOPING NO ONE VOULD HAVE TO DIE. CLUDING YOU. I HAD A PLAN HERE, YOU SEE.
LET MY PEOPLE GO, MEDUSA...
...AND I'M ALL YOURS.

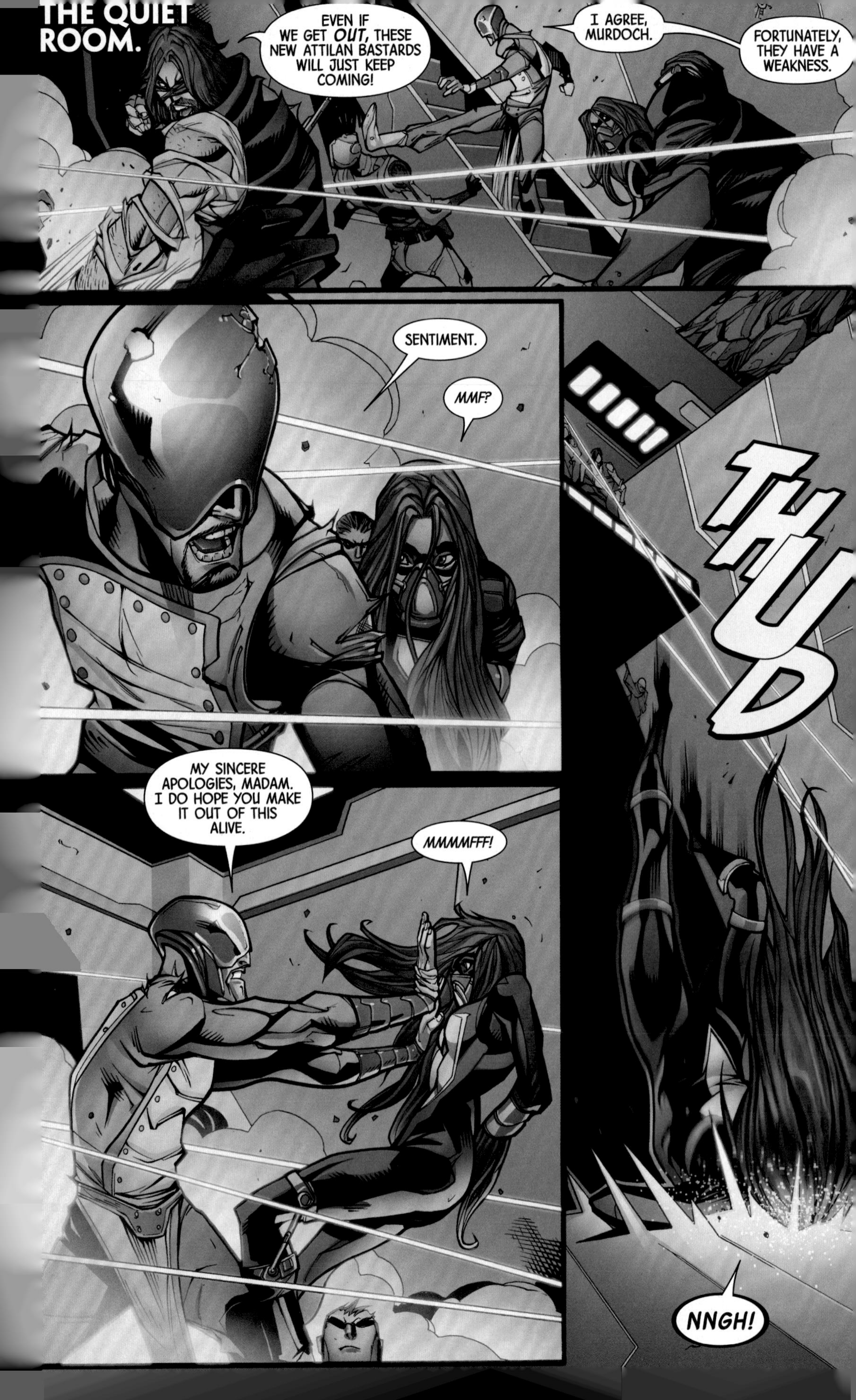
THE QUIET ROOM.
EVEN IF WE GET OUT, THESE NEW ATTILAN BASTARDS WILL JUST KEEP COMING!
I AGREE, MURDOCH.
FORTUNATELY, THEY HAVE A WEAKNESS.
SENTIMENT.
MMF?
MY SINCERE APOLOGIES, MADAM. I DO HOPE YOU MAKE IT OUT OF THIS ALIVE.
MMMMFFF!
THUD
NNGH!

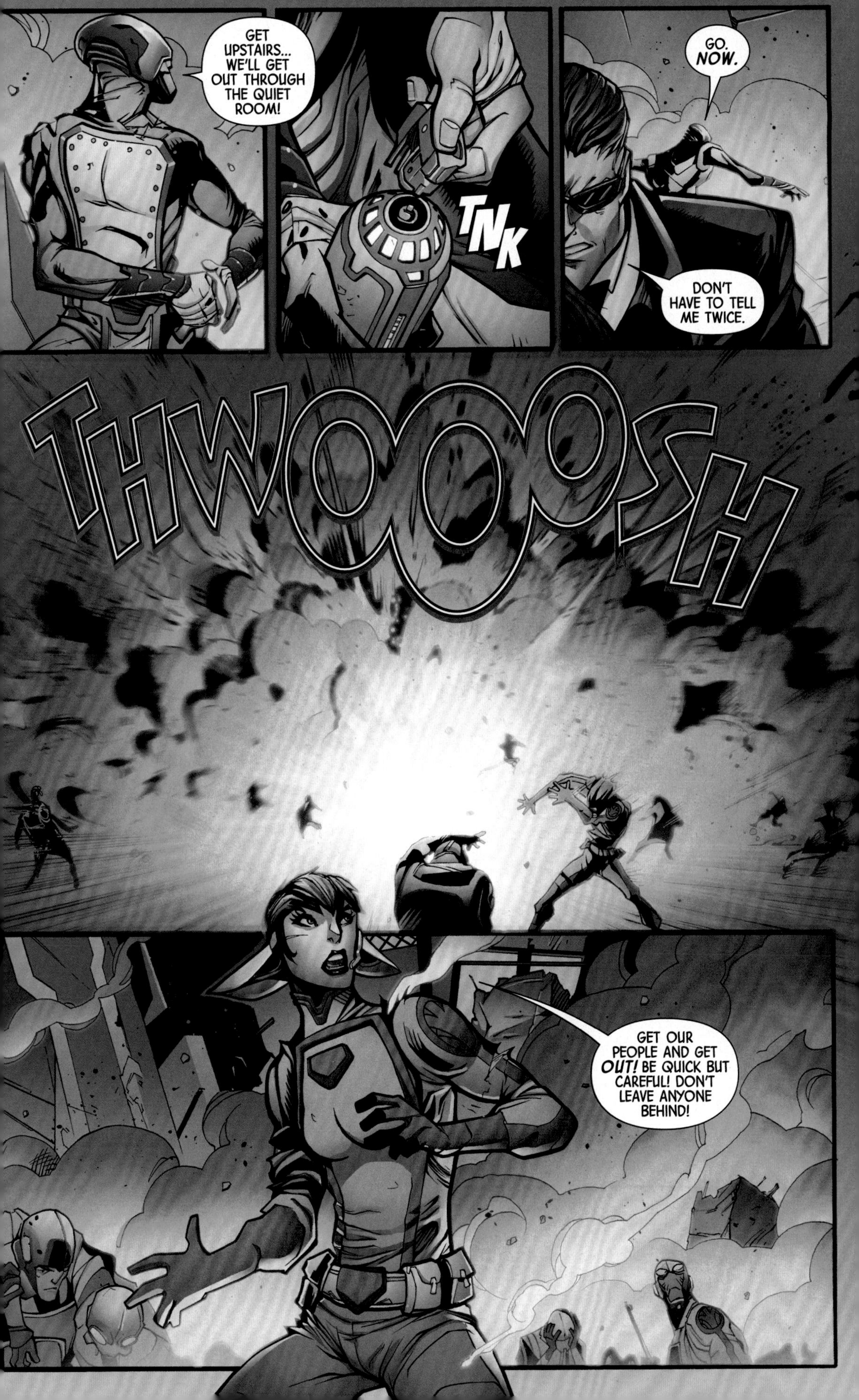
GET UPSTAIRS... WE'LL GET OUT THROUGH THE QUIET ROOM!
TNK
GO. NOW.
DON'T HAVE TO TELL ME TWICE.
THWOOOSH
GET OUR PEOPLE AND GET OUT! BE QUICK BUT CAREFUL! DON'T LEAVE ANYONE BEHIND!

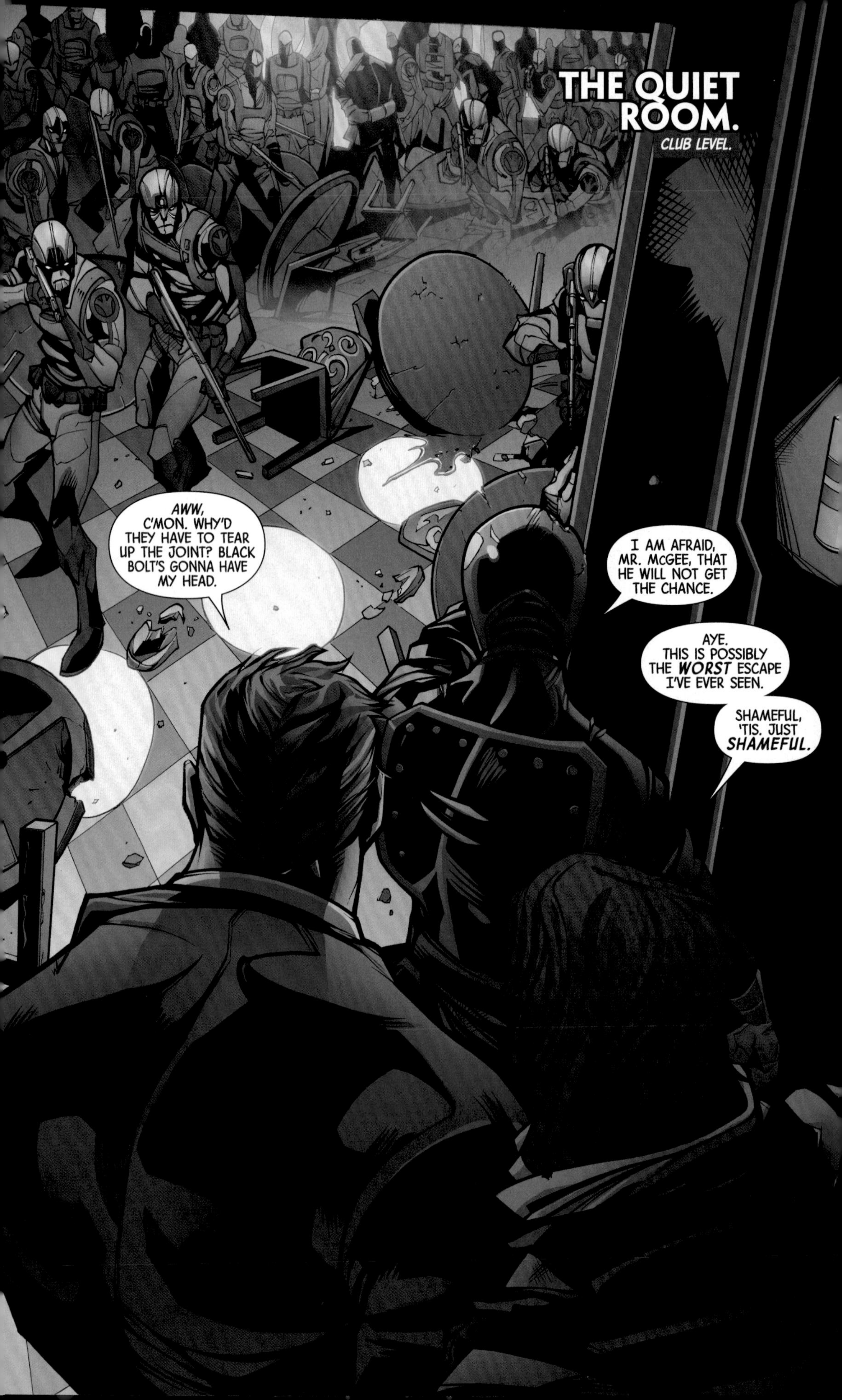
THE QUIET ROOM.
CLUB LEVEL.
AWW, C'MON. WHY'D THEY HAVE TO TEAR UP THE JOINT? BLACK BOLT'S GONNA HAVE MY HEAD.
I AM AFRAID, MR. McGEE, THAT HE WILL NOT GET THE CHANCE.
AYE. THIS IS POSSIBLY THE WORST ESCAPE I'VE EVER SEEN.
SHAMEFUL, 'TIS. JUST SHAMEFUL.

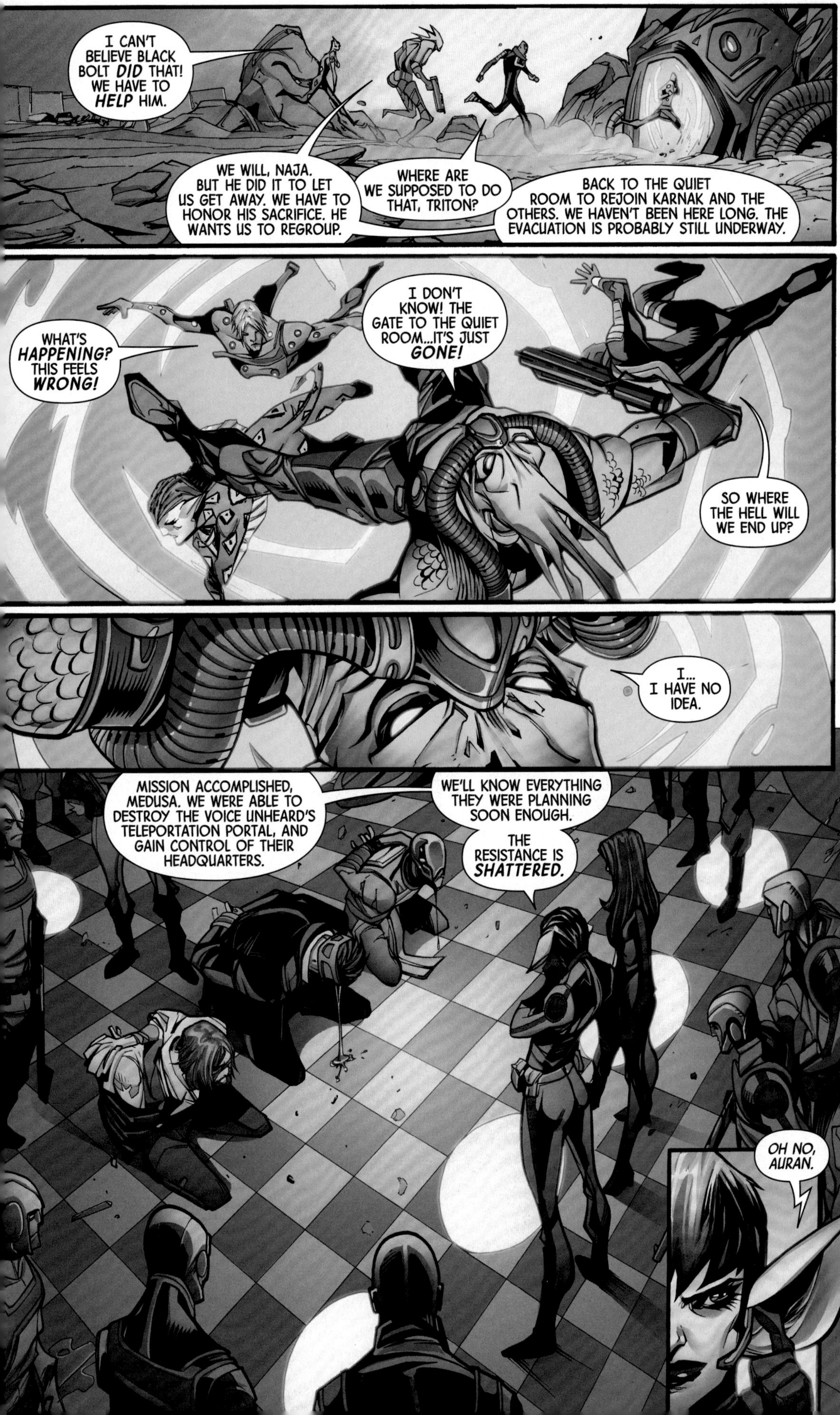

I CAN'T BELIEVE BLACK BOLT DID THAT! WE HAVE TO HELP HIM.
WE WILL, NAJA. BUT HE DID IT TO LET US GET AWAY. WE HAVE TO HONOR HIS SACRIFICE. HE WANTS US TO REGROUP.
WHERE ARE WE SUPPOSED TO DO THAT, TRITON?
BACK TO THE QUIET ROOM TO REJOIN KARNAK AND THE OTHERS. WE HAVEN'T BEEN HERE LONG. THE EVACUATION IS PROBABLY STILL UNDERWAY.
WHAT'S HAPPENING? THIS FEELS WRONG!
I DON'T KNOW! THE GATE TO THE QUIET ROOM...IT'S JUST GONE!
SO WHERE THE HELL WILL WE END UP?
I... I HAVE NO IDEA.
MISSION ACCOMPLISHED, MEDUSA. WE WERE ABLE TO DESTROY THE VOICE UNHEARD'S TELEPORTATION PORTAL, AND GAIN CONTROL OF THEIR HEADQUARTERS.
WE'LL KNOW EVERYTHING THEY WERE PLANNING SOON ENOUGH.
THE RESISTANCE IS SHATTERED.
OH NO, AURAN.

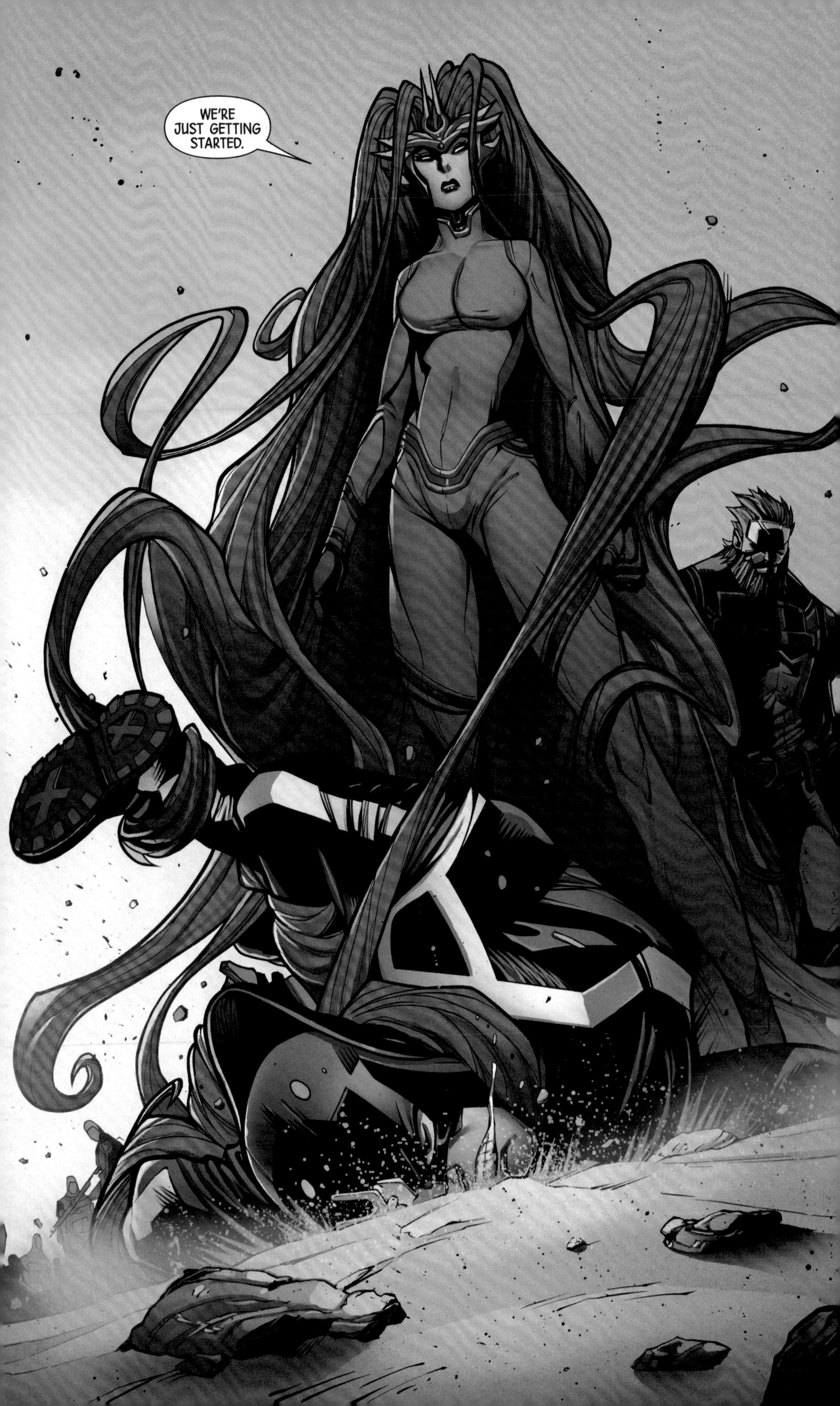
WE'RE JUST GETTING STARTED.

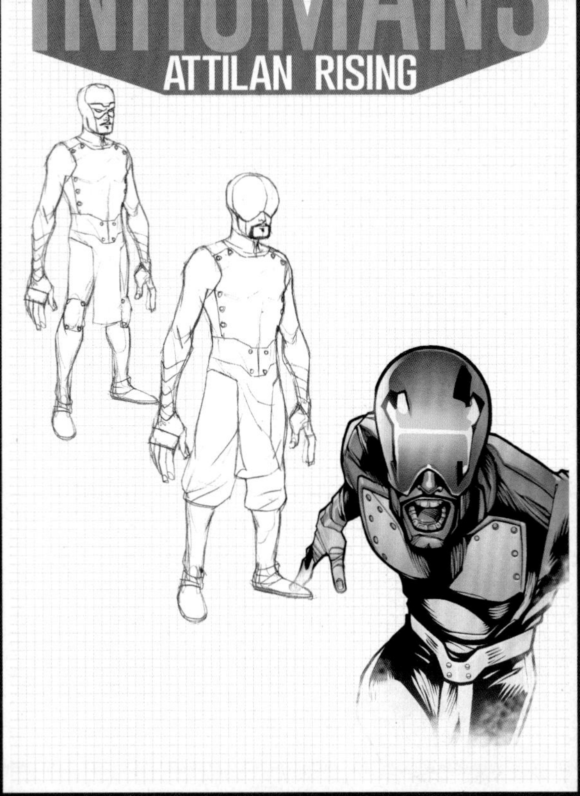
ATTILAN RISING

#4 DESIGN VARIANT BY DAVE

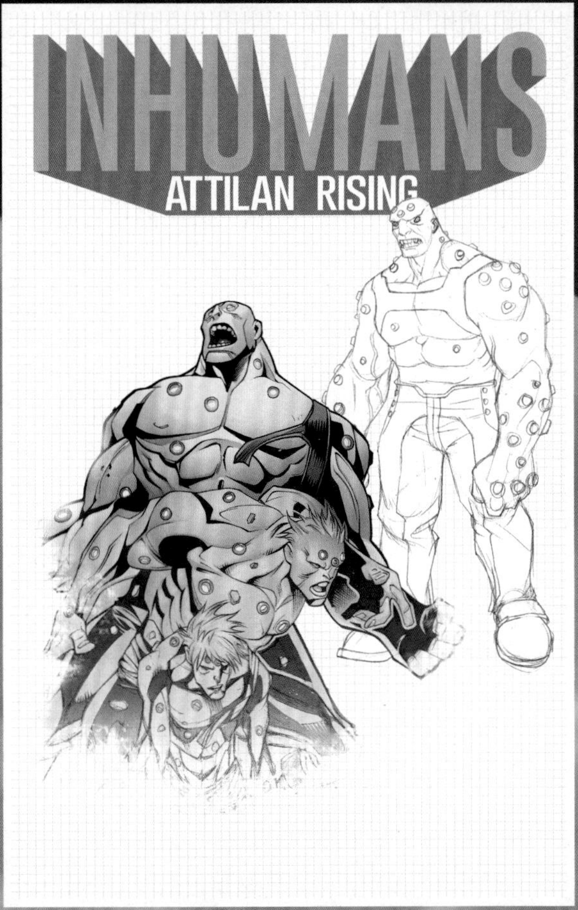
INHUMANS
ATTILAN RISING

 # 5 DESIGN VARIANT BY DAVE JOHNSON

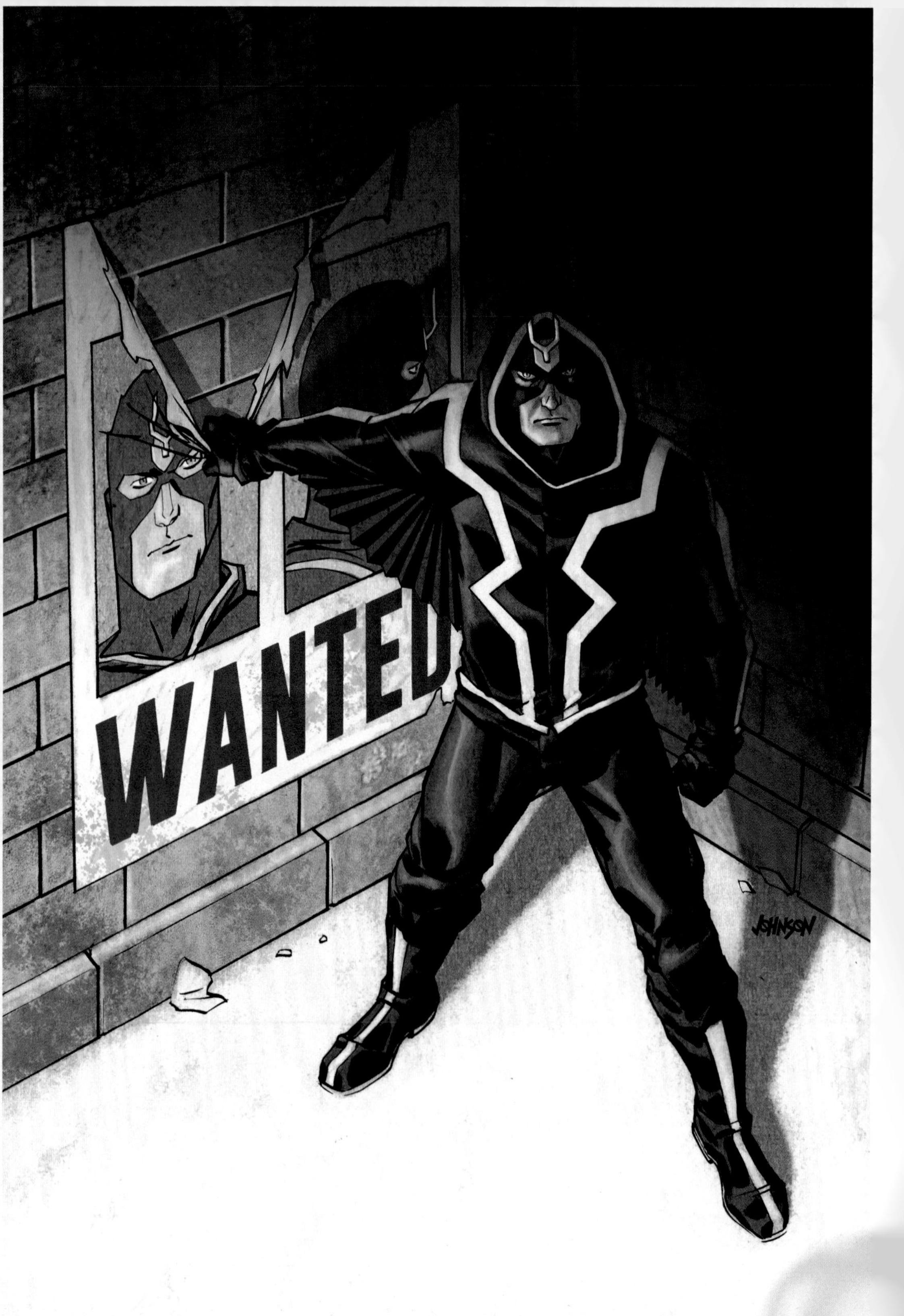
WANTED
JOHNSON

PART 4: THE SILENT HORROR

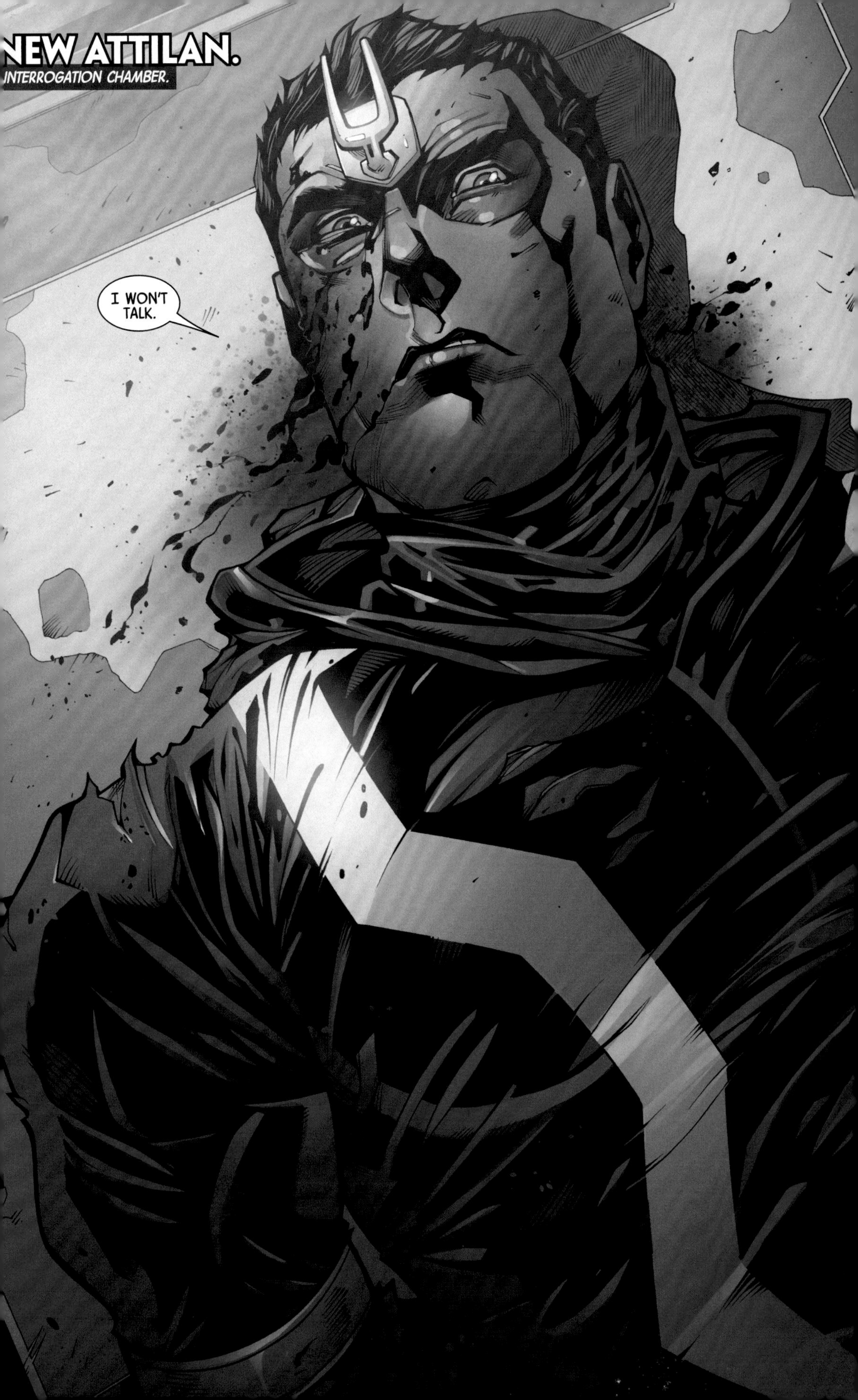
NEW ATTILAN.
INTERROGATION CHAMBER.
I WON'T TALK.

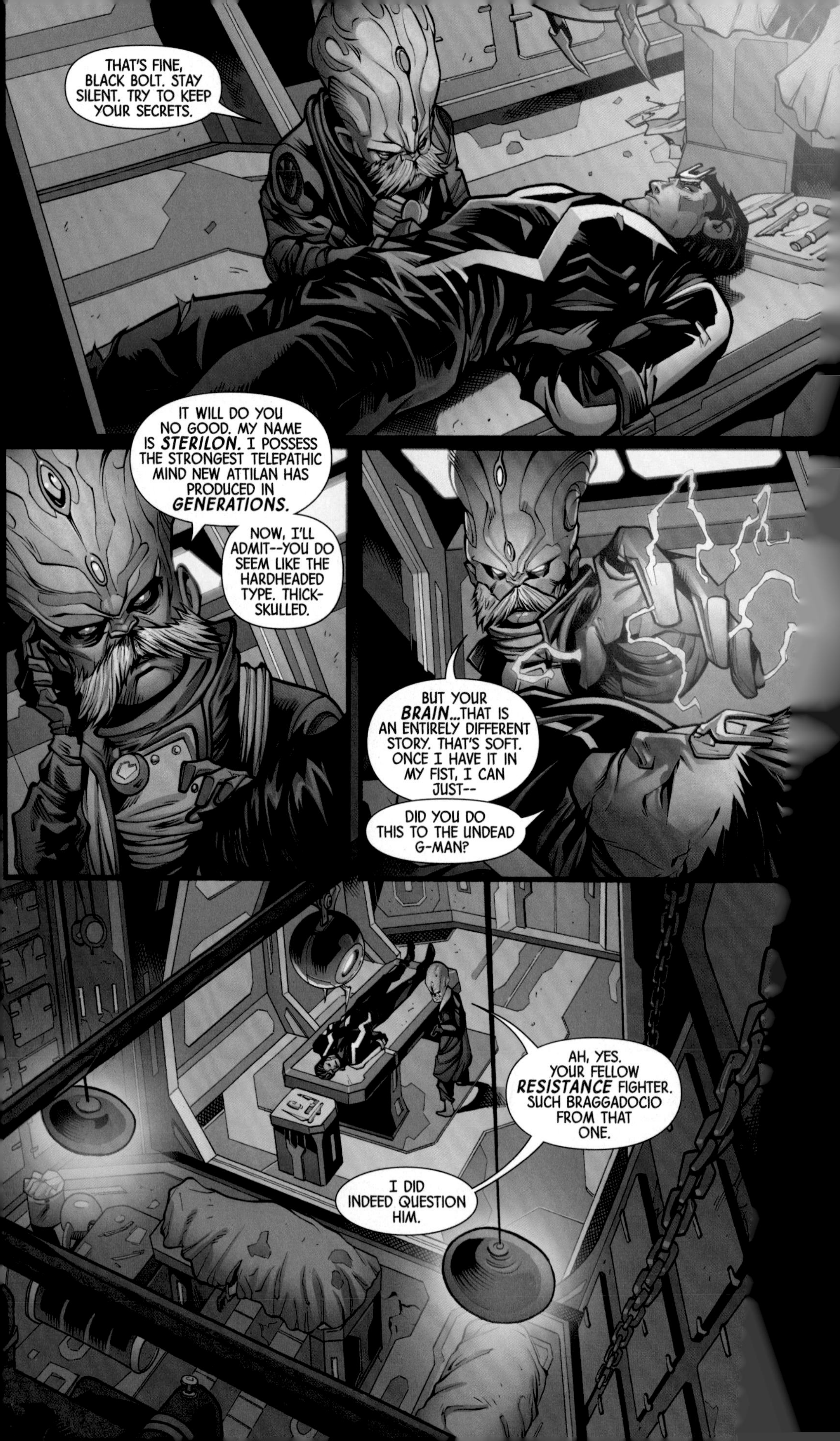
THAT'S FINE, BLACK BOLT. STAY SILENT. TRY TO KEEP YOUR SECRETS.
IT WILL DO YOU NO GOOD. MY NAME IS STERILON. I POSSESS THE STRONGEST TELEPATHIC MIND NEW ATTILAN HAS PRODUCED IN GENERATIONS.
NOW, I'LL ADMIT--YOU DO SEEM LIKE THE HARDHEADED TYPE. THICK-SKULLED.
BUT YOUR BRAIN...THAT IS AN ENTIRELY DIFFERENT STORY. THAT'S SOFT. ONCE I HAVE IT IN MY FIST, I CAN JUST--
DID YOU DO THIS TO THE UNDEAD G-MAN?
AH, YES. YOUR FELLOW RESISTANCE FIGHTER. SUCH BRAGGADOCIO FROM THAT ONE.
I DID INDEED QUESTION HIM.

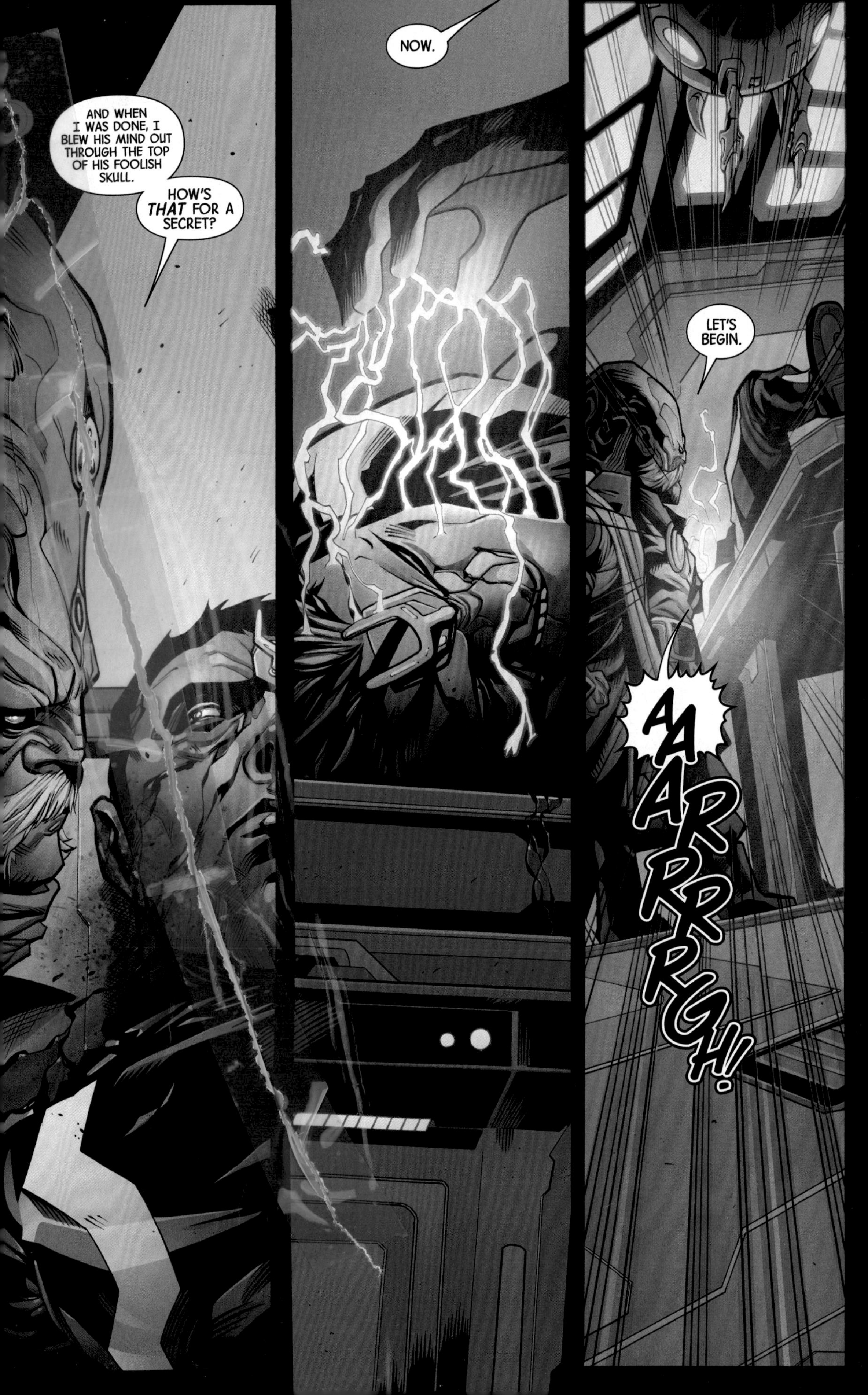
AND WHEN I WAS DONE, I BLEW HIS MIND OUT THROUGH THE TOP OF HIS FOOLISH SKULL.
HOW'S *THAT* FOR A SECRET?
NOW.
LET'S BEGIN.
AAARRRGH!

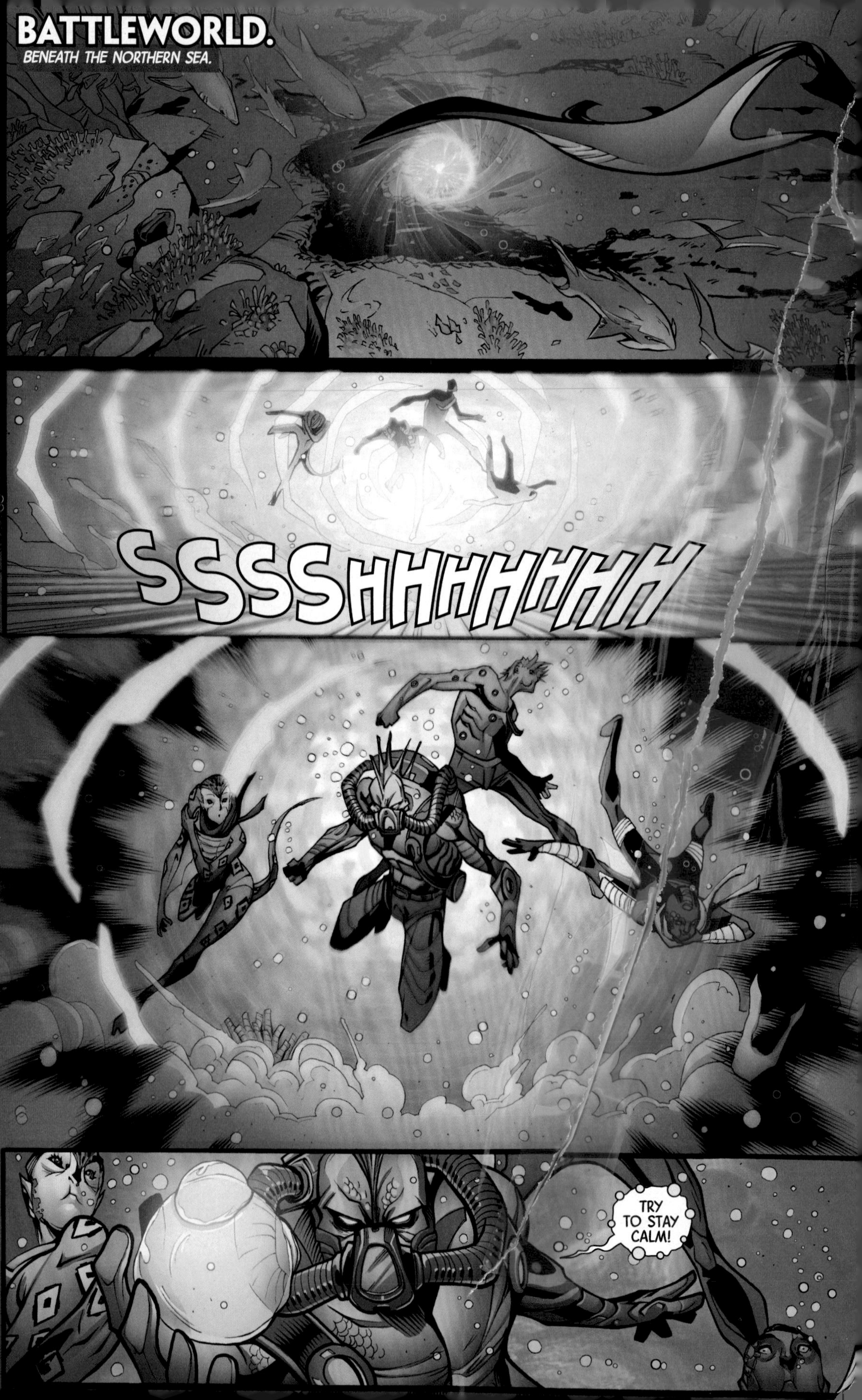
BATTLEWORLD.
BENEATH THE NORTHERN SEA.
SSSSHHHHHHHH
TRY TO STAY CALM!

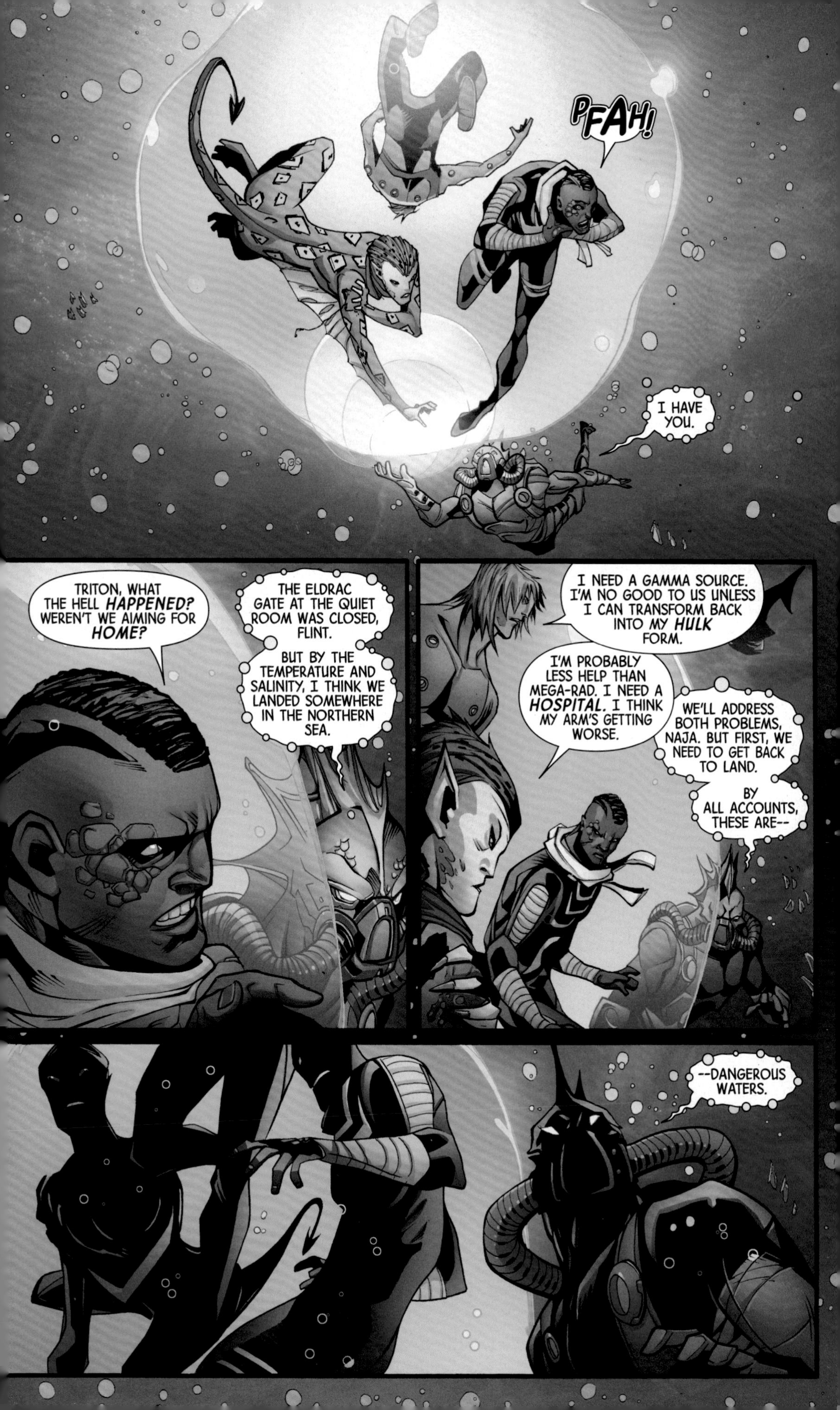
PFAH!
I HAVE YOU.
TRITON, WHAT THE HELL HAPPENED? WEREN'T WE AIMING FOR HOME?
THE ELDRAC GATE AT THE QUIET ROOM WAS CLOSED, FLINT.
BUT BY THE TEMPERATURE AND SALINITY, I THINK WE LANDED SOMEWHERE IN THE NORTHERN SEA.
I NEED A GAMMA SOURCE. I'M NO GOOD TO US UNLESS I CAN TRANSFORM BACK INTO MY HULK FORM.
I'M PROBABLY LESS HELP THAN MEGA-RAD. I NEED A HOSPITAL. I THINK MY ARM'S GETTING WORSE.
WE'LL ADDRESS BOTH PROBLEMS, NAJA. BUT FIRST, WE NEED TO GET BACK TO LAND.
BY ALL ACCOUNTS, THESE ARE--
--DANGEROUS WATERS.

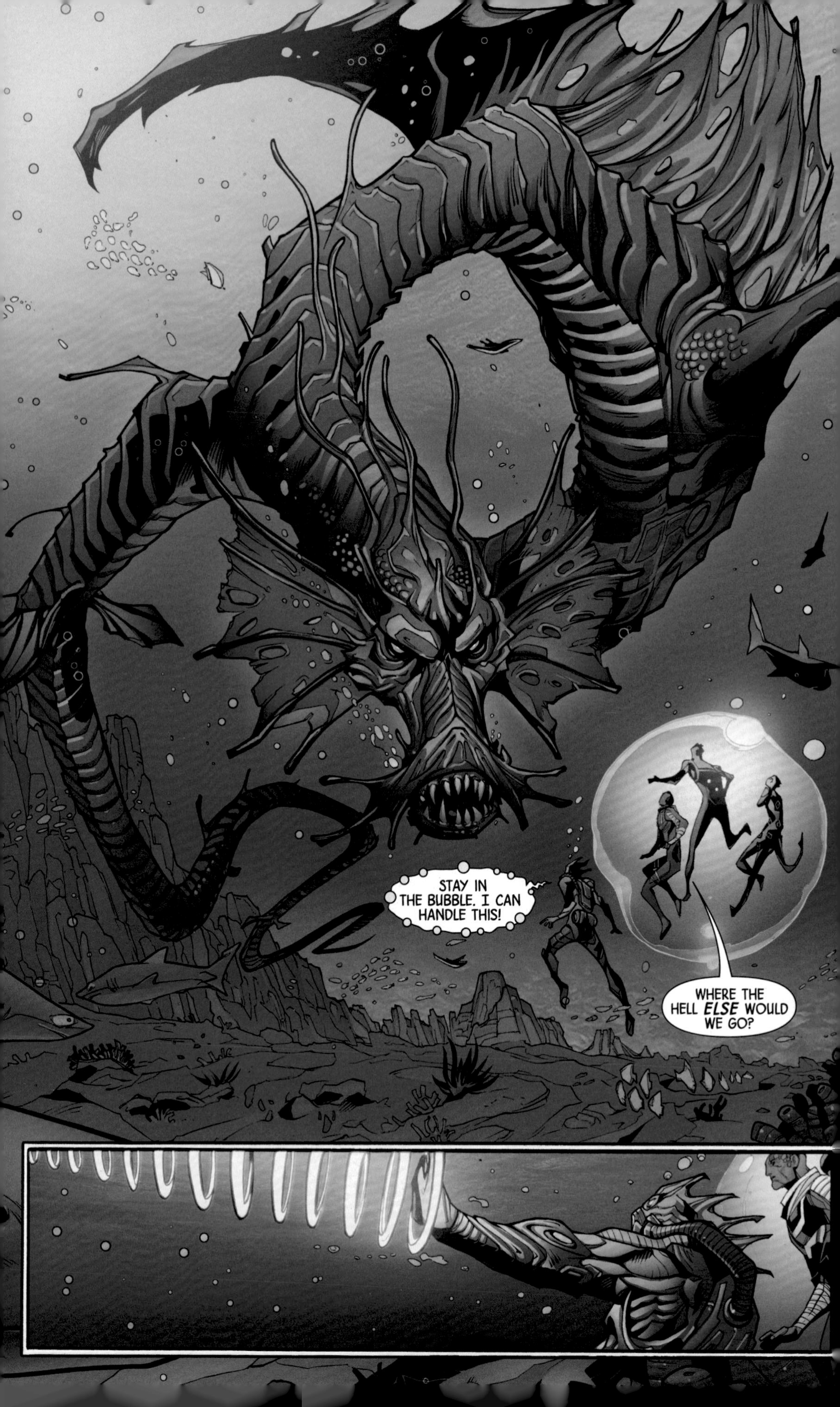
STAY IN THE BUBBLE. I CAN HANDLE THIS!
WHERE THE HELL *ELSE* WOULD WE GO?

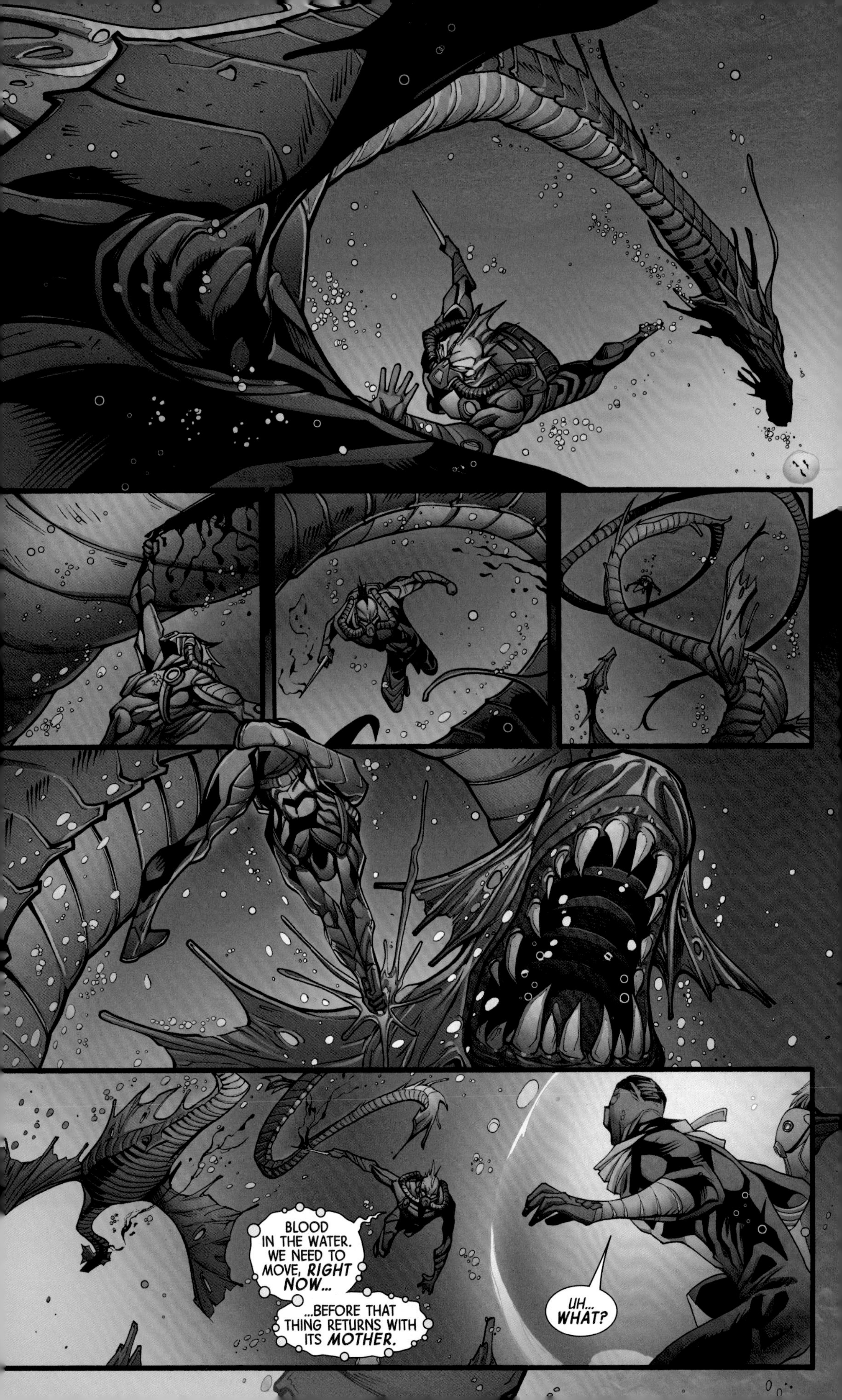
BLOOD IN THE WATER. WE NEED TO MOVE, RIGHT NOW...
...BEFORE THAT THING RETURNS WITH ITS MOTHER.
UH... WHAT?

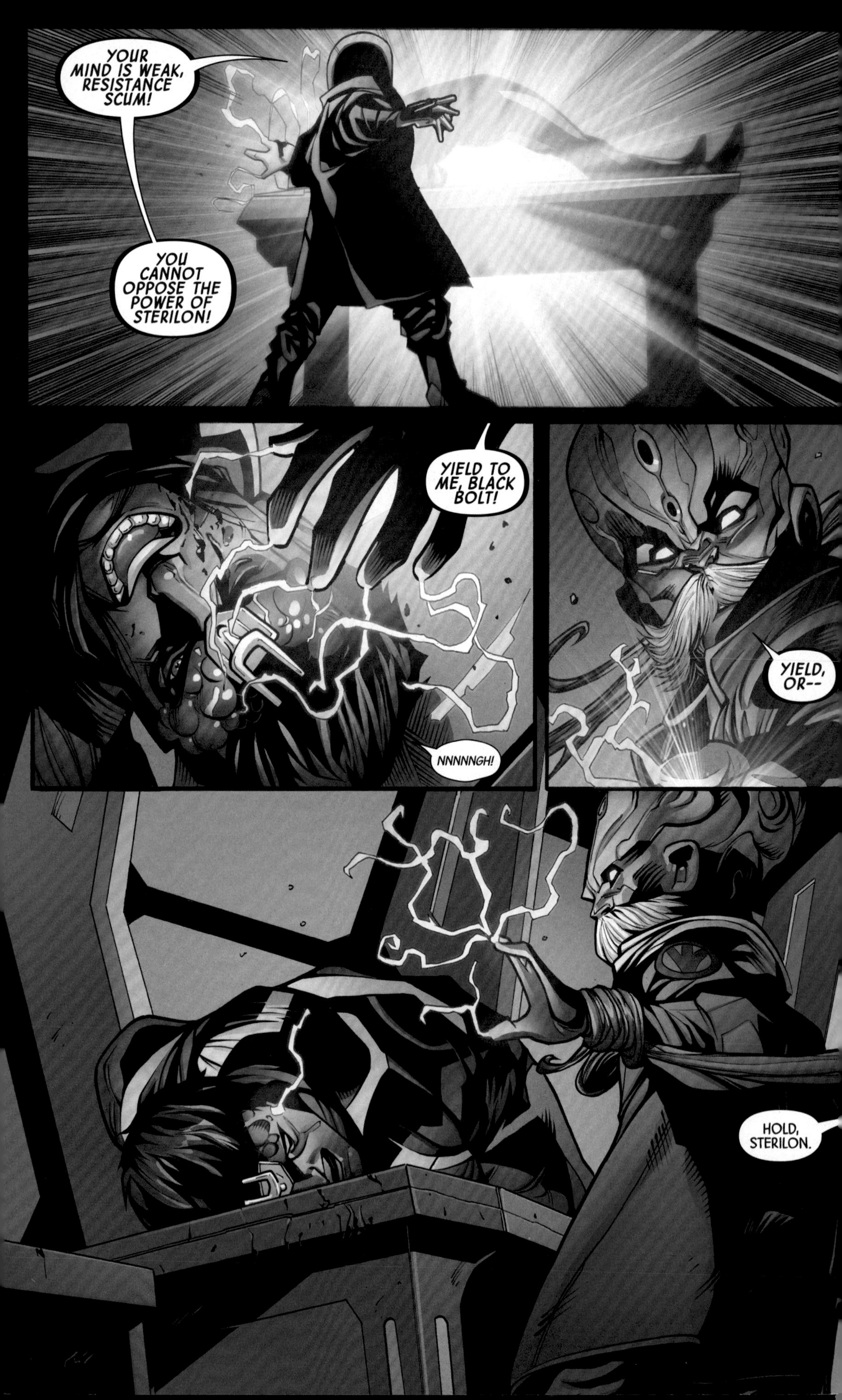
YOUR MIND IS WEAK, RESISTANCE SCUM!
YOU CANNOT OPPOSE THE POWER OF STERILON!
YIELD TO ME, BLACK BOLT!
NNNNNGH!
YIELD, OR--
HOLD, STERILON.

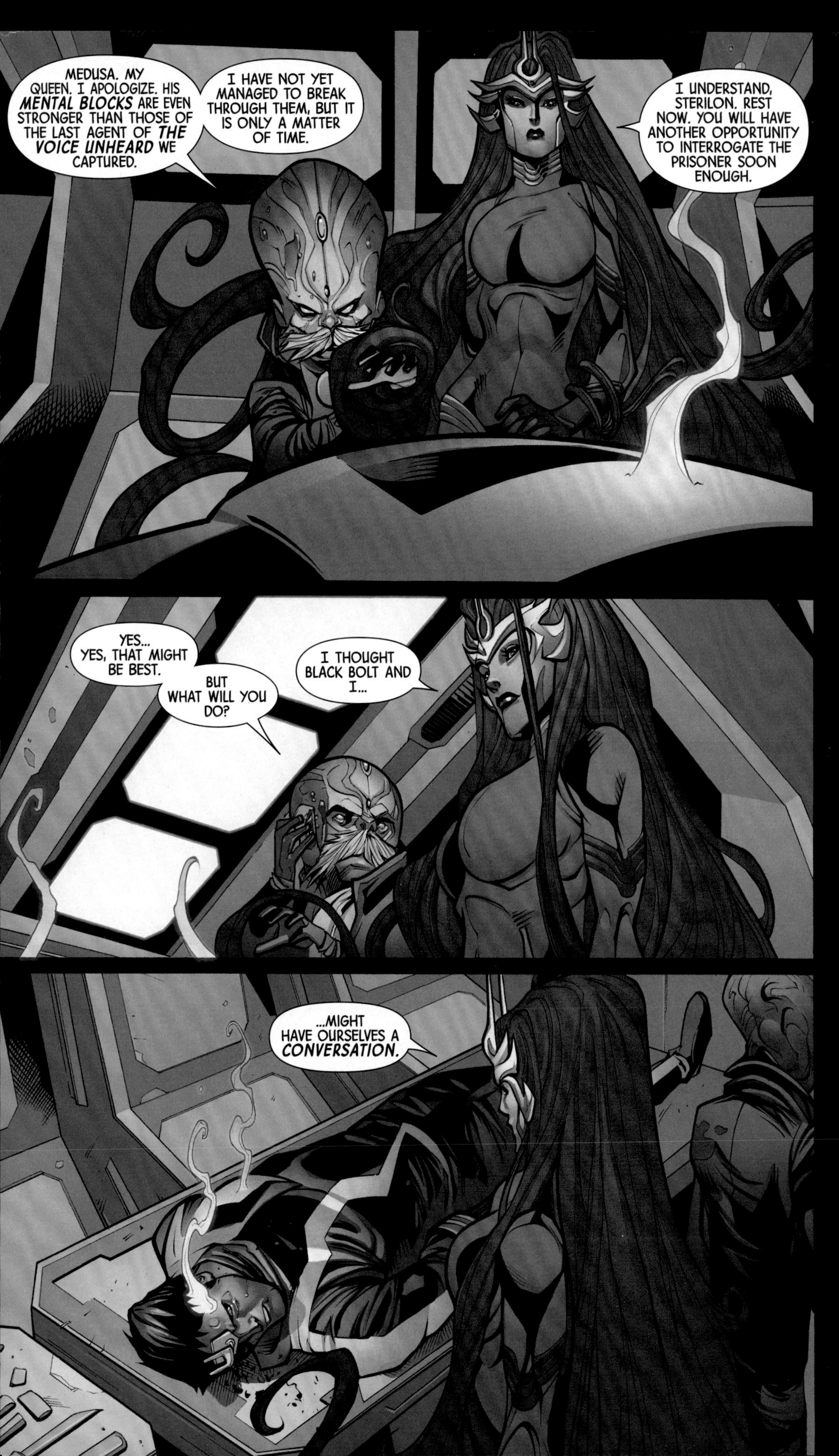
MEDUSA. MY QUEEN. I APOLOGIZE. HIS MENTAL BLOCKS ARE EVEN STRONGER THAN THOSE OF THE LAST AGENT OF THE VOICE UNHEARD WE CAPTURED.
I HAVE NOT YET MANAGED TO BREAK THROUGH THEM, BUT IT IS ONLY A MATTER OF TIME.
I UNDERSTAND, STERILON. REST NOW. YOU WILL HAVE ANOTHER OPPORTUNITY TO INTERROGATE THE PRISONER SOON ENOUGH.
YES... YES, THAT MIGHT BE BEST.
BUT WHAT WILL YOU DO?
I THOUGHT BLACK BOLT AND I...
...MIGHT HAVE OURSELVES A CONVERSATION.

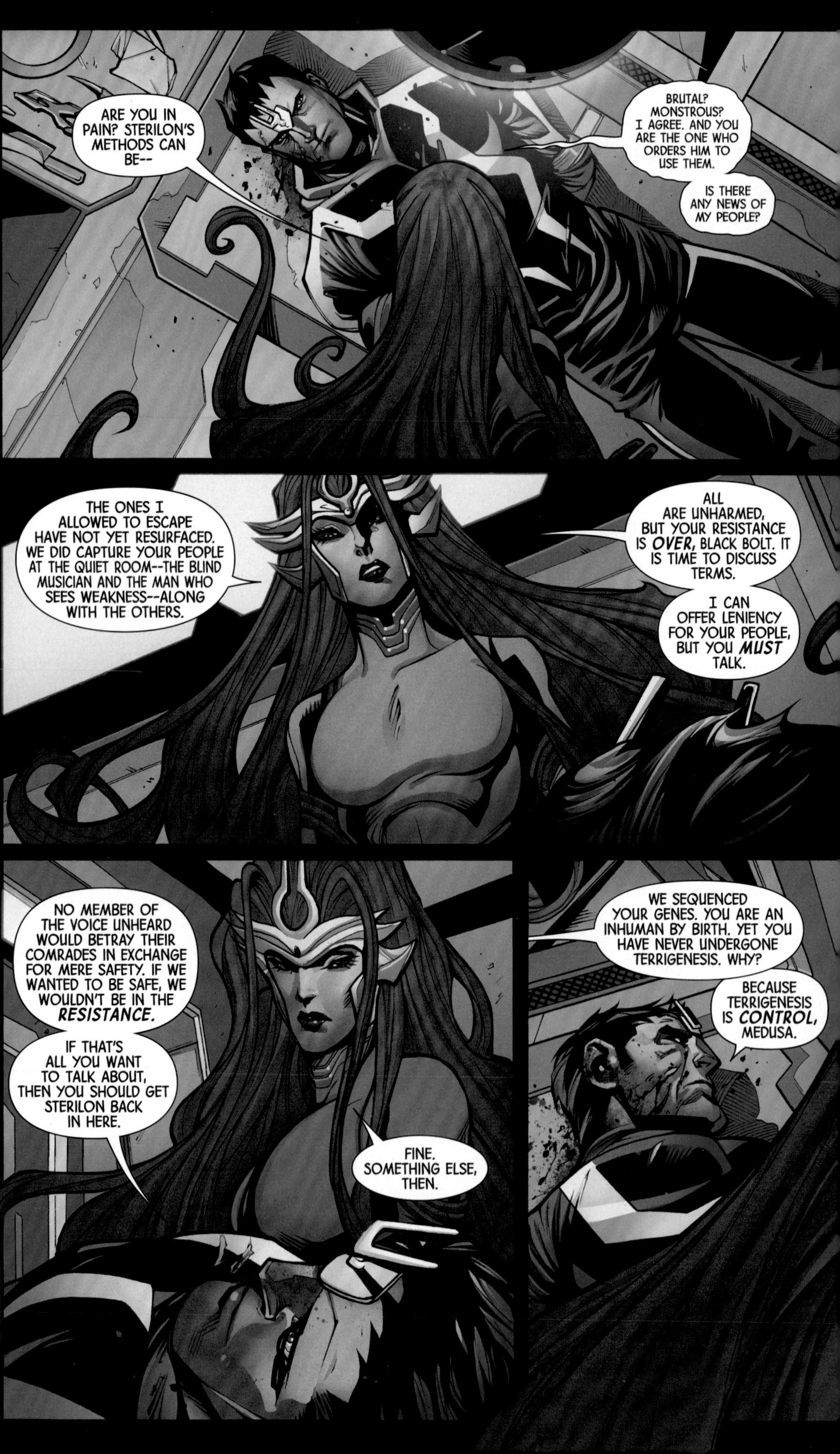
ARE YOU IN PAIN? STERILON'S METHODS CAN BE--
BRUTAL? MONSTROUS? I AGREE. AND YOU ARE THE ONE WHO ORDERS HIM TO USE THEM.
IS THERE ANY NEWS OF MY PEOPLE?
THE ONES I ALLOWED TO ESCAPE HAVE NOT YET RESURFACED. WE DID CAPTURE YOUR PEOPLE AT THE QUIET ROOM--THE BLIND MUSICIAN AND THE MAN WHO SEES WEAKNESS--ALONG WITH THE OTHERS.
ALL ARE UNHARMED, BUT YOUR RESISTANCE IS *OVER,* BLACK BOLT. IT IS TIME TO DISCUSS TERMS.
I CAN OFFER LENIENCY FOR YOUR PEOPLE, BUT YOU *MUST* TALK.
NO MEMBER OF THE VOICE UNHEARD WOULD BETRAY THEIR COMRADES IN EXCHANGE FOR MERE SAFETY. IF WE WANTED TO BE SAFE, WE WOULDN'T BE IN THE *RESISTANCE.*
IF THAT'S ALL YOU WANT TO TALK ABOUT, THEN YOU SHOULD GET STERILON BACK IN HERE.
FINE. SOMETHING ELSE, THEN.
WE SEQUENCED YOUR GENES. YOU ARE AN INHUMAN BY BIRTH. YET YOU HAVE NEVER UNDERGONE TERRIGENESIS. WHY?
BECAUSE TERRIGENESIS IS *CONTROL,* MEDUSA.

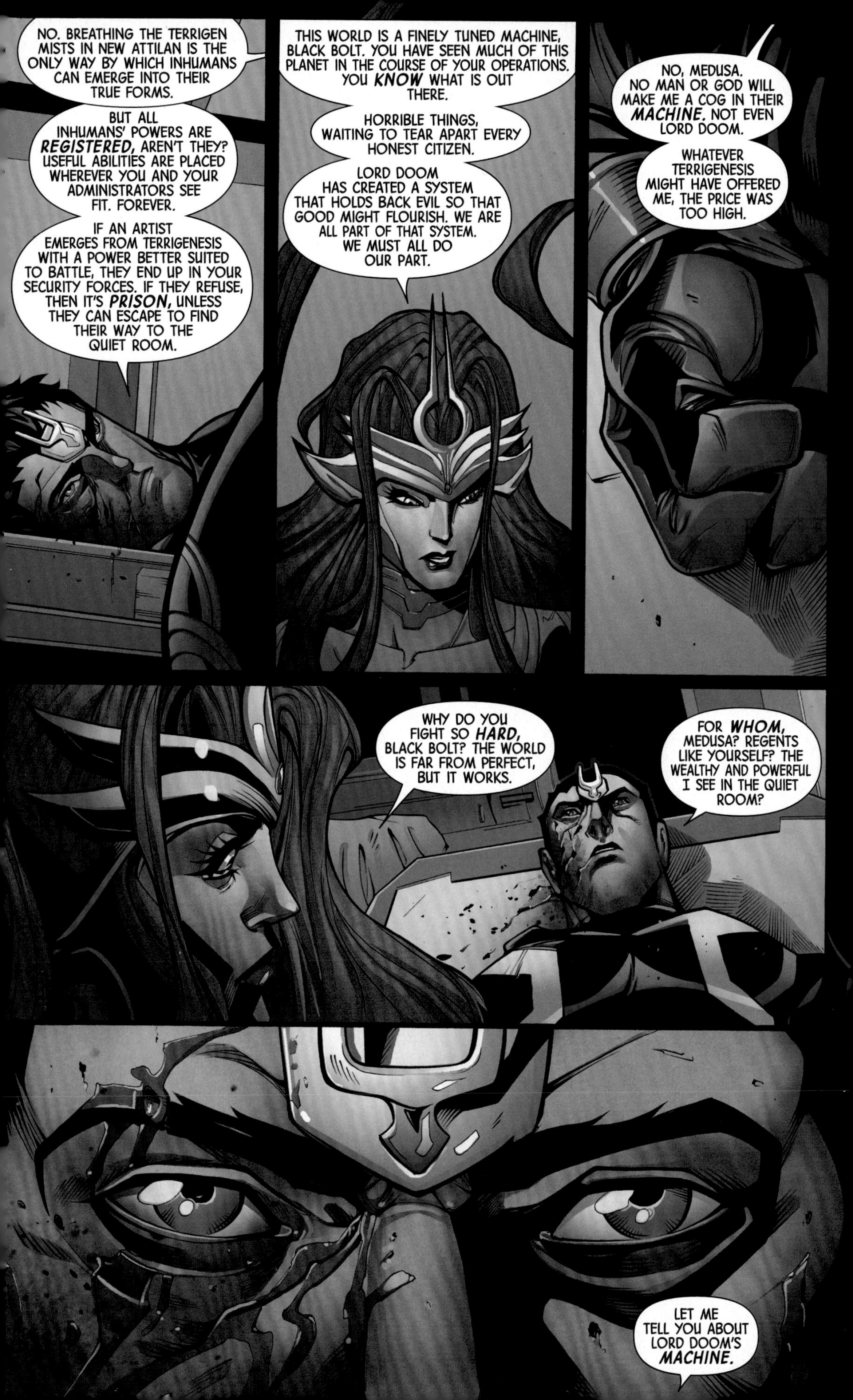
NO. BREATHING THE TERRIGEN MISTS IN NEW ATTILAN IS THE ONLY WAY BY WHICH INHUMANS CAN EMERGE INTO THEIR TRUE FORMS.
BUT ALL INHUMANS' POWERS ARE REGISTERED, AREN'T THEY? USEFUL ABILITIES ARE PLACED WHEREVER YOU AND YOUR ADMINISTRATORS SEE FIT. FOREVER.
IF AN ARTIST EMERGES FROM TERRIGENESIS WITH A POWER BETTER SUITED TO BATTLE, THEY END UP IN YOUR SECURITY FORCES. IF THEY REFUSE, THEN IT'S PRISON, UNLESS THEY CAN ESCAPE TO FIND THEIR WAY TO THE QUIET ROOM.
THIS WORLD IS A FINELY TUNED MACHINE, BLACK BOLT. YOU HAVE SEEN MUCH OF THIS PLANET IN THE COURSE OF YOUR OPERATIONS. YOU KNOW WHAT IS OUT THERE.
HORRIBLE THINGS, WAITING TO TEAR APART EVERY HONEST CITIZEN.
LORD DOOM HAS CREATED A SYSTEM THAT HOLDS BACK EVIL SO THAT GOOD MIGHT FLOURISH. WE ARE ALL PART OF THAT SYSTEM. WE MUST ALL DO OUR PART.
NO, MEDUSA. NO MAN OR GOD WILL MAKE ME A COG IN THEIR MACHINE. NOT EVEN LORD DOOM.
WHATEVER TERRIGENESIS MIGHT HAVE OFFERED ME, THE PRICE WAS TOO HIGH.
WHY DO YOU FIGHT SO HARD, BLACK BOLT? THE WORLD IS FAR FROM PERFECT, BUT IT WORKS.
FOR WHOM, MEDUSA? REGENTS LIKE YOURSELF? THE WEALTHY AND POWERFUL I SEE IN THE QUIET ROOM?
LET ME TELL YOU ABOUT LORD DOOM'S MACHINE.

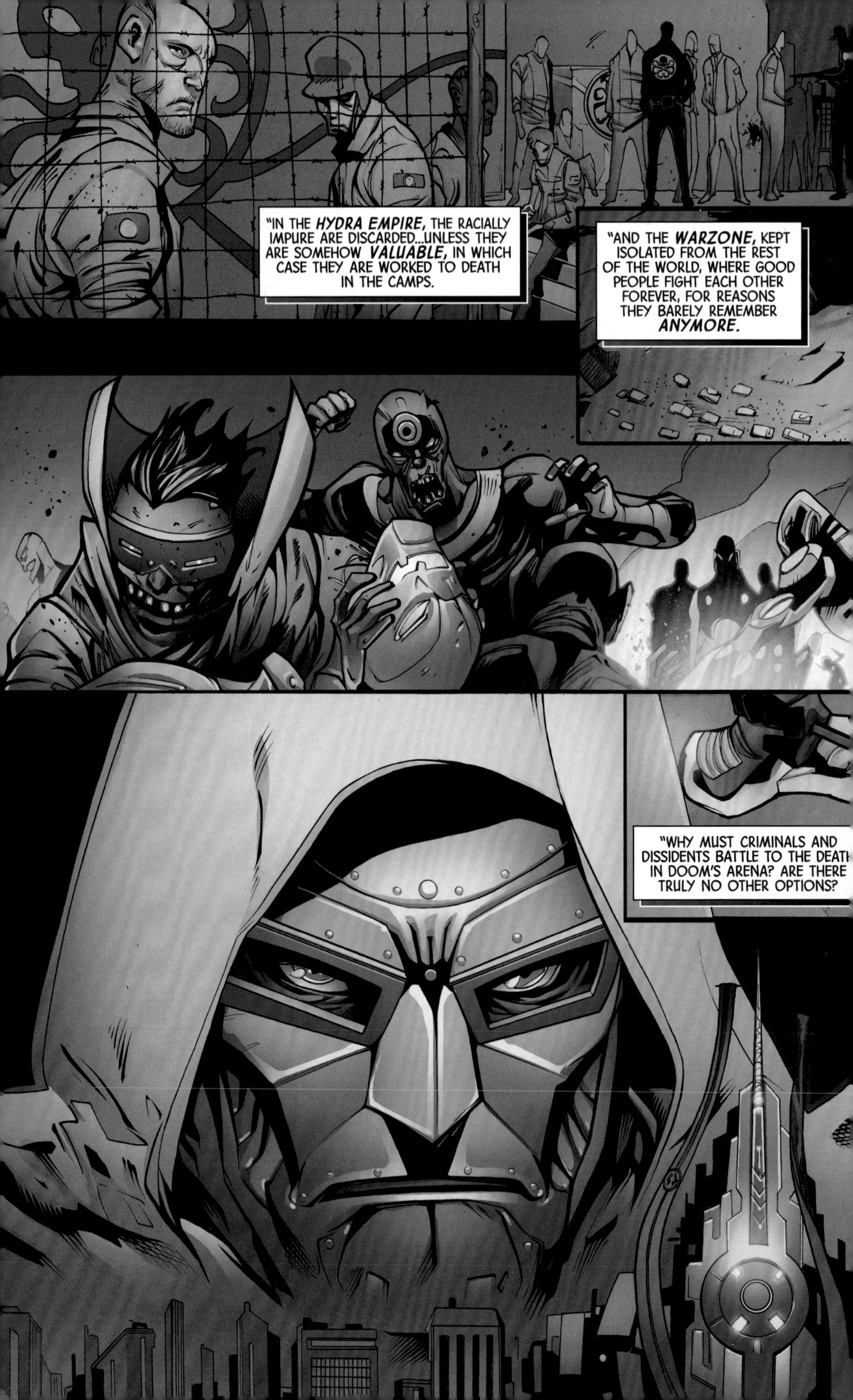
"IN THE HYDRA EMPIRE, THE RACIALLY IMPURE ARE DISCARDED...UNLESS THEY ARE SOMEHOW VALUABLE, IN WHICH CASE THEY ARE WORKED TO DEATH IN THE CAMPS.
"AND THE WARZONE, KEPT ISOLATED FROM THE REST OF THE WORLD, WHERE GOOD PEOPLE FIGHT EACH OTHER FOREVER, FOR REASONS THEY BARELY REMEMBER ANYMORE.
"WHY MUST CRIMINALS AND DISSIDENTS BATTLE TO THE DEATH IN DOOM'S ARENA? ARE THERE TRULY NO OTHER OPTIONS?

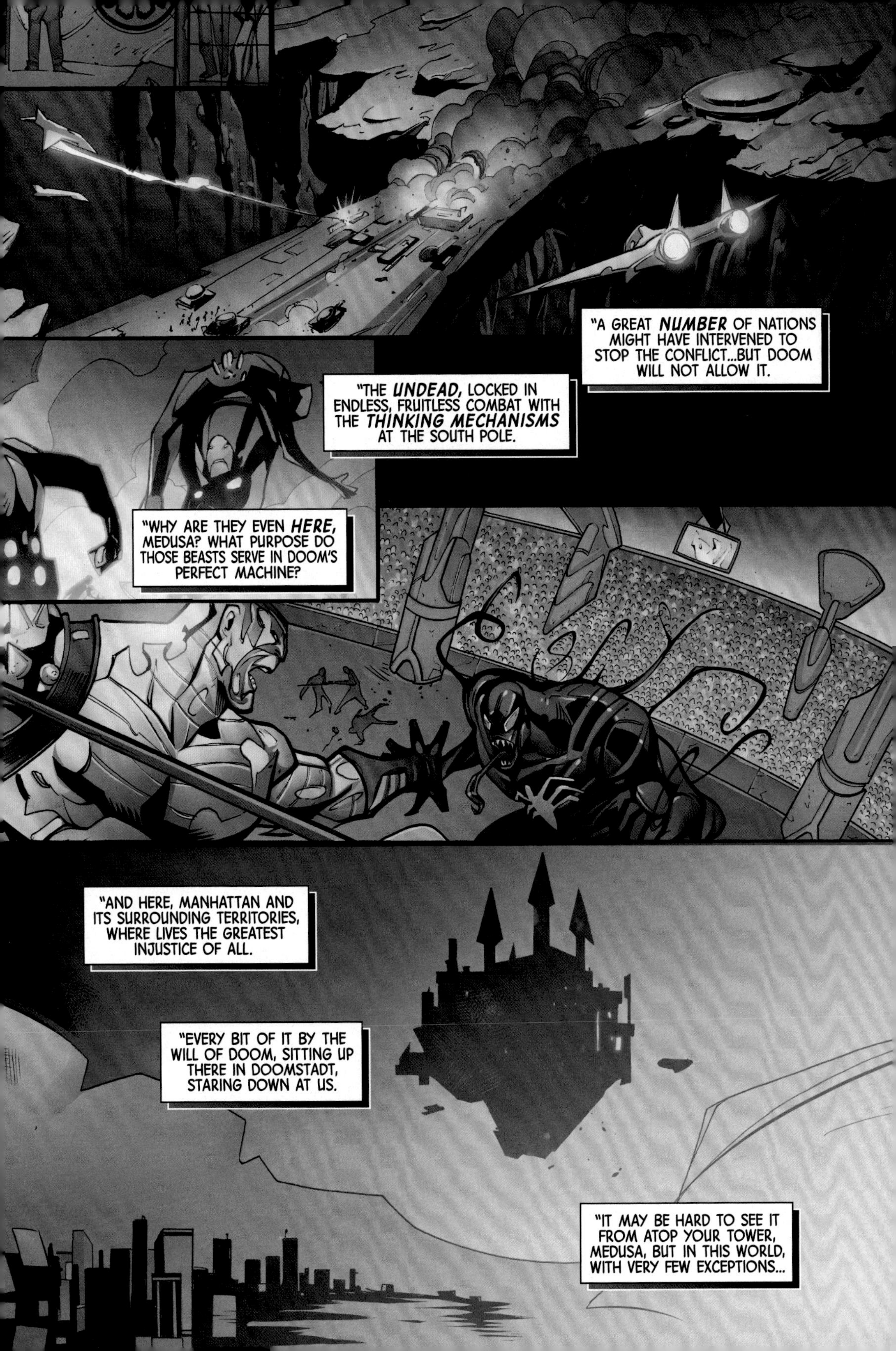
"A GREAT NUMBER OF NATIONS MIGHT HAVE INTERVENED TO STOP THE CONFLICT...BUT DOOM WILL NOT ALLOW IT.
"THE UNDEAD, LOCKED IN ENDLESS, FRUITLESS COMBAT WITH THE THINKING MECHANISMS AT THE SOUTH POLE.
"WHY ARE THEY EVEN HERE, MEDUSA? WHAT PURPOSE DO THOSE BEASTS SERVE IN DOOM'S PERFECT MACHINE?
"AND HERE, MANHATTAN AND ITS SURROUNDING TERRITORIES, WHERE LIVES THE GREATEST INJUSTICE OF ALL.
"EVERY BIT OF IT BY THE WILL OF DOOM, SITTING UP THERE IN DOOMSTADT, STARING DOWN AT US.
"IT MAY BE HARD TO SEE IT FROM ATOP YOUR TOWER, MEDUSA, BUT IN THIS WORLD, WITH VERY FEW EXCEPTIONS...

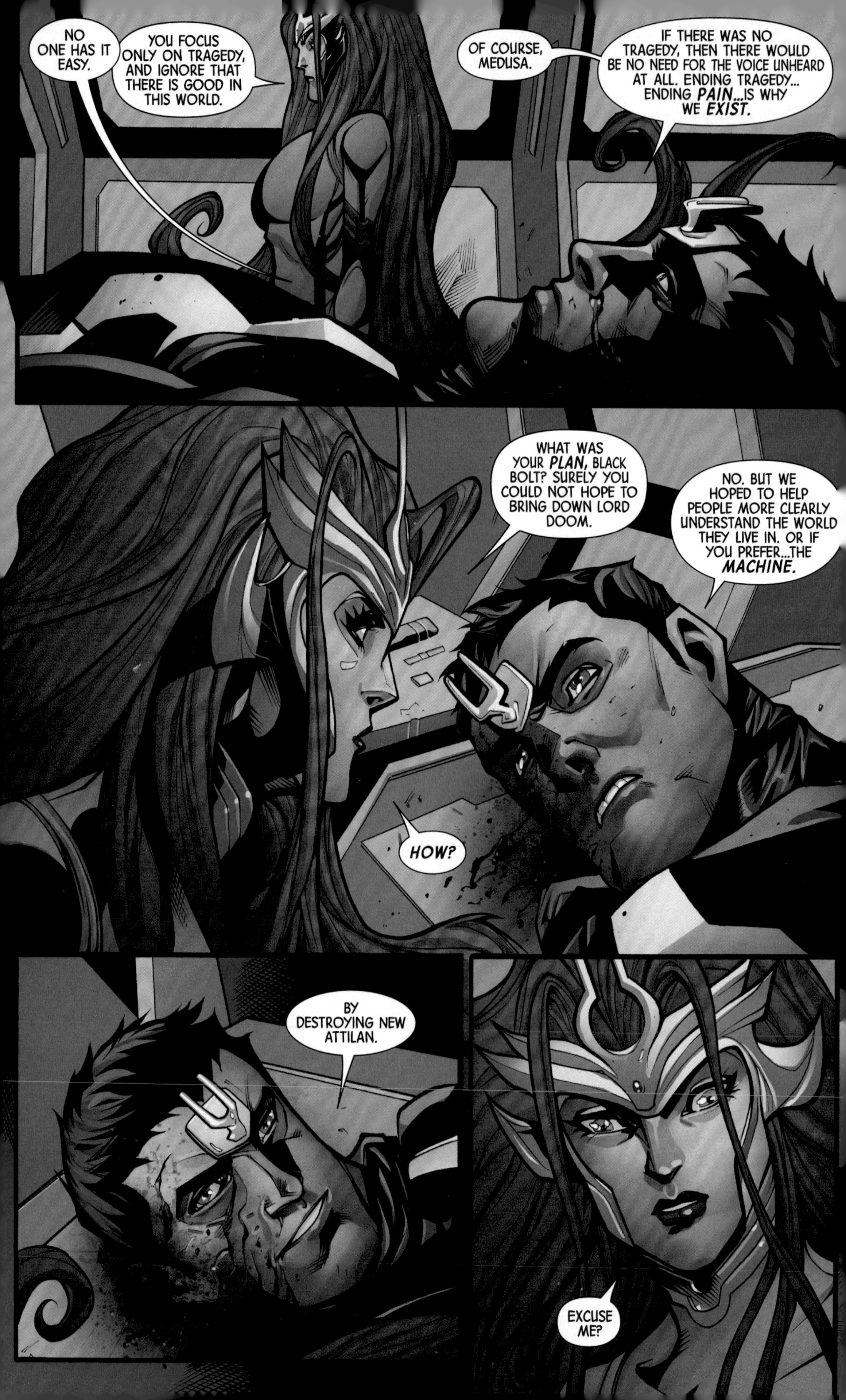
NO ONE HAS IT EASY.
YOU FOCUS ONLY ON TRAGEDY, AND IGNORE THAT THERE IS GOOD IN THIS WORLD.
OF COURSE, MEDUSA.
IF THERE WAS NO TRAGEDY, THEN THERE WOULD BE NO NEED FOR THE VOICE UNHEARD AT ALL. ENDING TRAGEDY... ENDING PAIN...IS WHY WE EXIST.
WHAT WAS YOUR PLAN, BLACK BOLT? SURELY YOU COULD NOT HOPE TO BRING DOWN LORD DOOM.
NO. BUT WE HOPED TO HELP PEOPLE MORE CLEARLY UNDERSTAND THE WORLD THEY LIVE IN. OR IF YOU PREFER...THE MACHINE.
HOW?
BY DESTROYING NEW ATTILAN.
EXCUSE ME?

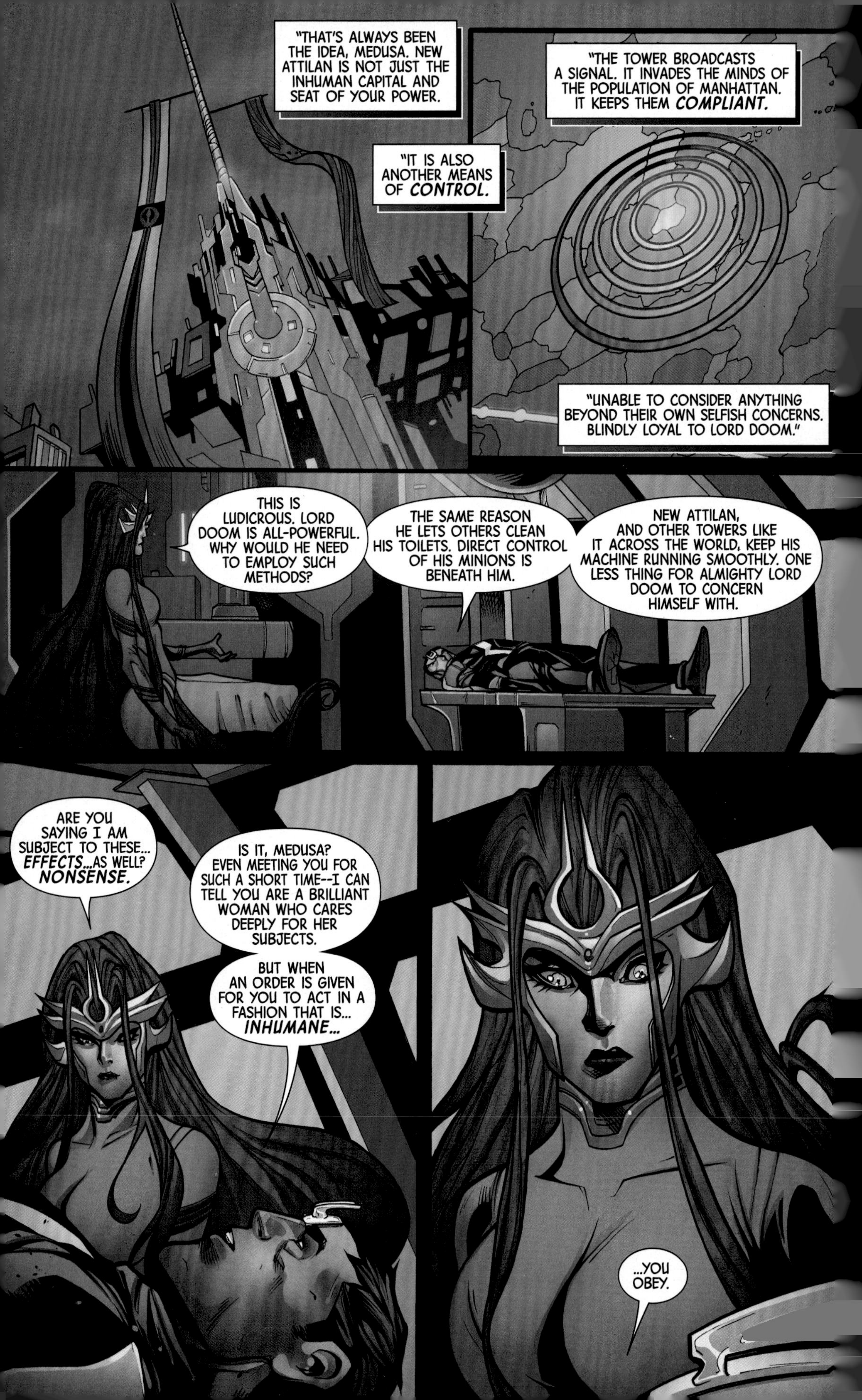
"THAT'S ALWAYS BEEN THE IDEA, MEDUSA. NEW ATTILAN IS NOT JUST THE INHUMAN CAPITAL AND SEAT OF YOUR POWER.
"IT IS ALSO ANOTHER MEANS OF CONTROL.
"THE TOWER BROADCASTS A SIGNAL. IT INVADES THE MINDS OF THE POPULATION OF MANHATTAN. IT KEEPS THEM COMPLIANT.
"UNABLE TO CONSIDER ANYTHING BEYOND THEIR OWN SELFISH CONCERNS. BLINDLY LOYAL TO LORD DOOM."
THIS IS LUDICROUS. LORD DOOM IS ALL-POWERFUL. WHY WOULD HE NEED TO EMPLOY SUCH METHODS?
THE SAME REASON HE LETS OTHERS CLEAN HIS TOILETS. DIRECT CONTROL OF HIS MINIONS IS BENEATH HIM.
NEW ATTILAN, AND OTHER TOWERS LIKE IT ACROSS THE WORLD, KEEP HIS MACHINE RUNNING SMOOTHLY. ONE LESS THING FOR ALMIGHTY LORD DOOM TO CONCERN HIMSELF WITH.
ARE YOU SAYING I AM SUBJECT TO THESE... EFFECTS...AS WELL? NONSENSE.
IS IT, MEDUSA? EVEN MEETING YOU FOR SUCH A SHORT TIME--I CAN TELL YOU ARE A BRILLIANT WOMAN WHO CARES DEEPLY FOR HER SUBJECTS.
BUT WHEN AN ORDER IS GIVEN FOR YOU TO ACT IN A FASHION THAT IS... INHUMANE...
...YOU OBEY.

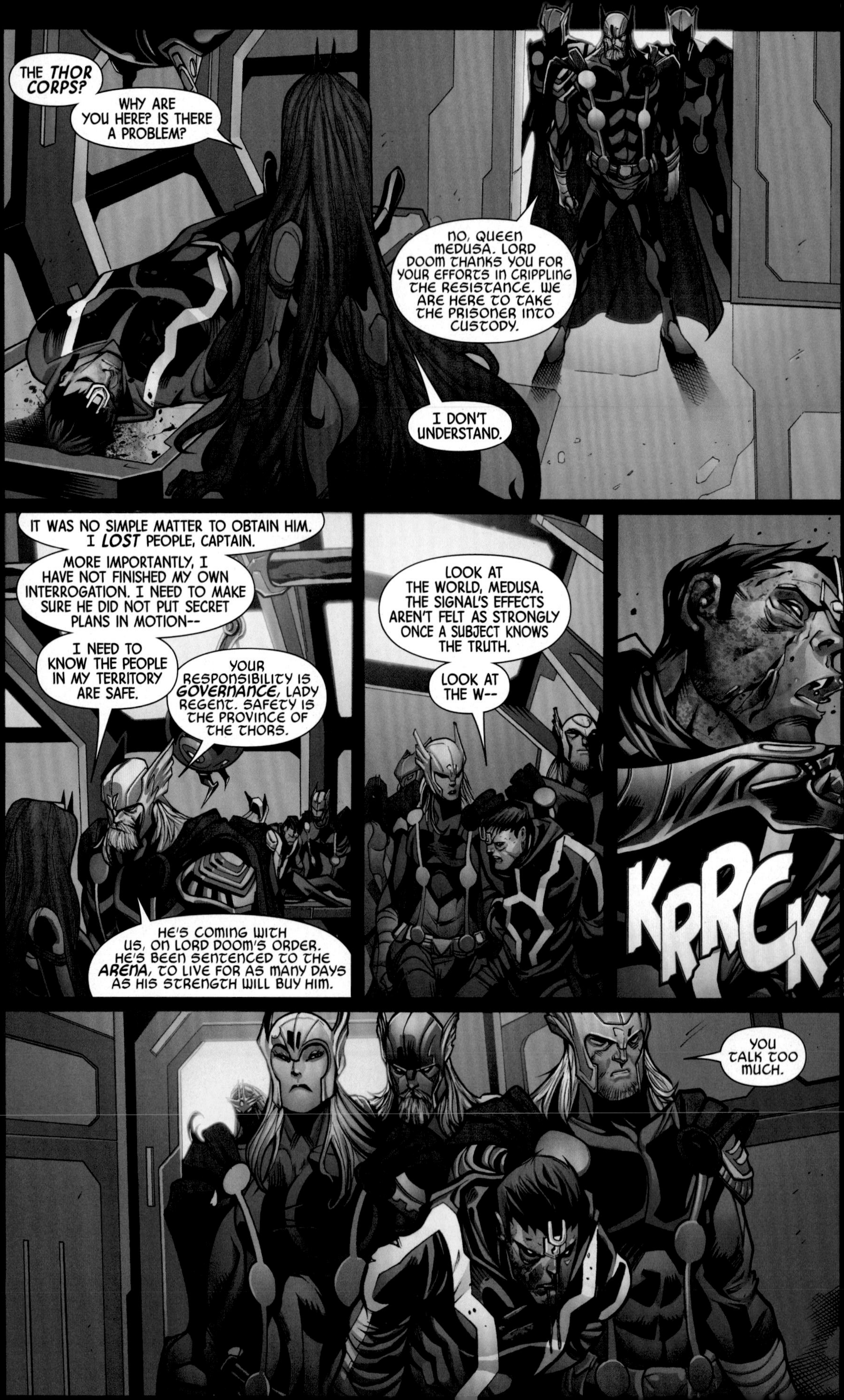

THE THOR CORPS?
WHY ARE YOU HERE? IS THERE A PROBLEM?
NO, QUEEN MEDUSA. LORD DOOM THANKS YOU FOR YOUR EFFORTS IN CRIPPLING THE RESISTANCE. WE ARE HERE TO TAKE THE PRISONER INTO CUSTODY.
I DON'T UNDERSTAND.
IT WAS NO SIMPLE MATTER TO OBTAIN HIM. I LOST PEOPLE, CAPTAIN.
MORE IMPORTANTLY, I HAVE NOT FINISHED MY OWN INTERROGATION. I NEED TO MAKE SURE HE DID NOT PUT SECRET PLANS IN MOTION--
I NEED TO KNOW THE PEOPLE IN MY TERRITORY ARE SAFE.
YOUR RESPONSIBILITY IS GOVERNANCE, LADY REGENT. SAFETY IS THE PROVINCE OF THE THORS.
HE'S COMING WITH US, ON LORD DOOM'S ORDER. HE'S BEEN SENTENCED TO THE ARENA, TO LIVE FOR AS MANY DAYS AS HIS STRENGTH WILL BUY HIM.
LOOK AT THE WORLD, MEDUSA. THE SIGNAL'S EFFECTS AREN'T FELT AS STRONGLY ONCE A SUBJECT KNOWS THE TRUTH.
LOOK AT THE W--
KRRCK
YOU TALK TOO MUCH.

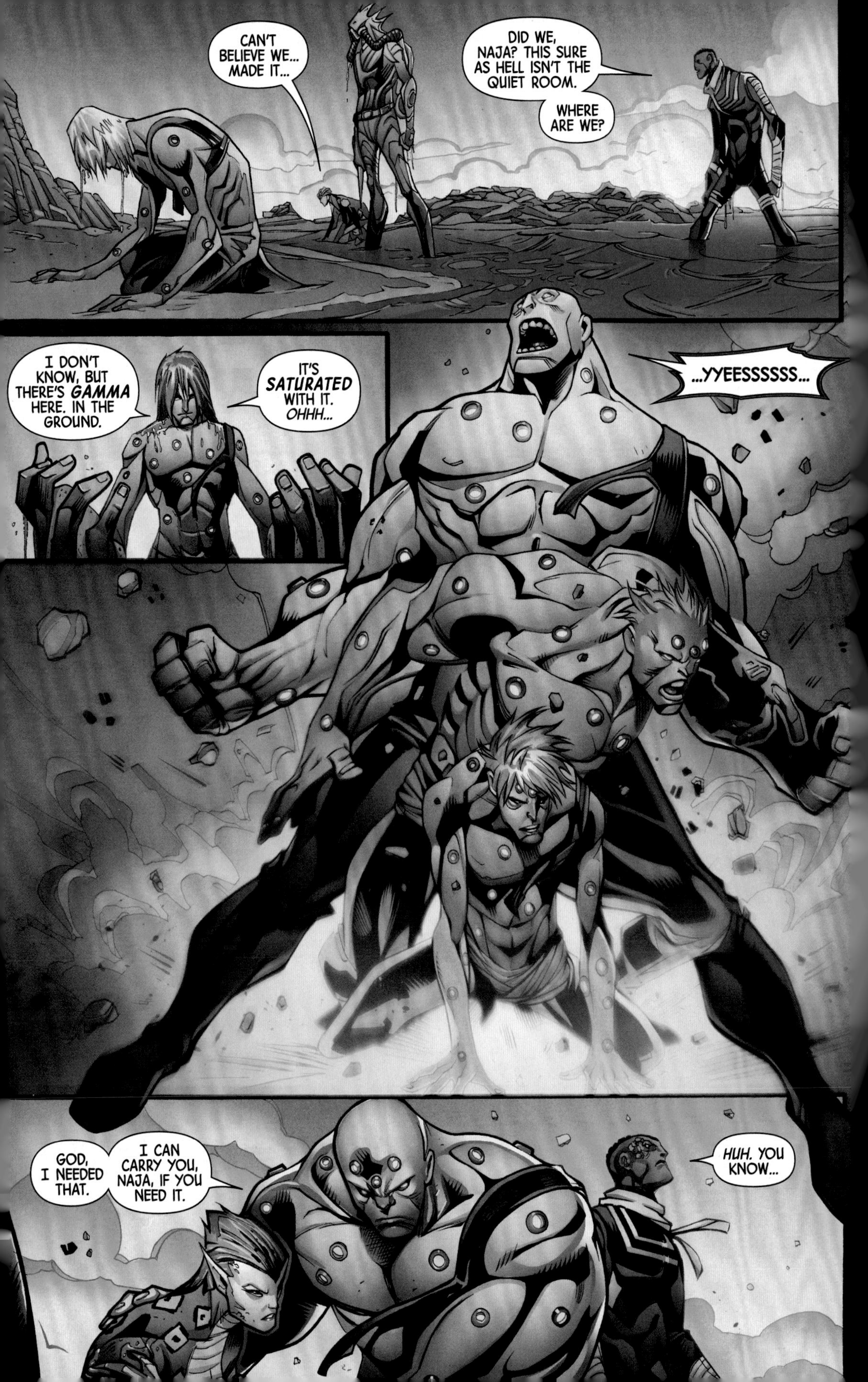
CAN'T BELIEVE WE... MADE IT...
DID WE, NAJA? THIS SURE AS HELL ISN'T THE QUIET ROOM.
WHERE ARE WE?
I DON'T KNOW, BUT THERE'S *GAMMA* HERE. IN THE GROUND.
IT'S *SATURATED* WITH IT. *OHHH...*
...YYEESSSSSS...
GOD, I NEEDED THAT.
I CAN CARRY YOU, NAJA, IF YOU NEED IT.
HUH. YOU KNOW...

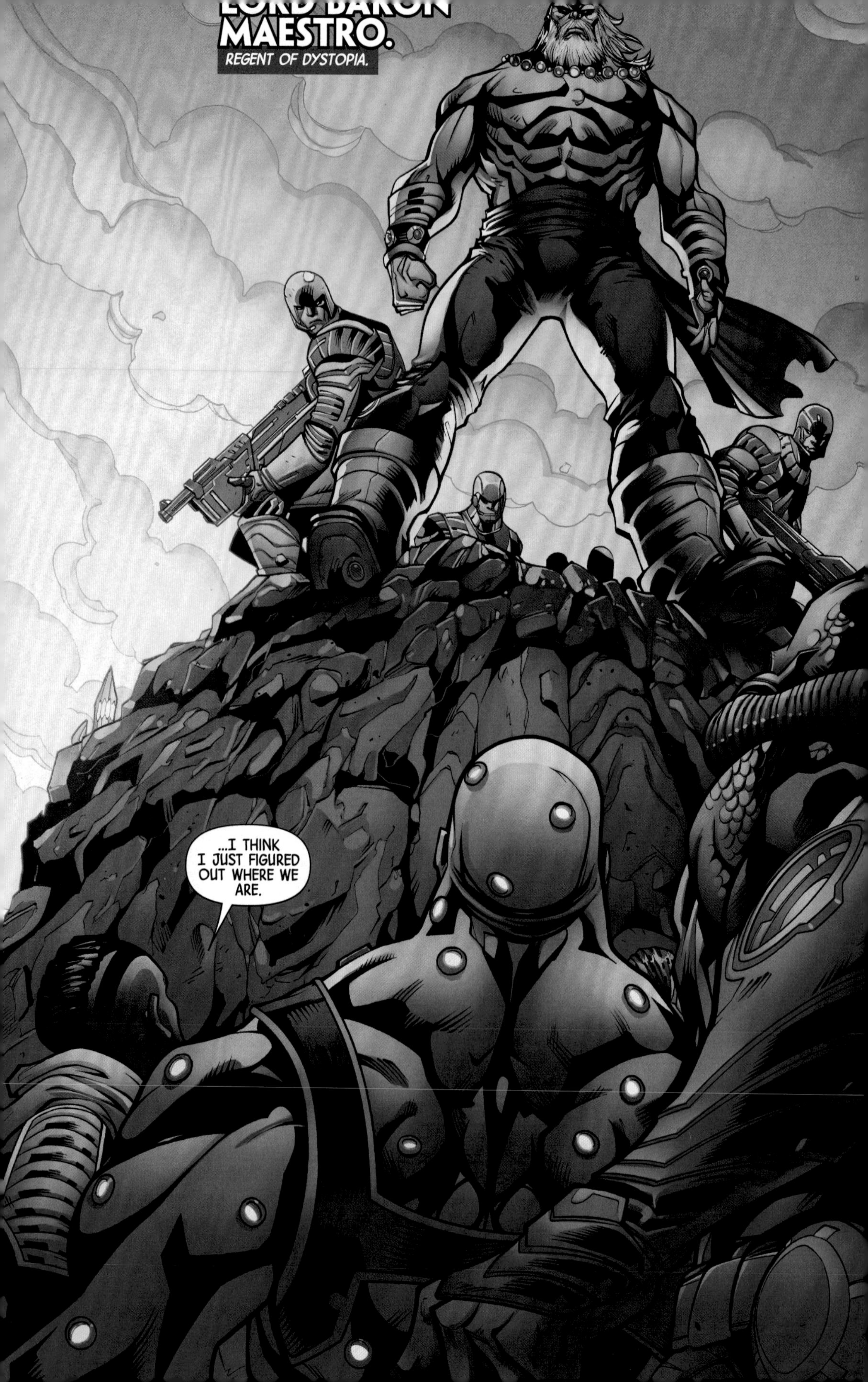
LORD BARON
MAESTRO.
REGENT OF DYSTOPIA.
...I THINK I JUST FIGURED OUT WHERE WE ARE.

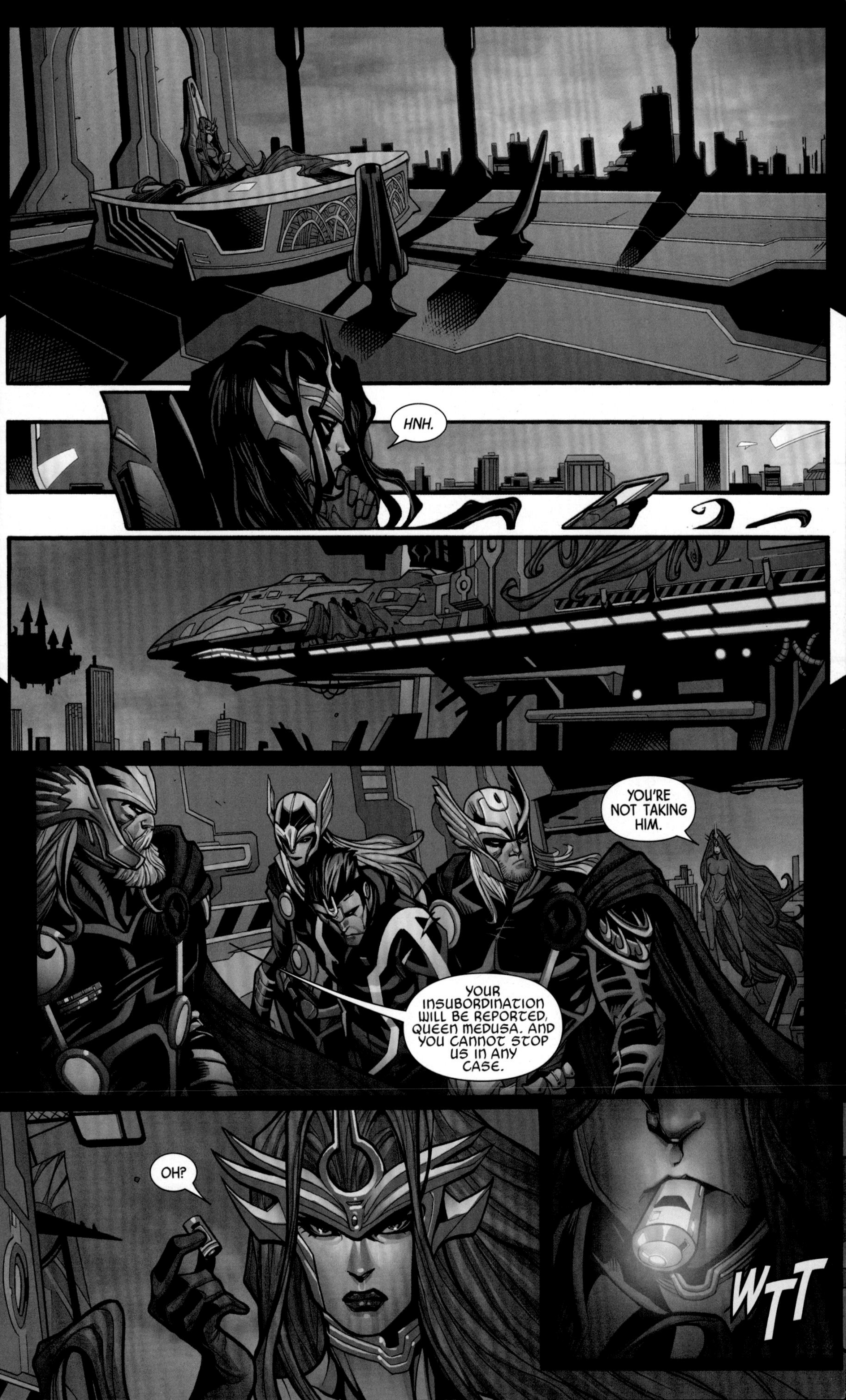
HNH.
YOU'RE NOT TAKING HIM.
YOUR INSUBORDINATION WILL BE REPORTED, QUEEN MEDUSA. AND YOU CANNOT STOP US IN ANY CASE.
OH?
WTT

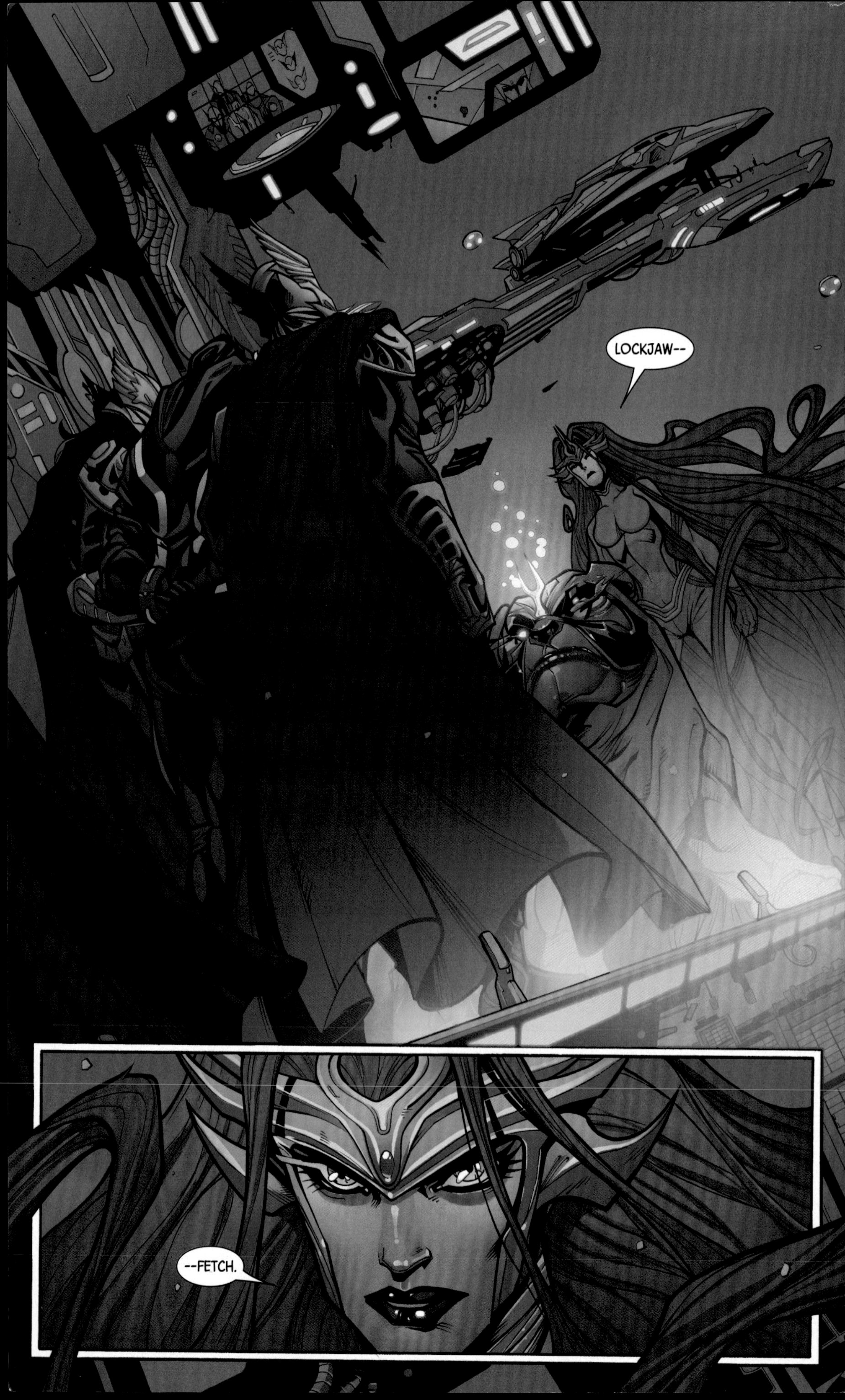
LOCKJAW--
--FETCH.

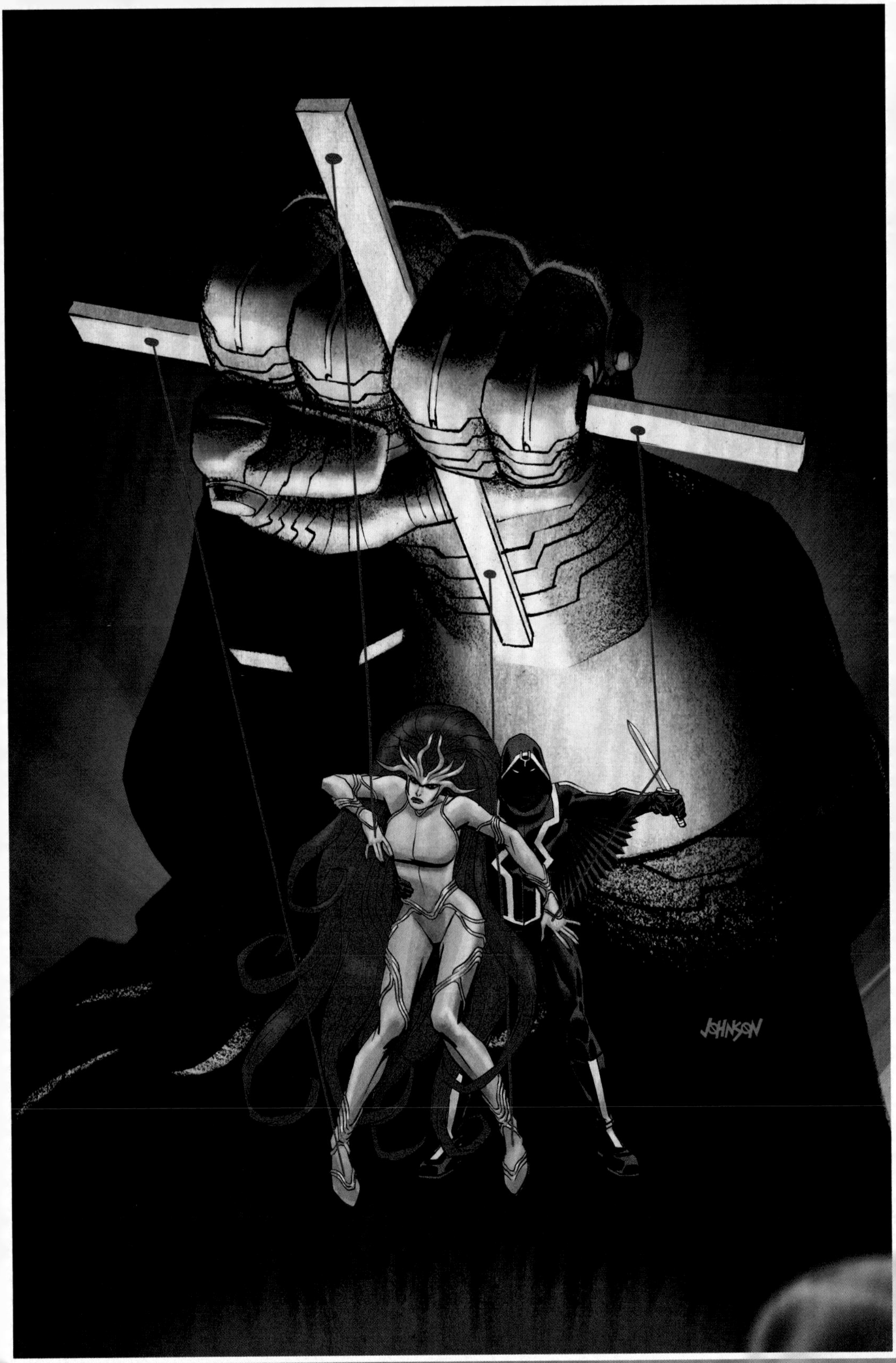
JOHNSON

PART 5: THE DYING OF THE LIGHT

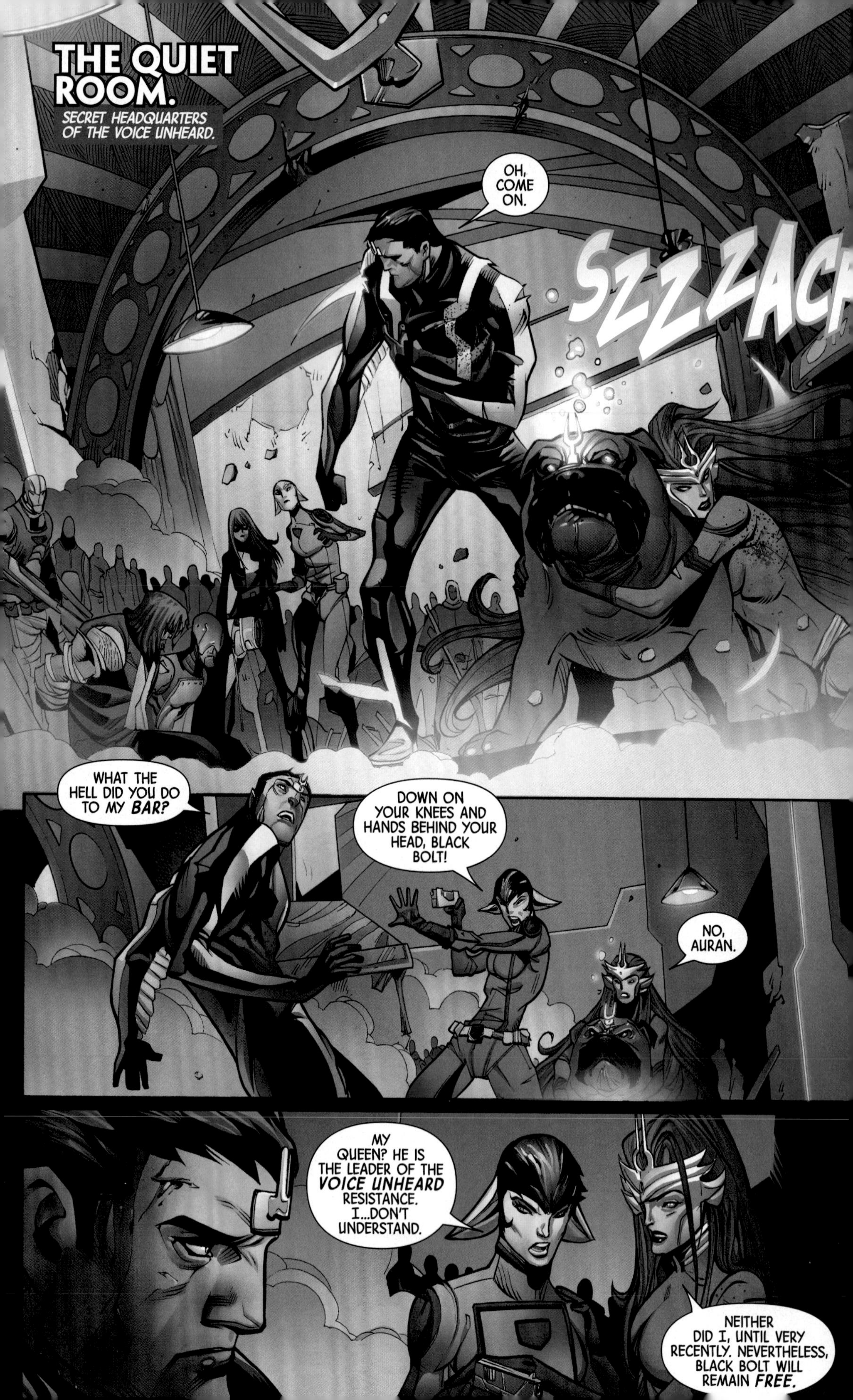
THE QUIET ROOM.
SECRET HEADQUARTERS OF THE VOICE UNHEARD.
OH, COME ON.
SZZZACK
WHAT THE HELL DID YOU DO TO MY BAR?
DOWN ON YOUR KNEES AND HANDS BEHIND YOUR HEAD, BLACK BOLT!
NO, AURAN.
MY QUEEN? HE IS THE LEADER OF THE VOICE UNHEARD RESISTANCE. I...DON'T UNDERSTAND.
NEITHER DID I, UNTIL VERY RECENTLY. NEVERTHELESS, BLACK BOLT WILL REMAIN FREE.

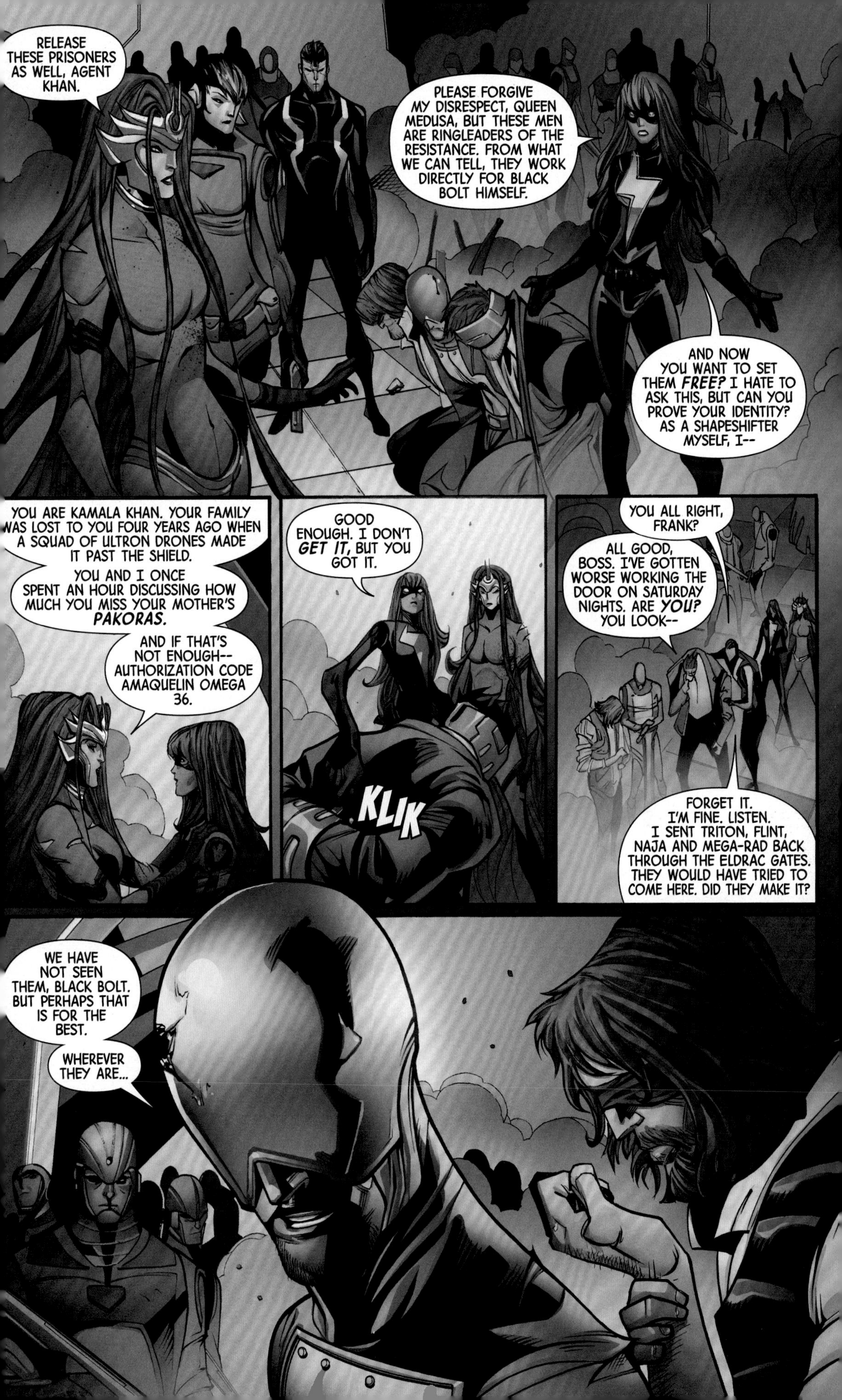
RELEASE THESE PRISONERS AS WELL, AGENT KHAN.
PLEASE FORGIVE MY DISRESPECT, QUEEN MEDUSA, BUT THESE MEN ARE RINGLEADERS OF THE RESISTANCE. FROM WHAT WE CAN TELL, THEY WORK DIRECTLY FOR BLACK BOLT HIMSELF.
AND NOW YOU WANT TO SET THEM *FREE?* I HATE TO ASK THIS, BUT CAN YOU PROVE YOUR IDENTITY? AS A SHAPESHIFTER MYSELF, I--
YOU ARE KAMALA KHAN. YOUR FAMILY WAS LOST TO YOU FOUR YEARS AGO WHEN A SQUAD OF ULTRON DRONES MADE IT PAST THE SHIELD.
YOU AND I ONCE SPENT AN HOUR DISCUSSING HOW MUCH YOU MISS YOUR MOTHER'S *PAKORAS.*
AND IF THAT'S NOT ENOUGH-- AUTHORIZATION CODE AMAQUELIN OMEGA 36.
GOOD ENOUGH. I DON'T *GET IT,* BUT YOU GOT IT.
KLIK
YOU ALL RIGHT, FRANK?
ALL GOOD, BOSS. I'VE GOTTEN WORSE WORKING THE DOOR ON SATURDAY NIGHTS. ARE *YOU?* YOU LOOK--
FORGET IT. I'M FINE. LISTEN. I SENT TRITON, FLINT, NAJA AND MEGA-RAD BACK THROUGH THE ELDRAC GATES. THEY WOULD HAVE TRIED TO COME HERE. DID THEY MAKE IT?
WE HAVE NOT SEEN THEM, BLACK BOLT. BUT PERHAPS THAT IS FOR THE BEST.
WHEREVER THEY ARE...

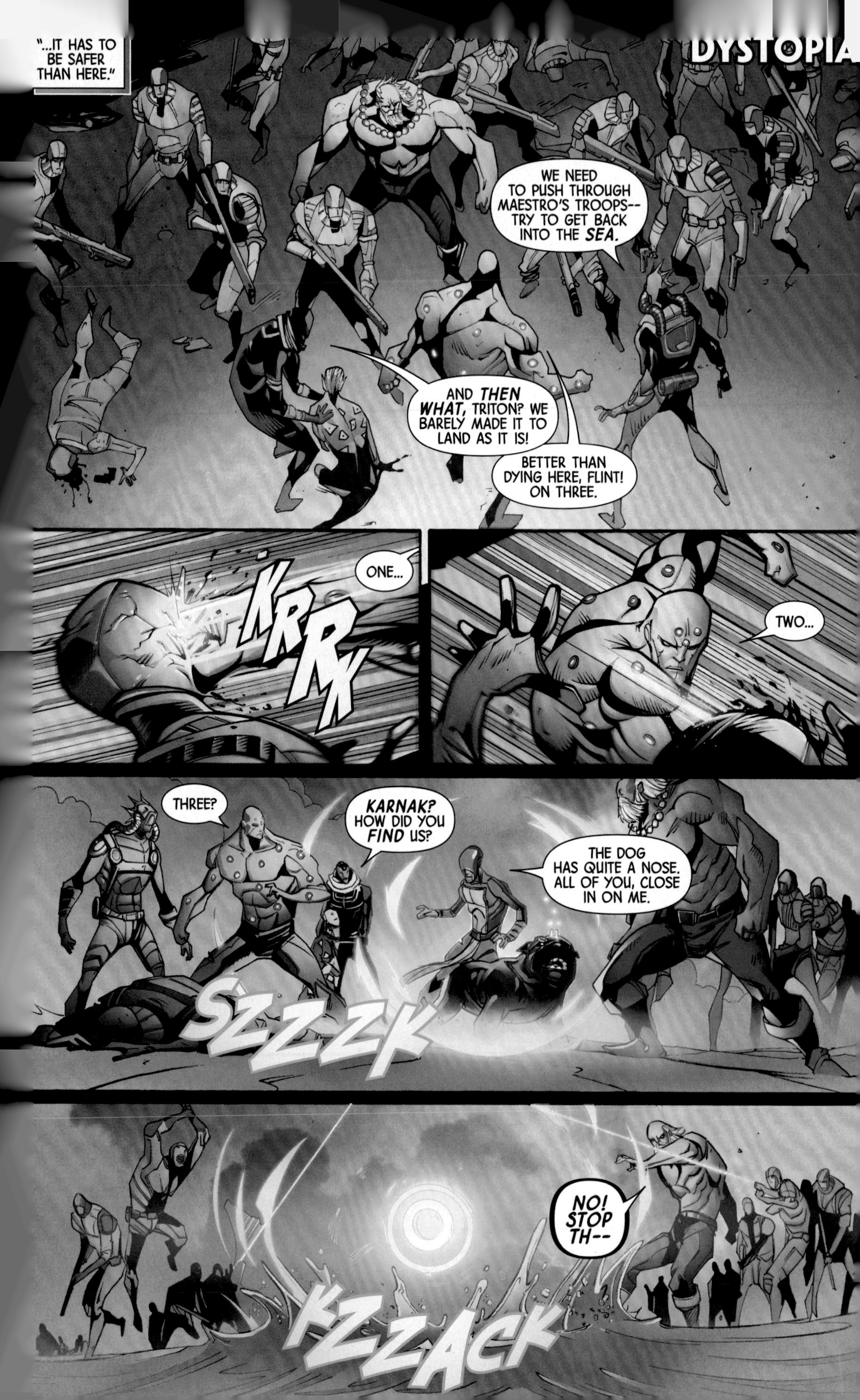

"...IT HAS TO BE SAFER THAN HERE."
DYSTOPIA
WE NEED TO PUSH THROUGH MAESTRO'S TROOPS-- TRY TO GET BACK INTO THE SEA.
AND THEN WHAT, TRITON? WE BARELY MADE IT TO LAND AS IT IS!
BETTER THAN DYING HERE, FLINT! ON THREE.
ONE...
KRRRK
TWO...
THREE?
KARNAK? HOW DID YOU FIND US?
THE DOG HAS QUITE A NOSE. ALL OF YOU, CLOSE IN ON ME.
SZZZK
NO! STOP TH--
KZZACK

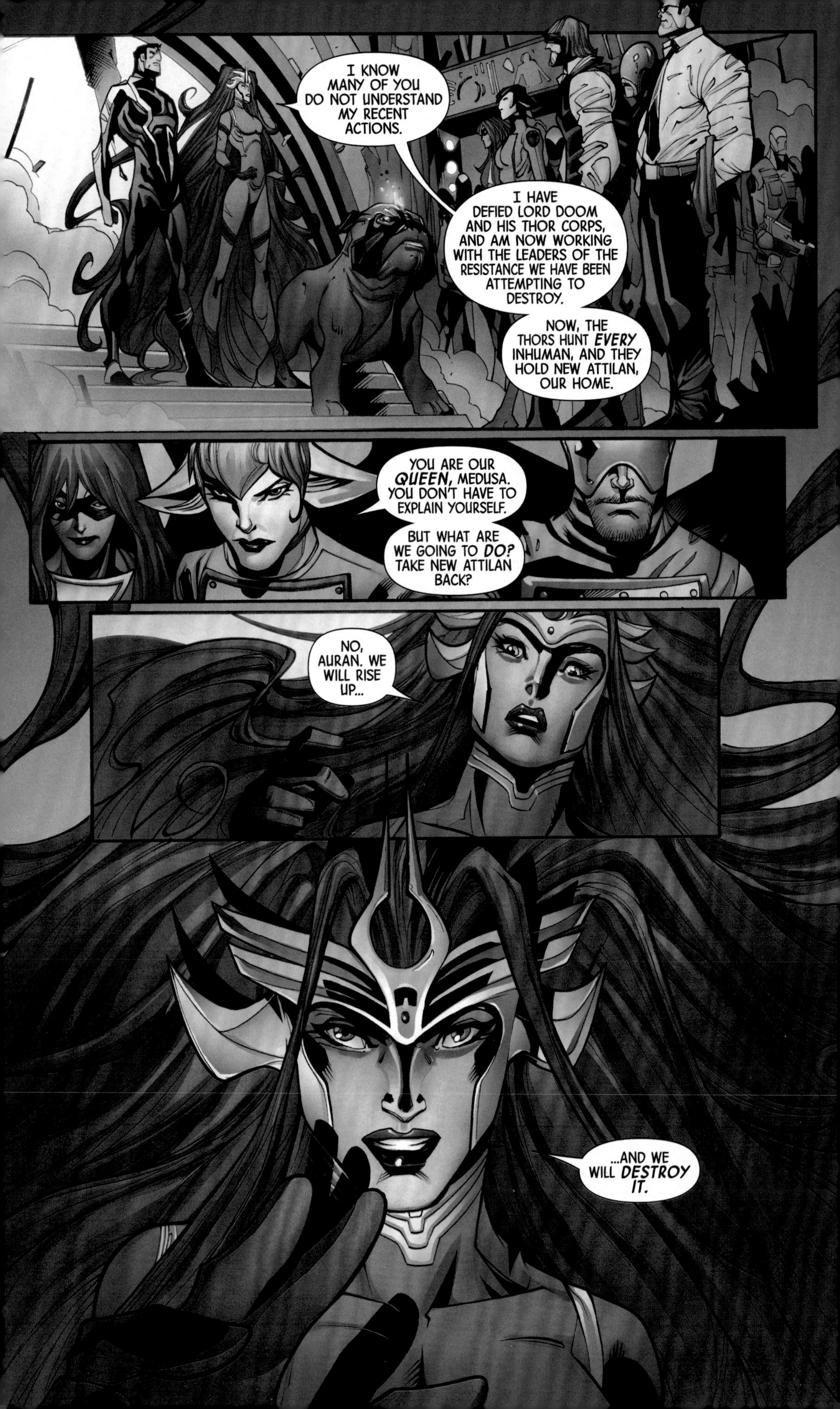

I KNOW MANY OF YOU DO NOT UNDERSTAND MY RECENT ACTIONS.
I HAVE DEFIED LORD DOOM AND HIS THOR CORPS, AND AM NOW WORKING WITH THE LEADERS OF THE RESISTANCE WE HAVE BEEN ATTEMPTING TO DESTROY.
NOW, THE THORS HUNT *EVERY* INHUMAN, AND THEY HOLD NEW ATTILAN, OUR HOME.
YOU ARE OUR ***QUEEN,*** MEDUSA. YOU DON'T HAVE TO EXPLAIN YOURSELF.
BUT WHAT ARE WE GOING TO *DO?* TAKE NEW ATTILAN BACK?
NO, AURAN. WE WILL RISE UP...
...AND WE WILL *DESTROY IT.*

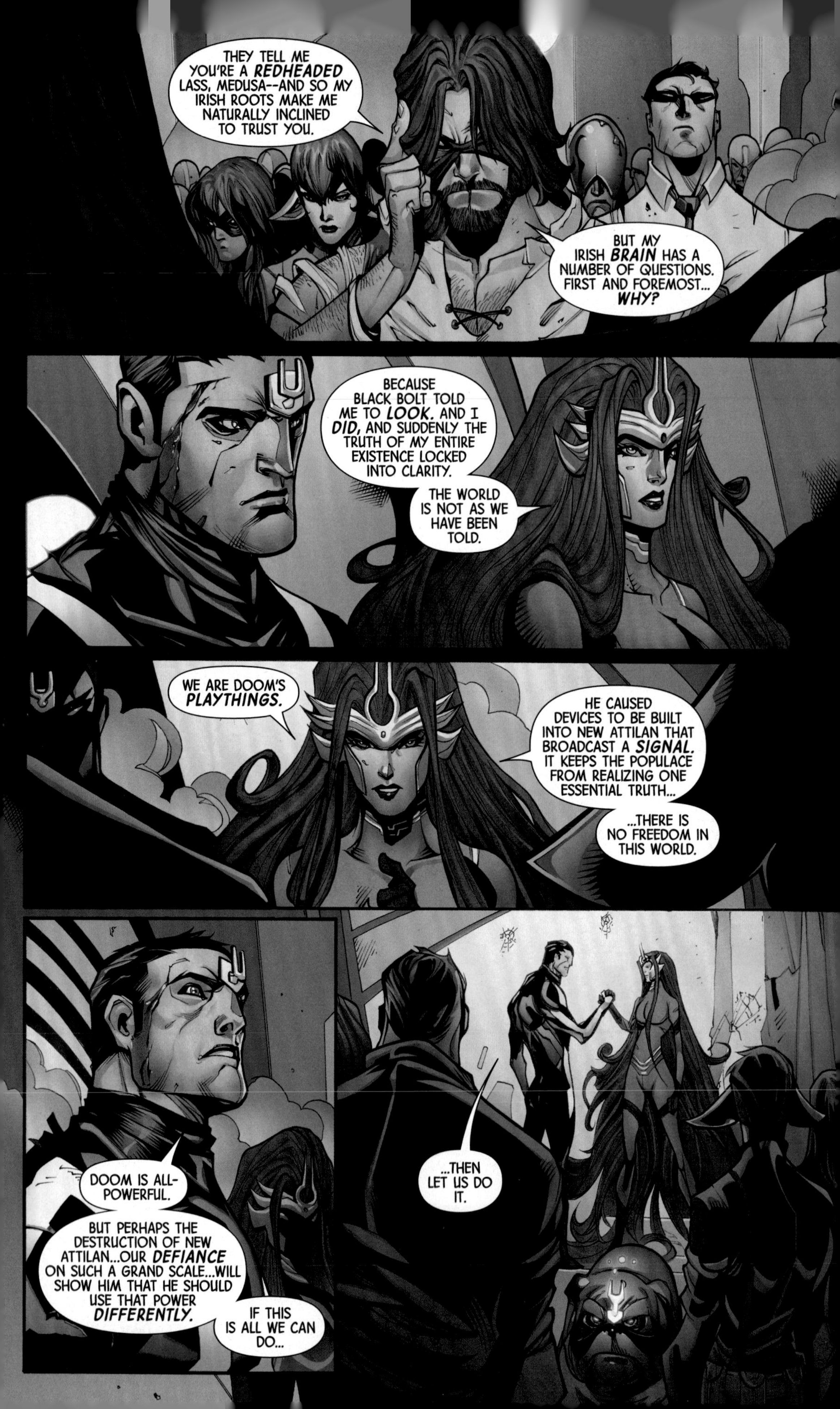
THEY TELL ME YOU'RE A REDHEADED LASS, MEDUSA--AND SO MY IRISH ROOTS MAKE ME NATURALLY INCLINED TO TRUST YOU.
BUT MY IRISH BRAIN HAS A NUMBER OF QUESTIONS. FIRST AND FOREMOST... WHY?
BECAUSE BLACK BOLT TOLD ME TO LOOK. AND I DID, AND SUDDENLY THE TRUTH OF MY ENTIRE EXISTENCE LOCKED INTO CLARITY.
THE WORLD IS NOT AS WE HAVE BEEN TOLD.
WE ARE DOOM'S PLAYTHINGS.
HE CAUSED DEVICES TO BE BUILT INTO NEW ATTILAN THAT BROADCAST A SIGNAL. IT KEEPS THE POPULACE FROM REALIZING ONE ESSENTIAL TRUTH...
...THERE IS NO FREEDOM IN THIS WORLD.
DOOM IS ALL-POWERFUL.
BUT PERHAPS THE DESTRUCTION OF NEW ATTILAN...OUR DEFIANCE ON SUCH A GRAND SCALE...WILL SHOW HIM THAT HE SHOULD USE THAT POWER DIFFERENTLY.
IF THIS IS ALL WE CAN DO...
...THEN LET US DO IT.

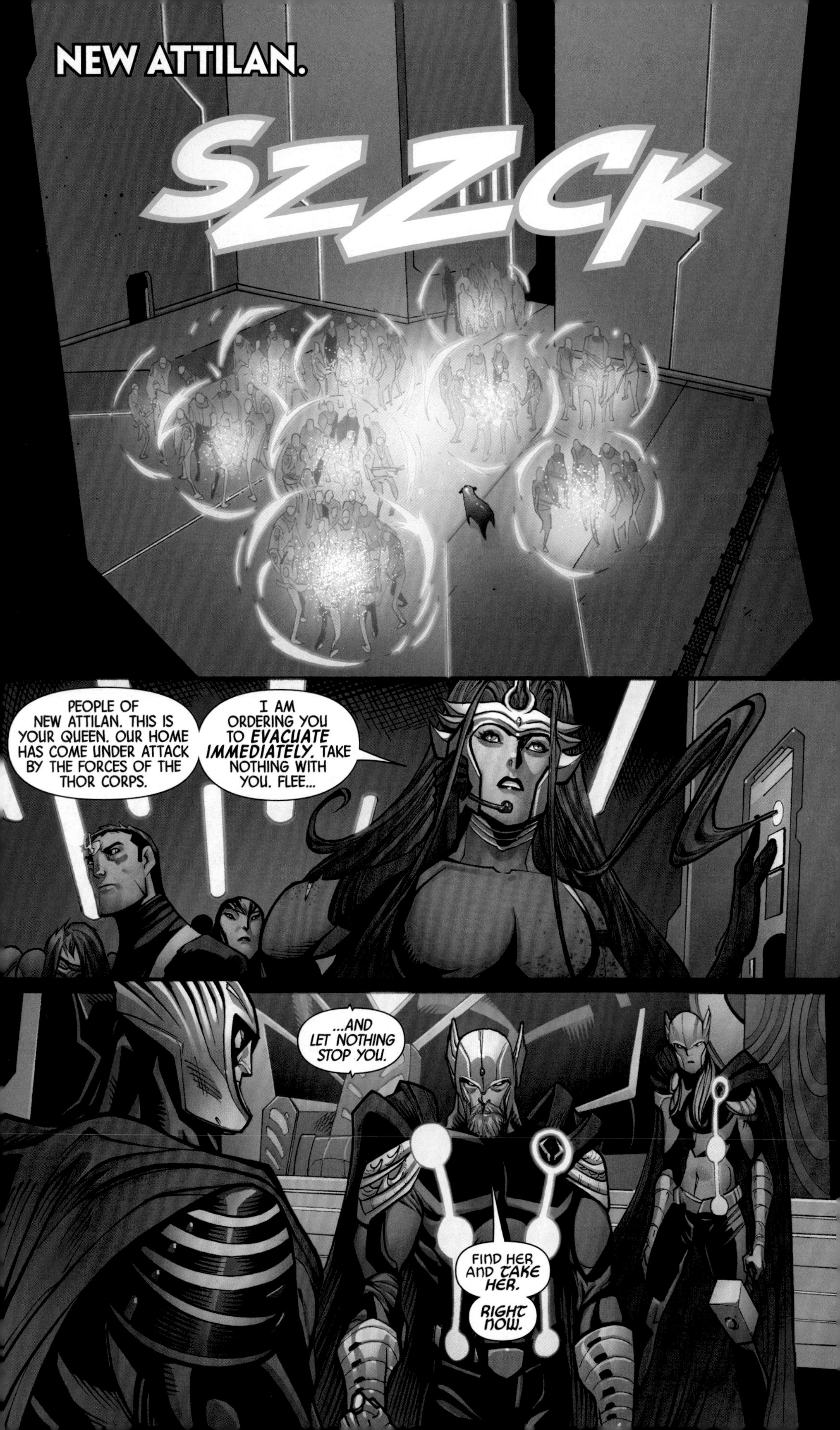
NEW ATTILAN.
SZZCK
PEOPLE OF NEW ATTILAN. THIS IS YOUR QUEEN. OUR HOME HAS COME UNDER ATTACK BY THE FORCES OF THE THOR CORPS.
I AM ORDERING YOU TO EVACUATE IMMEDIATELY. TAKE NOTHING WITH YOU. FLEE...
...AND LET NOTHING STOP YOU.
FIND HER AND TAKE HER.
RIGHT NOW.

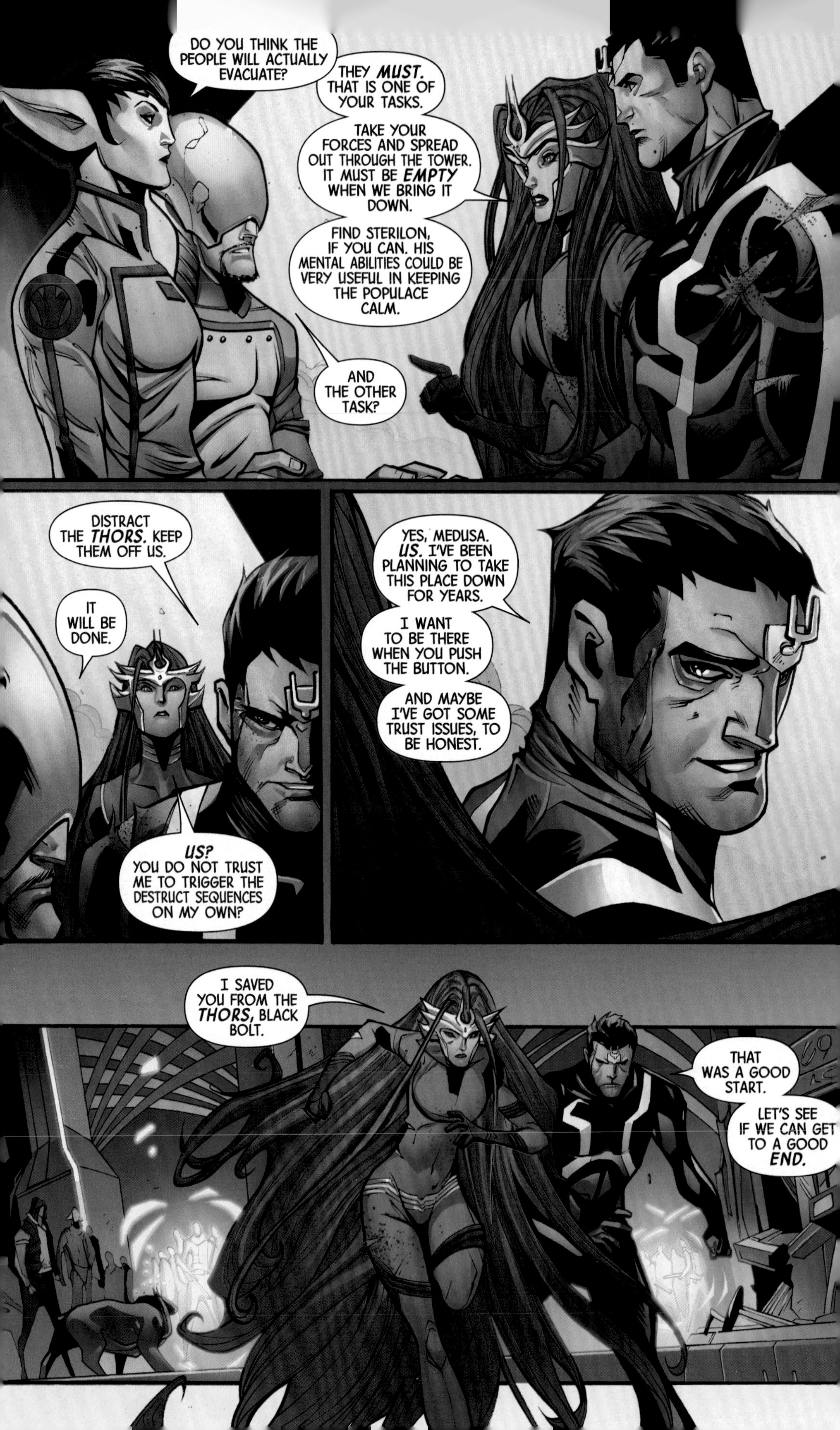
DO YOU THINK THE PEOPLE WILL ACTUALLY EVACUATE?
THEY MUST. THAT IS ONE OF YOUR TASKS.
TAKE YOUR FORCES AND SPREAD OUT THROUGH THE TOWER. IT MUST BE EMPTY WHEN WE BRING IT DOWN.
FIND STERILON, IF YOU CAN. HIS MENTAL ABILITIES COULD BE VERY USEFUL IN KEEPING THE POPULACE CALM.
AND THE OTHER TASK?
DISTRACT THE THORS. KEEP THEM OFF US.
IT WILL BE DONE.
US? YOU DO NOT TRUST ME TO TRIGGER THE DESTRUCT SEQUENCES ON MY OWN?
YES, MEDUSA. US. I'VE BEEN PLANNING TO TAKE THIS PLACE DOWN FOR YEARS.
I WANT TO BE THERE WHEN YOU PUSH THE BUTTON.
AND MAYBE I'VE GOT SOME TRUST ISSUES, TO BE HONEST.
I SAVED YOU FROM THE THORS, BLACK BOLT.
THAT WAS A GOOD START.
LET'S SEE IF WE CAN GET TO A GOOD END.

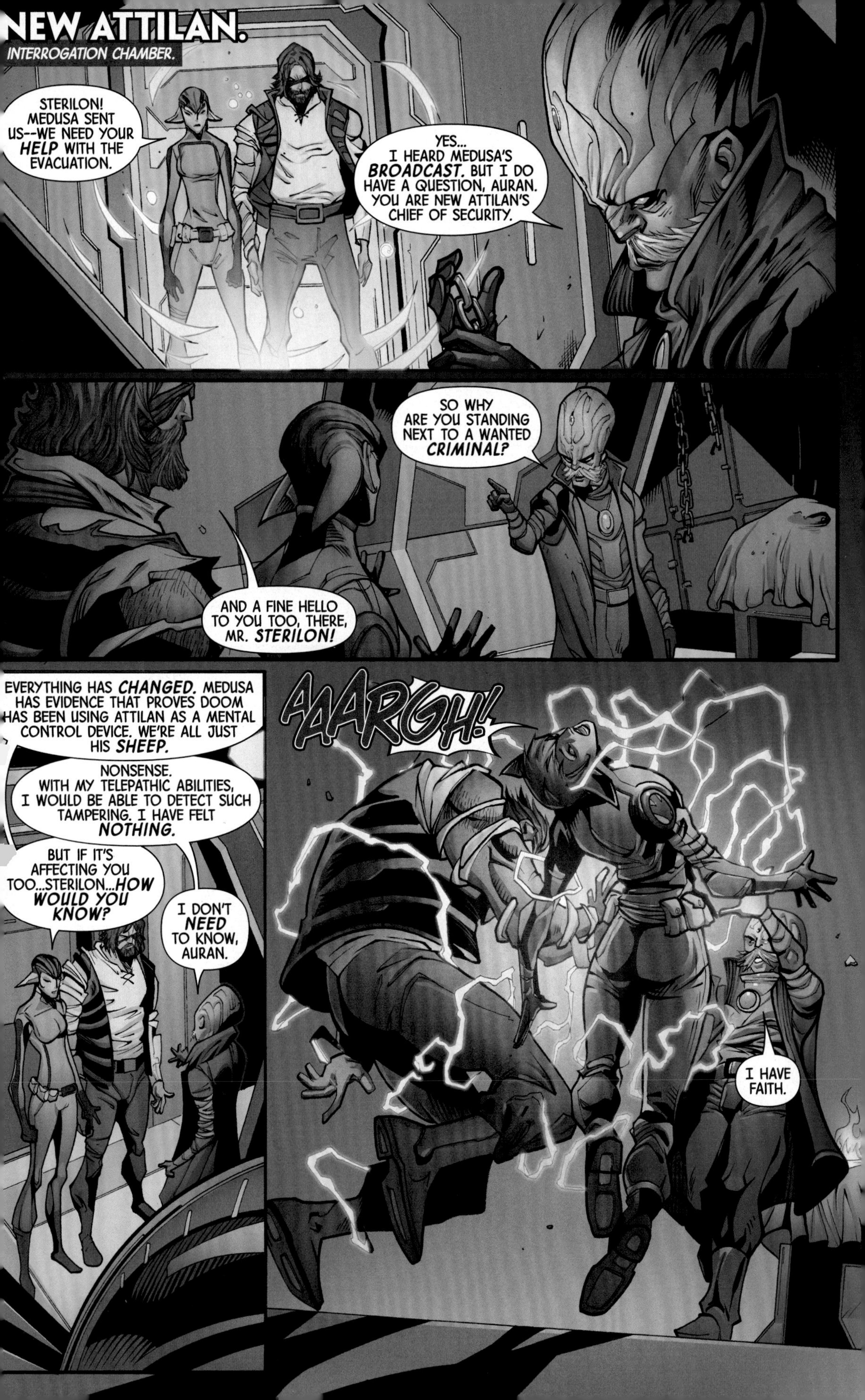
NEW ATTILAN.
INTERROGATION CHAMBER.
STERILON! MEDUSA SENT US--WE NEED YOUR HELP WITH THE EVACUATION.
YES... I HEARD MEDUSA'S BROADCAST. BUT I DO HAVE A QUESTION, AURAN. YOU ARE NEW ATTILAN'S CHIEF OF SECURITY.
SO WHY ARE YOU STANDING NEXT TO A WANTED CRIMINAL?
AND A FINE HELLO TO YOU TOO, THERE, MR. STERILON!
EVERYTHING HAS CHANGED. MEDUSA HAS EVIDENCE THAT PROVES DOOM HAS BEEN USING ATTILAN AS A MENTAL CONTROL DEVICE. WE'RE ALL JUST HIS SHEEP.
NONSENSE. WITH MY TELEPATHIC ABILITIES, I WOULD BE ABLE TO DETECT SUCH TAMPERING. I HAVE FELT NOTHING.
BUT IF IT'S AFFECTING YOU TOO...STERILON...HOW WOULD YOU KNOW?
I DON'T NEED TO KNOW, AURAN.
AAARGH!
I HAVE FAITH.

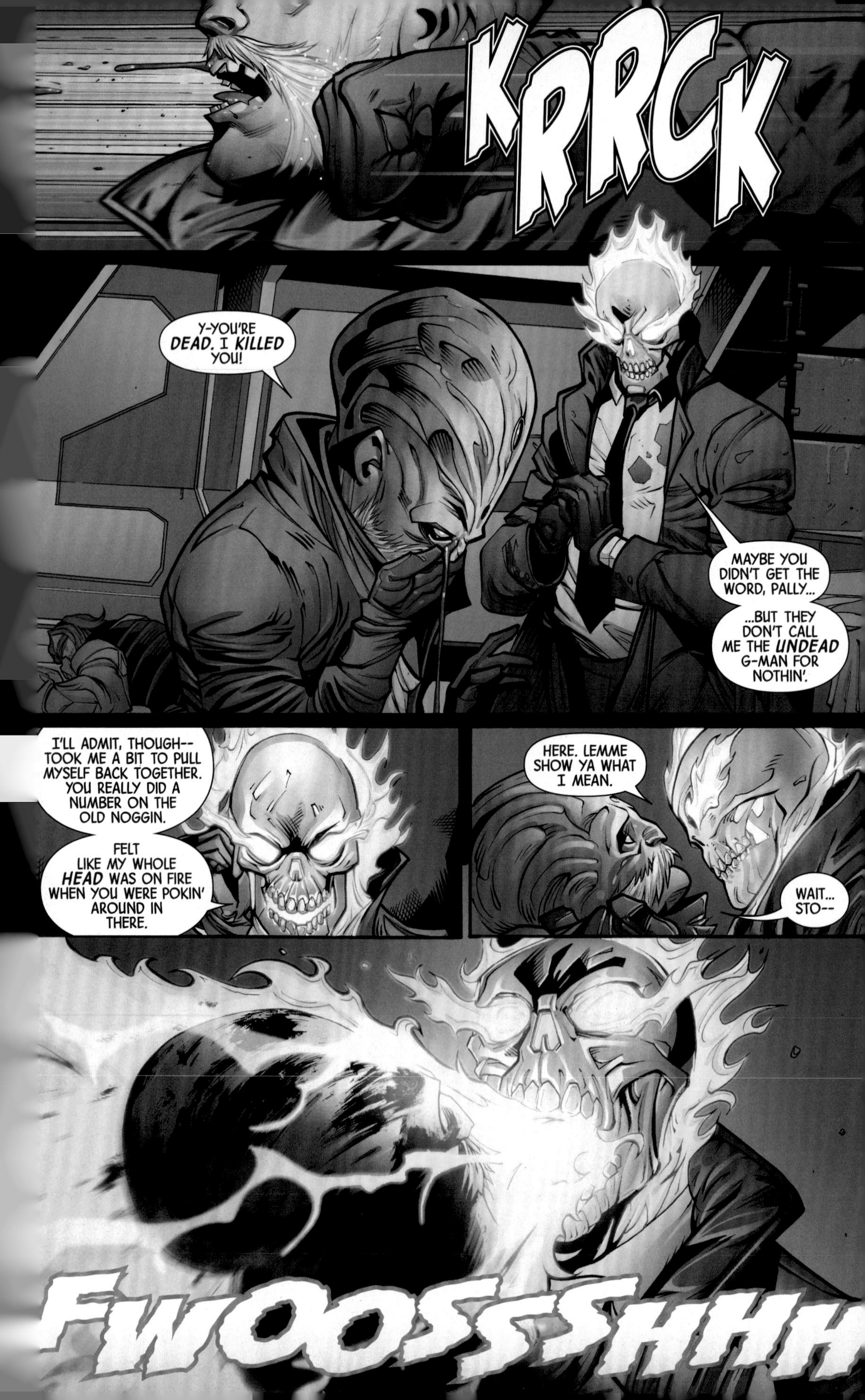
KRRCK
Y-YOU'RE DEAD. I KILLED YOU!
MAYBE YOU DIDN'T GET THE WORD, PALLY...
...BUT THEY DON'T CALL ME THE UNDEAD G-MAN FOR NOTHIN'.
I'LL ADMIT, THOUGH-- TOOK ME A BIT TO PULL MYSELF BACK TOGETHER. YOU REALLY DID A NUMBER ON THE OLD NOGGIN.
FELT LIKE MY WHOLE HEAD WAS ON FIRE WHEN YOU WERE POKIN' AROUND IN THERE.
HERE. LEMME SHOW YA WHAT I MEAN.
WAIT... STO--
FWOOSSHHH

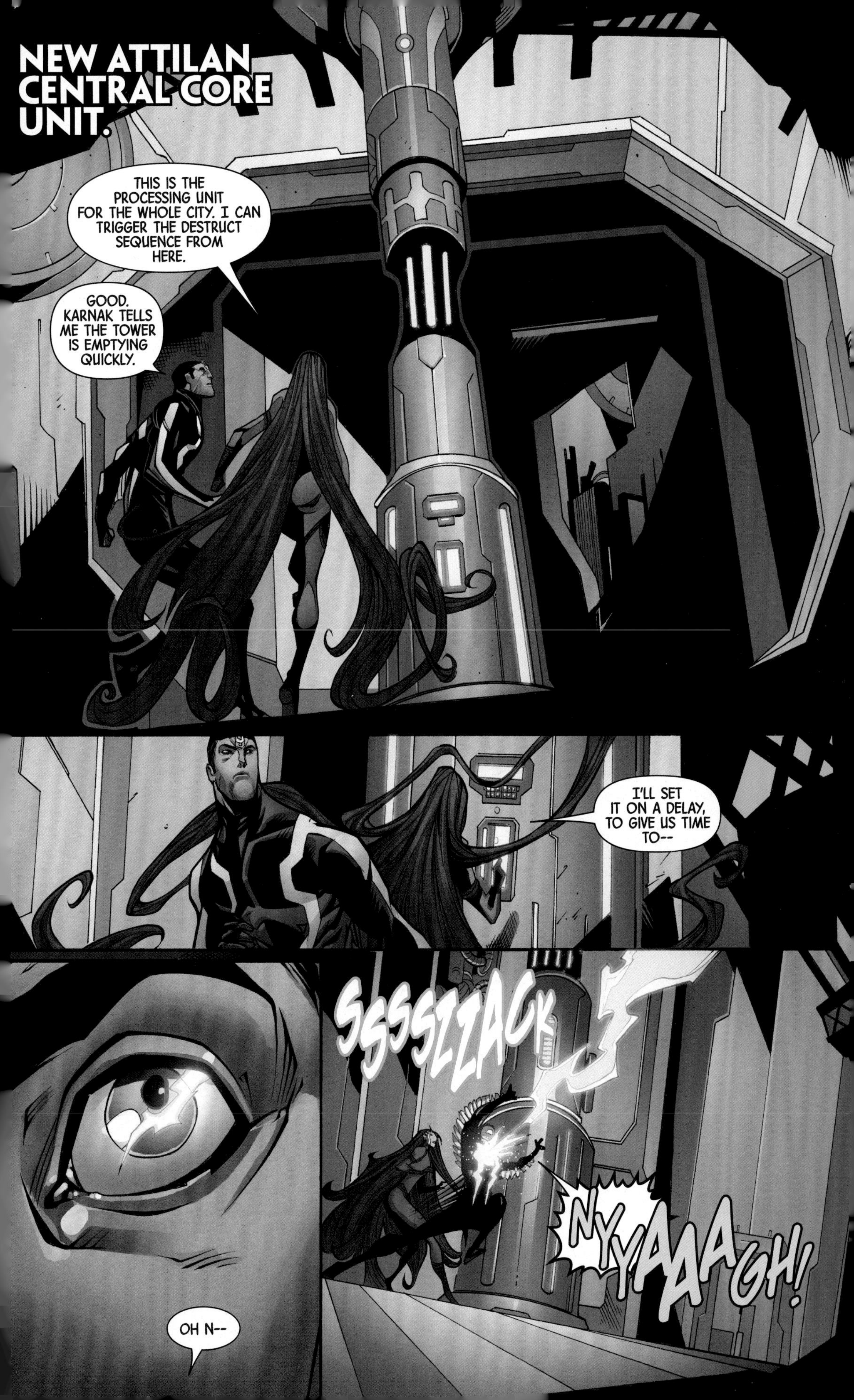
NEW ATTILAN CENTRAL CORE UNIT.
THIS IS THE PROCESSING UNIT FOR THE WHOLE CITY. I CAN TRIGGER THE DESTRUCT SEQUENCE FROM HERE.
GOOD. KARNAK TELLS ME THE TOWER IS EMPTYING QUICKLY.
I'LL SET IT ON A DELAY, TO GIVE US TIME TO--
SSSSZZACK
NYYAAAAGH!
OH N--

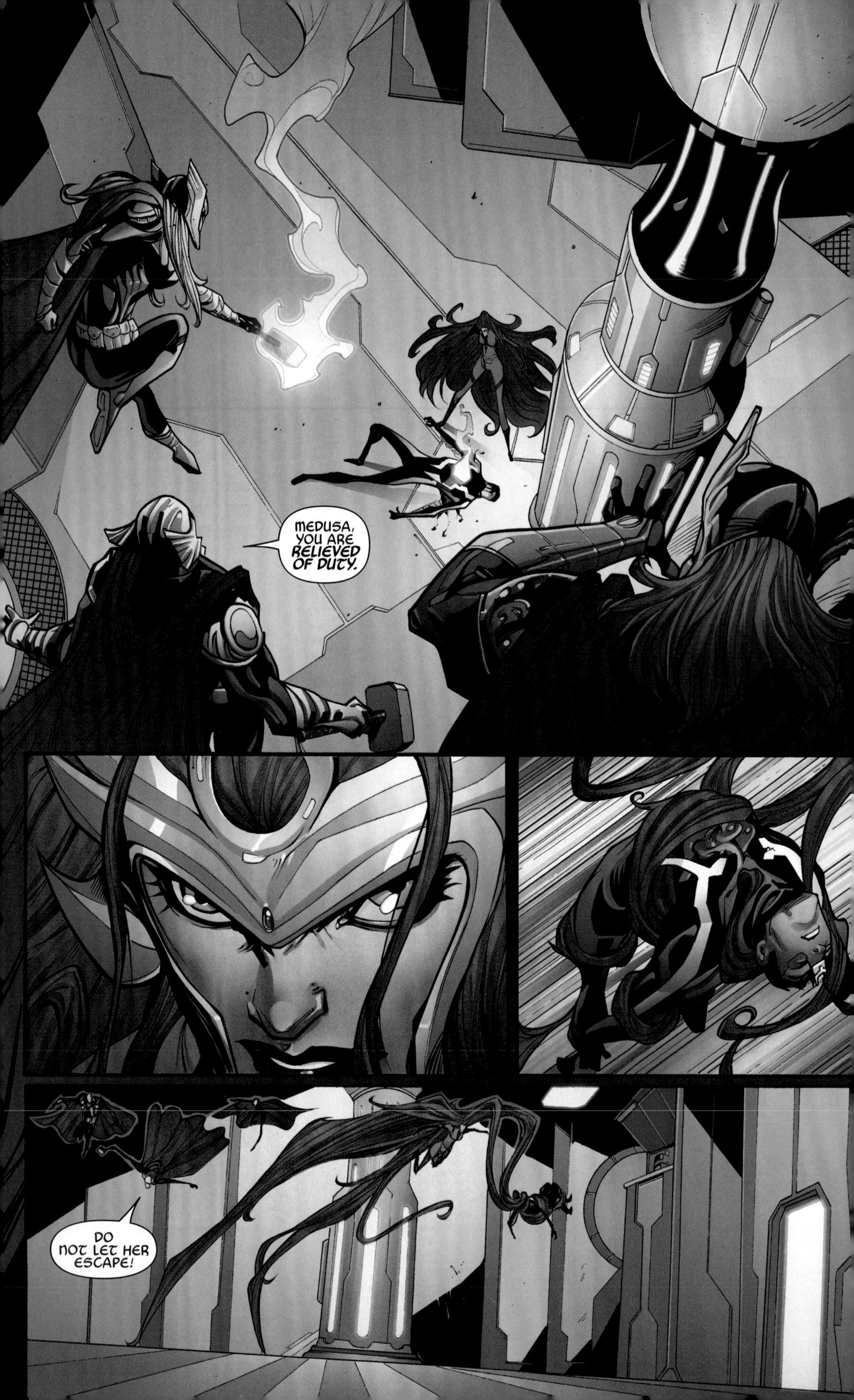
MEDUSA, YOU ARE RELIEVED OF DUTY.
DO NOT LET HER ESCAPE!

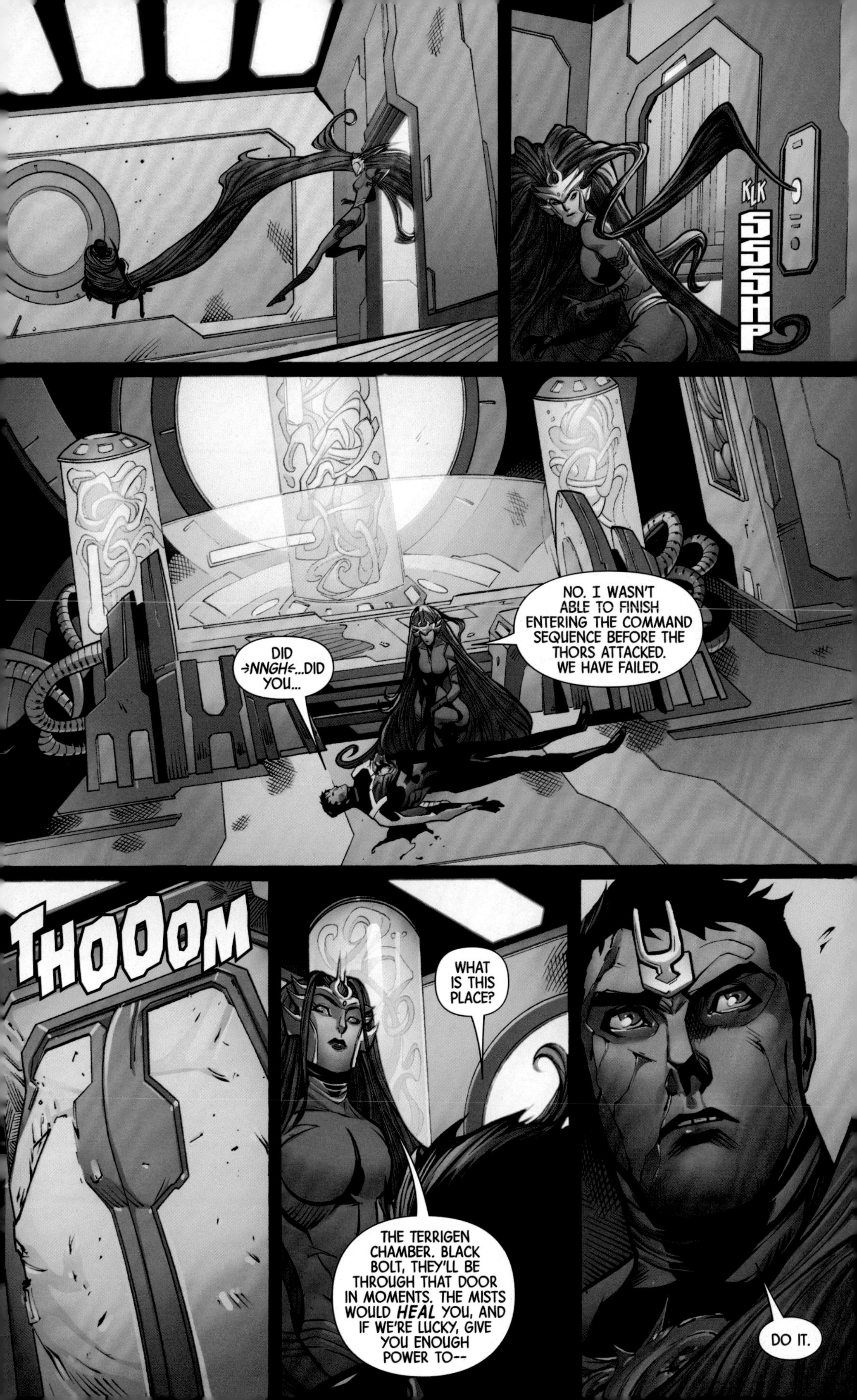
KLK
SSSHP
DID -NNGH-...DID YOU...
NO. I WASN'T ABLE TO FINISH ENTERING THE COMMAND SEQUENCE BEFORE THE THORS ATTACKED. WE HAVE FAILED.
THOOOM
WHAT IS THIS PLACE?
THE TERRIGEN CHAMBER. BLACK BOLT, THEY'LL BE THROUGH THAT DOOR IN MOMENTS. THE MISTS WOULD *HEAL* YOU, AND IF WE'RE LUCKY, GIVE YOU ENOUGH POWER TO--
DO IT.

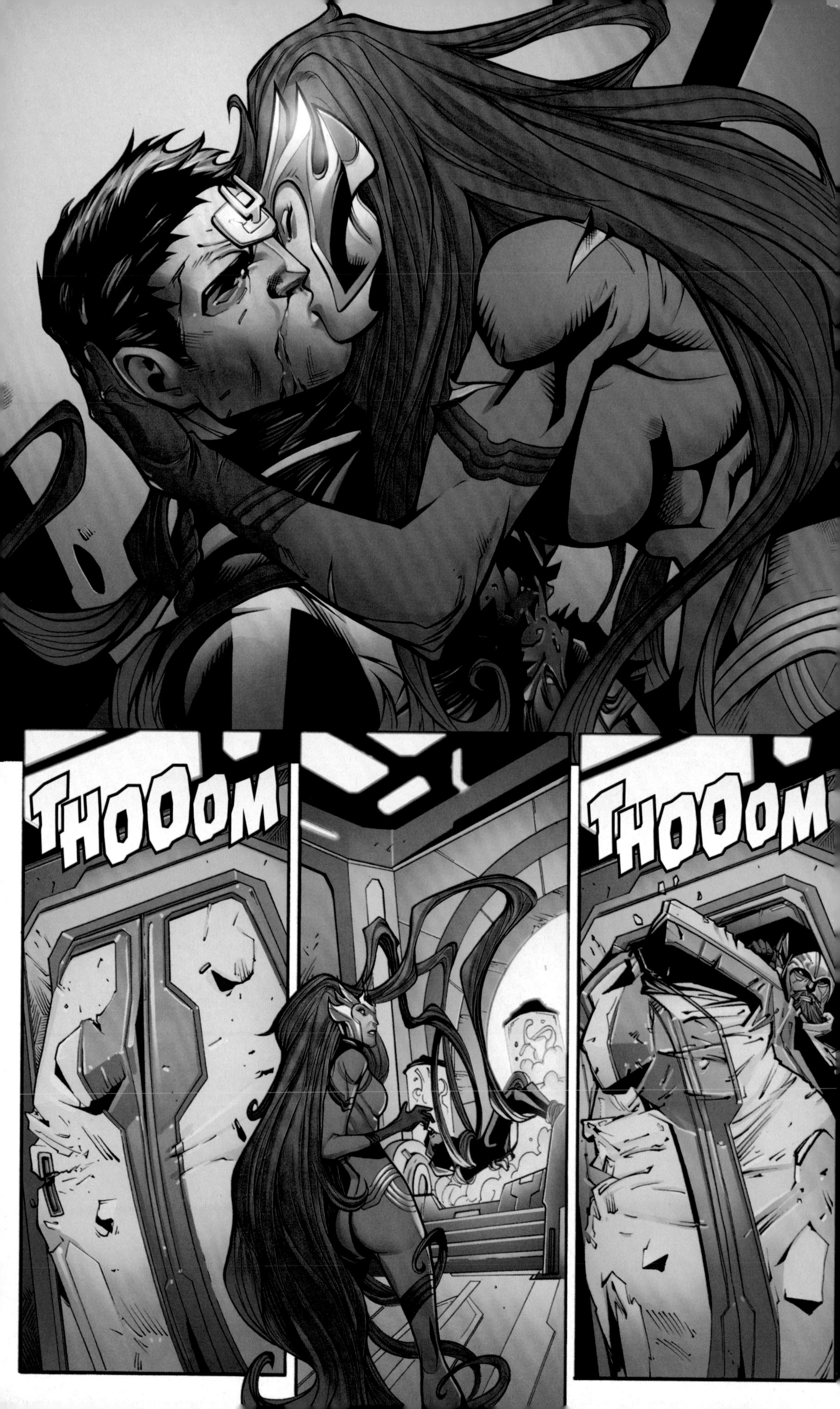
THOOOM
THOOOM

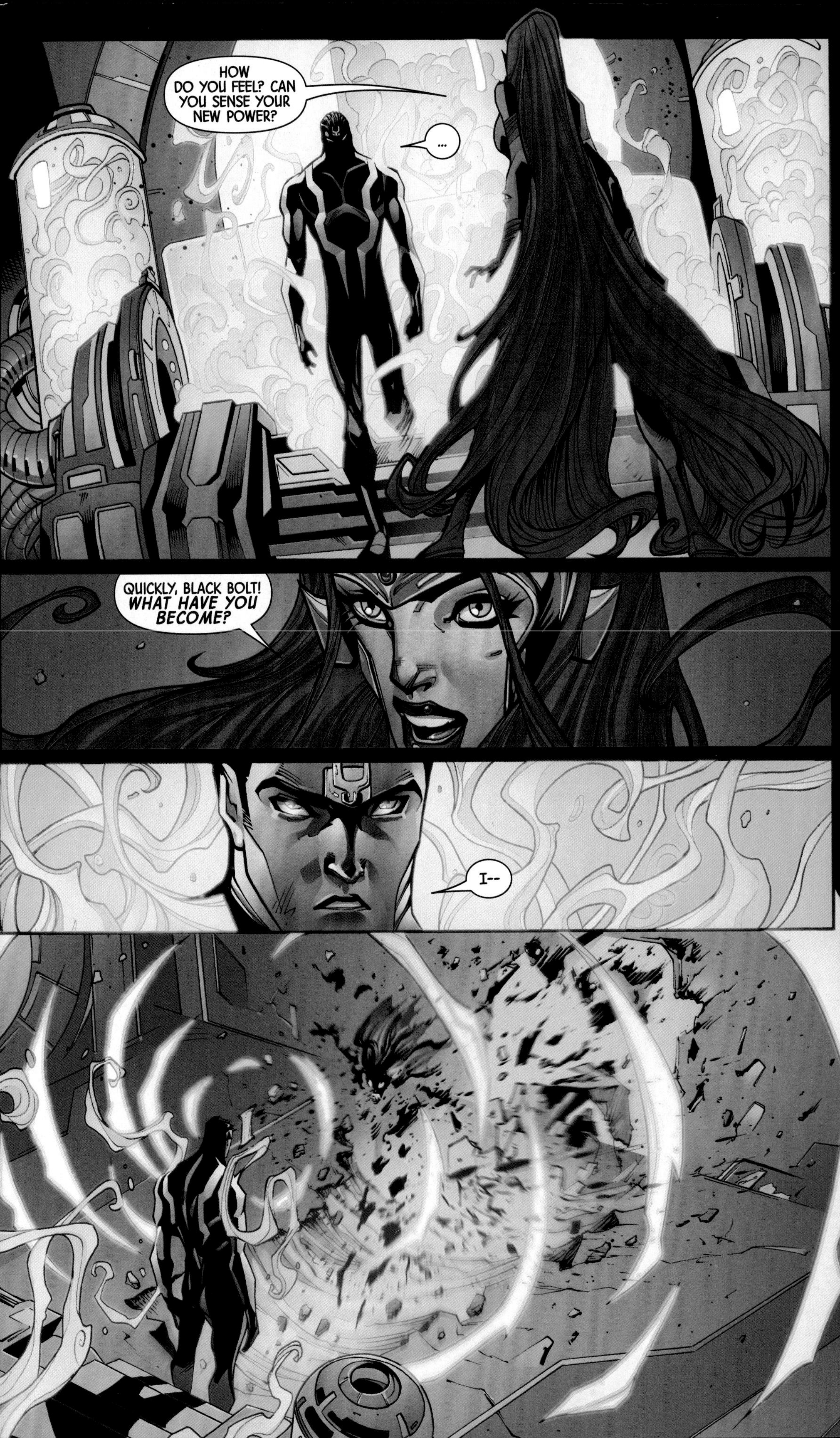
HOW DO YOU FEEL? CAN YOU SENSE YOUR NEW POWER?
...
QUICKLY, BLACK BOLT! WHAT HAVE YOU BECOME?
I--

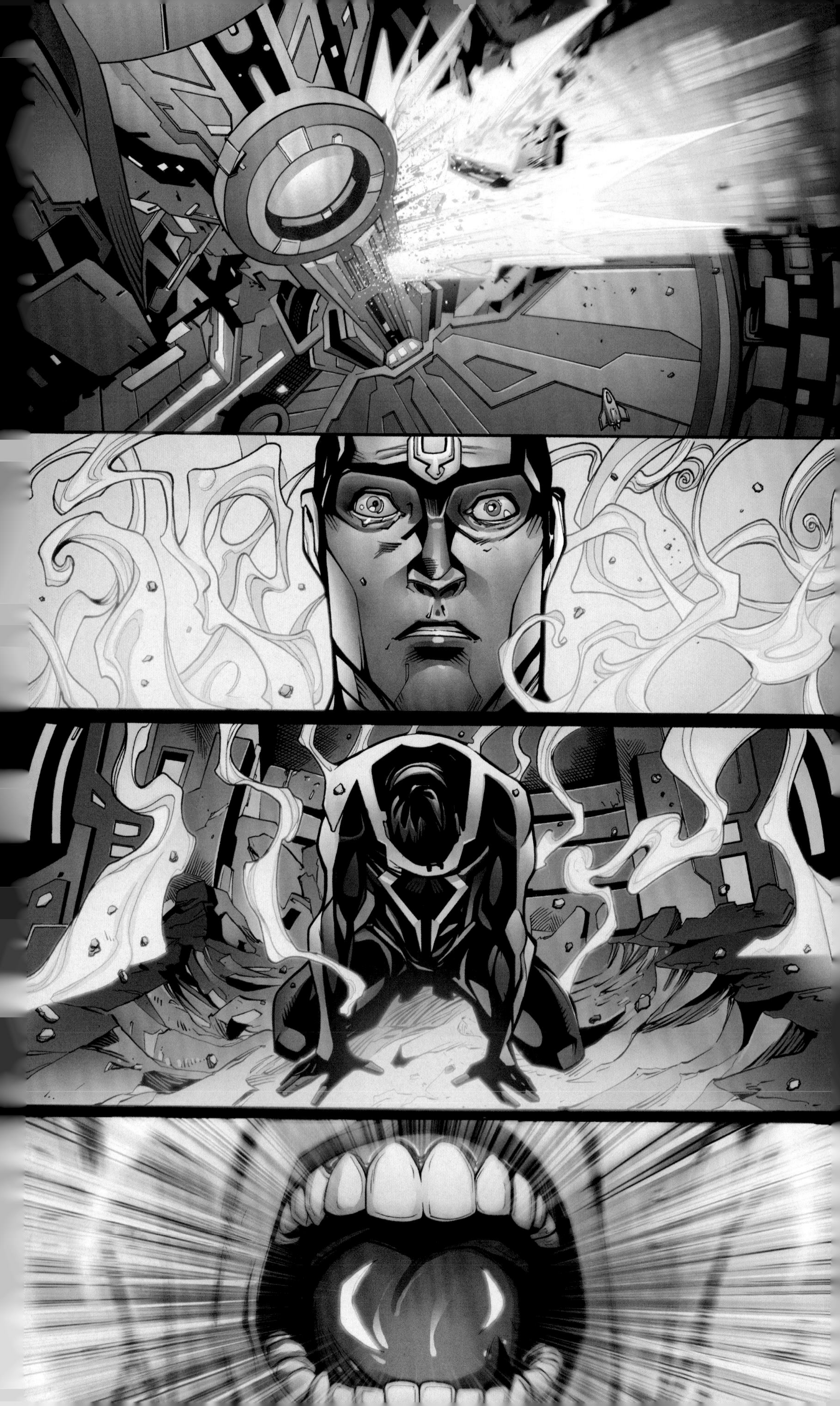

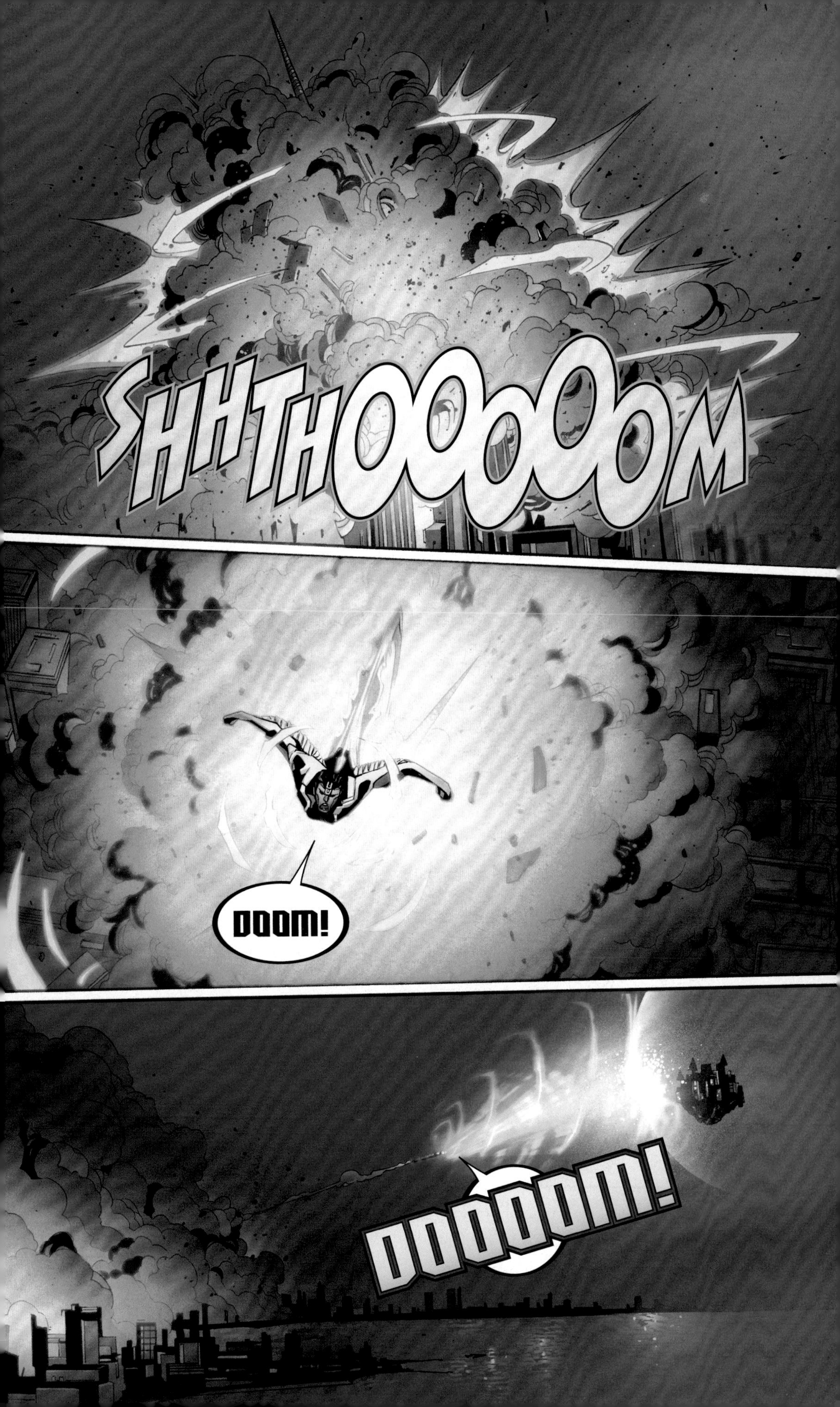
SHHTHOOOOOOM
DOOM!
DOOOOOM!

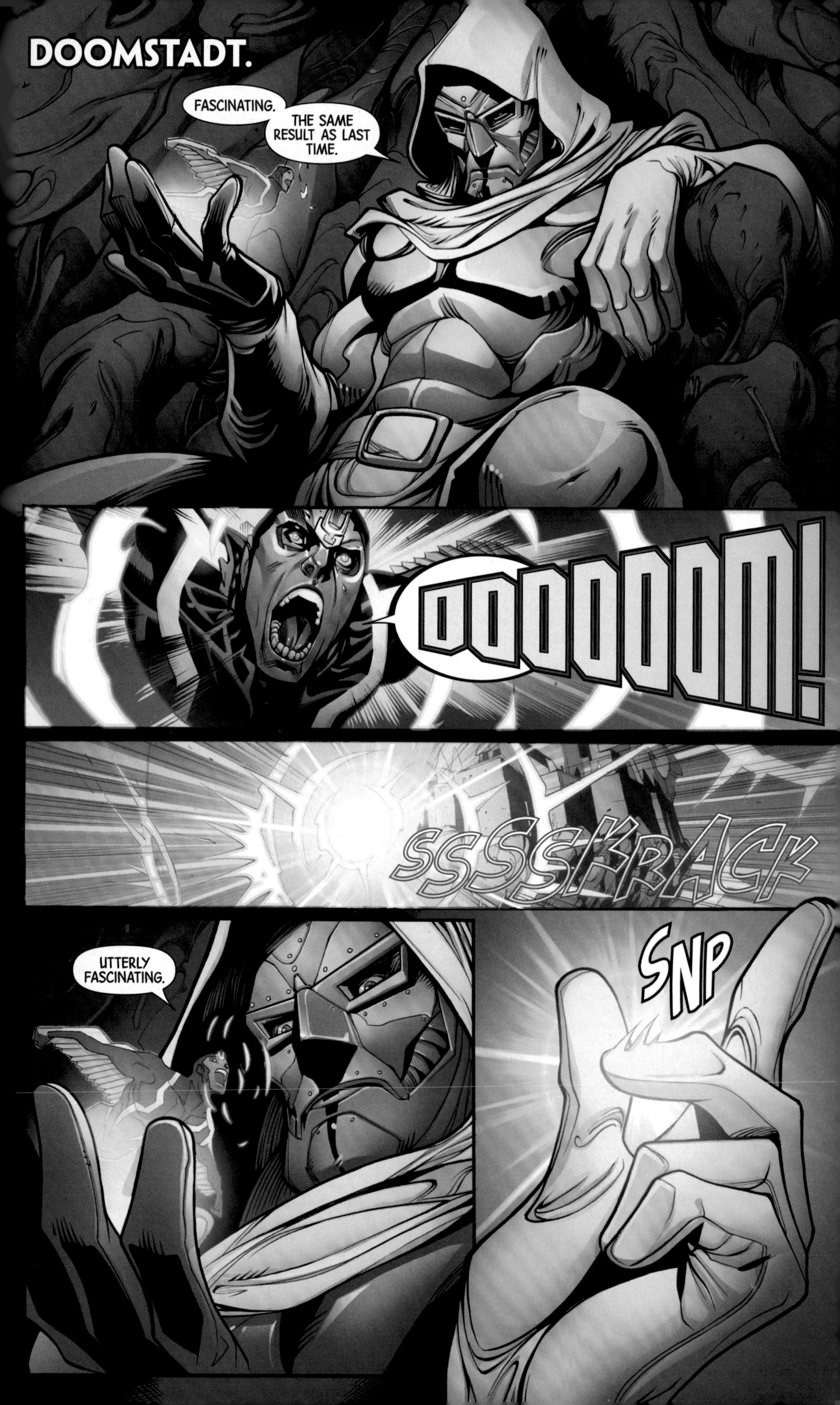
DOOMSTADT.
FASCINATING.
THE SAME RESULT AS LAST TIME.
DOOOOOOM!
SSSSK'RACK
UTTERLY FASCINATING.
SNP

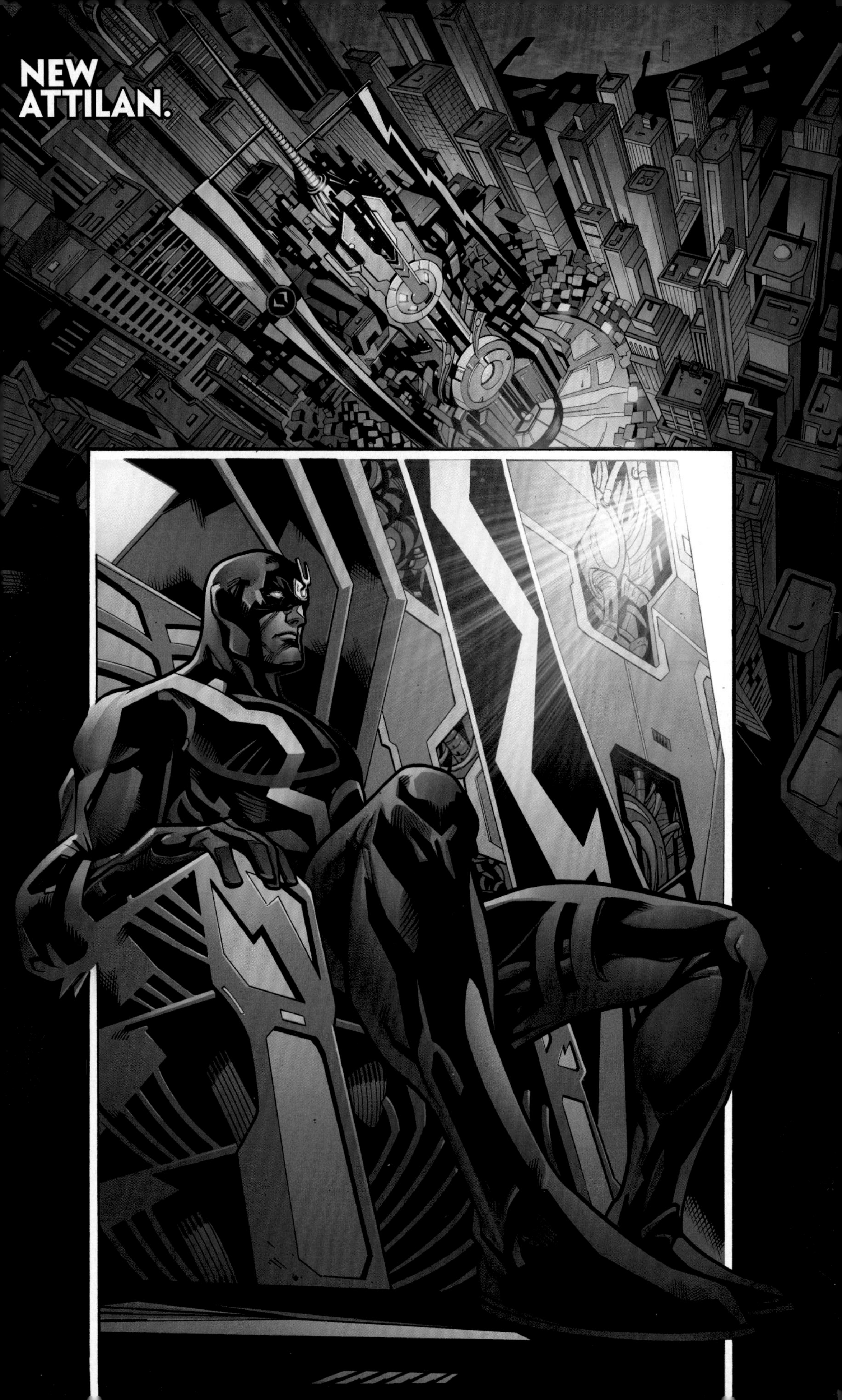
NEW ATTILAN.

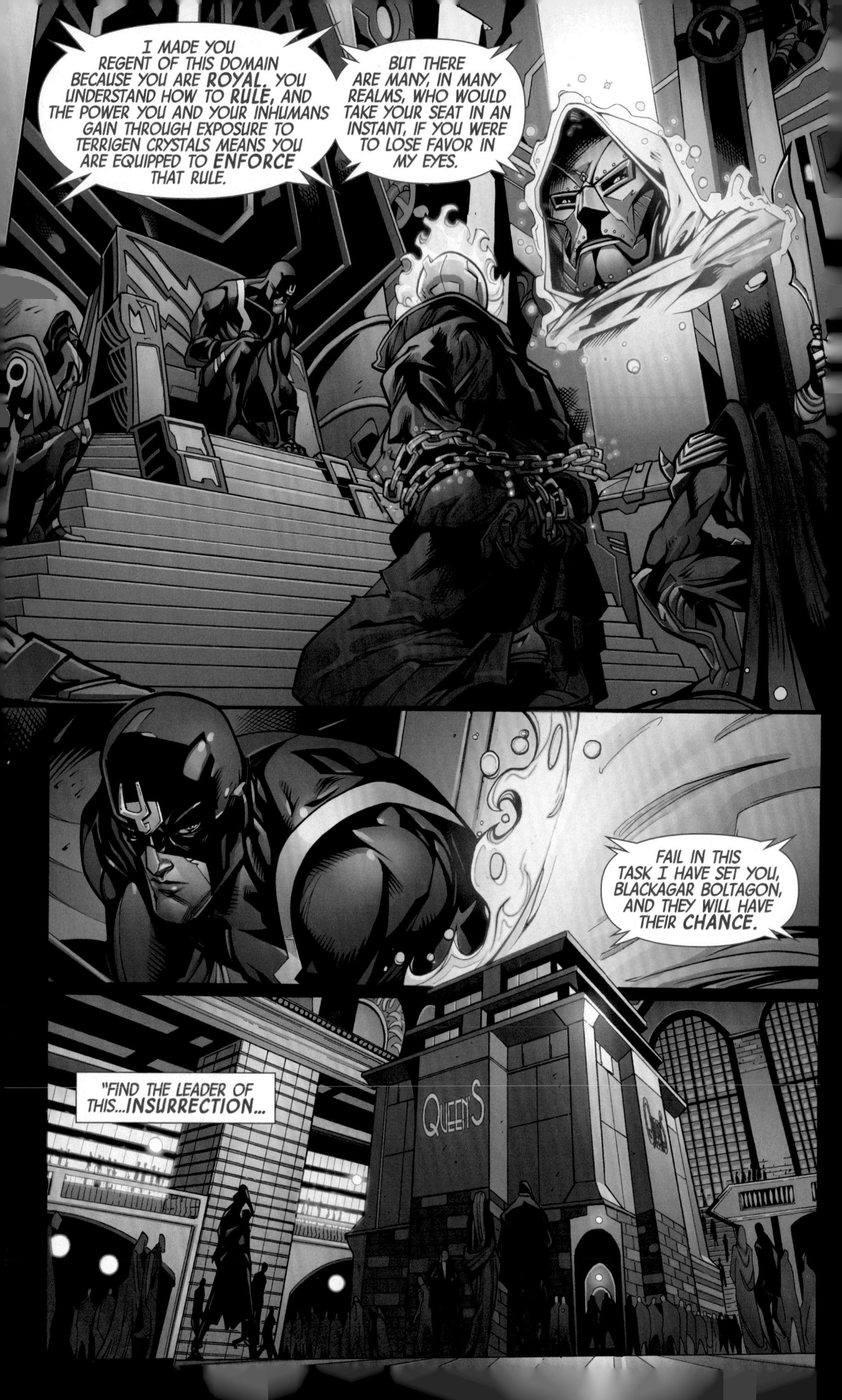
I MADE YOU REGENT OF THIS DOMAIN BECAUSE YOU ARE ROYAL. YOU UNDERSTAND HOW TO RULE, AND THE POWER YOU AND YOUR INHUMANS GAIN THROUGH EXPOSURE TO TERRIGEN CRYSTALS MEANS YOU ARE EQUIPPED TO ENFORCE THAT RULE.
BUT THERE ARE MANY, IN MANY REALMS, WHO WOULD TAKE YOUR SEAT IN AN INSTANT, IF YOU WERE TO LOSE FAVOR IN MY EYES.
FAIL IN THIS TASK I HAVE SET YOU, BLACKAGAR BOLTAGON, AND THEY WILL HAVE THEIR CHANCE.
"FIND THE LEADER OF THIS...INSURRECTION...
QUEEN'S

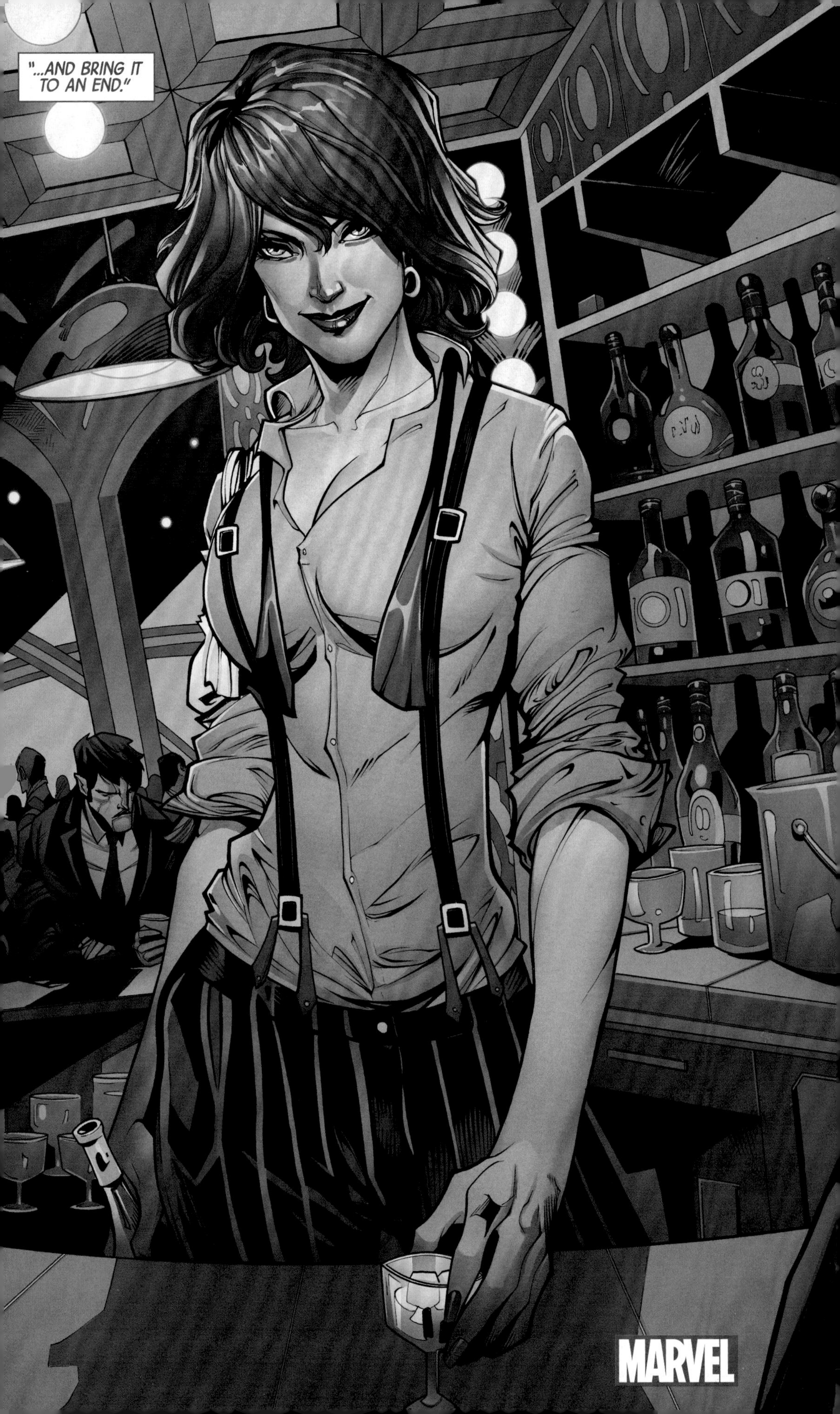
"...AND BRING IT
TO AN END."
MARVEL

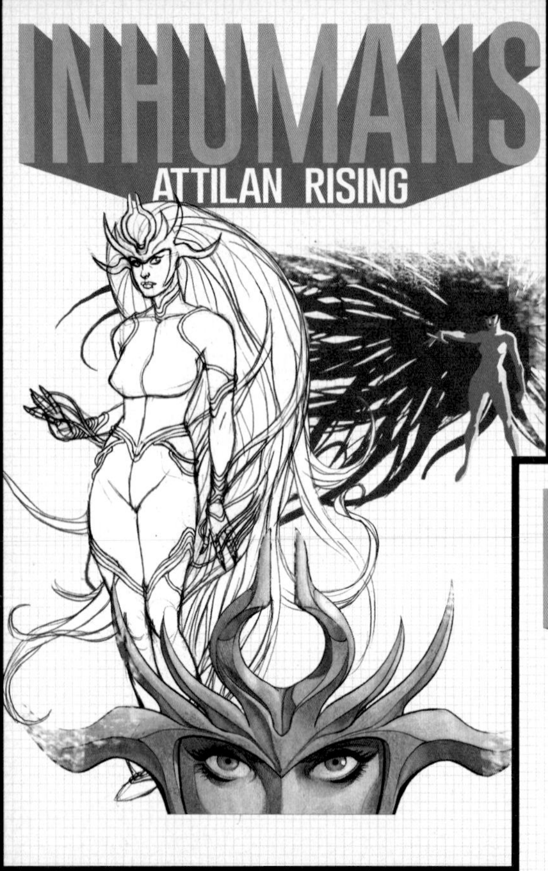
INHUMANS
ATTILAN RISING
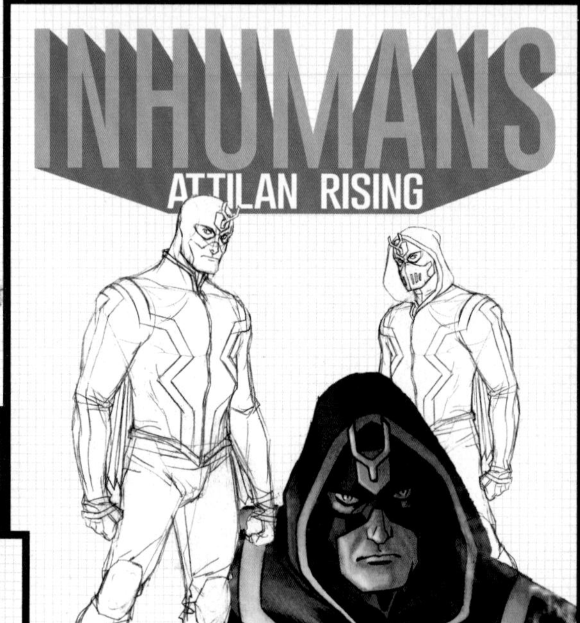
INHUMANS
ATTILAN RISING
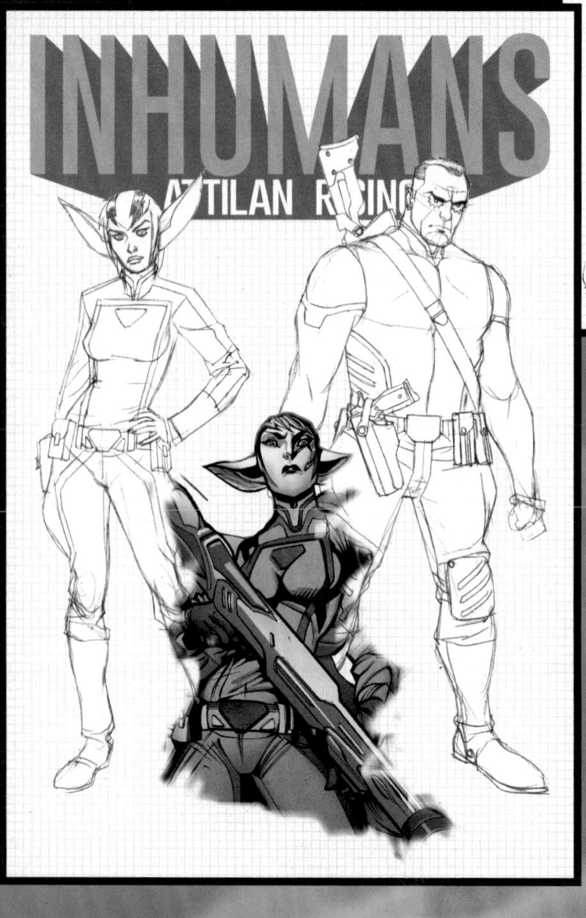
INHUMANS

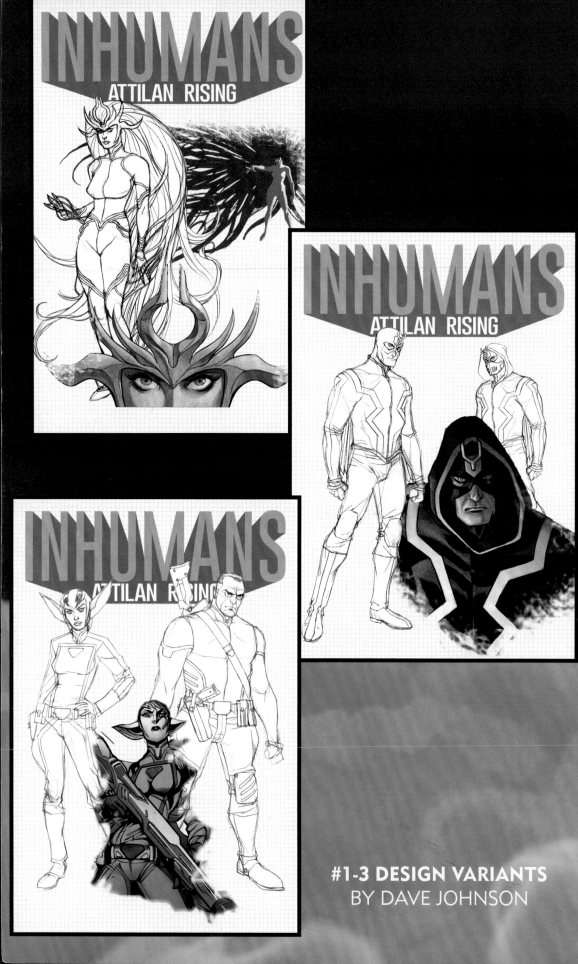

#1-3 DESIGN VARIANTS
BY DAVE JOHNSON

#1 VARIANT BY W. SCOTT FORBES

ATTILAN RISING

#1 VARIANT BY SKOTTIE YOUNG

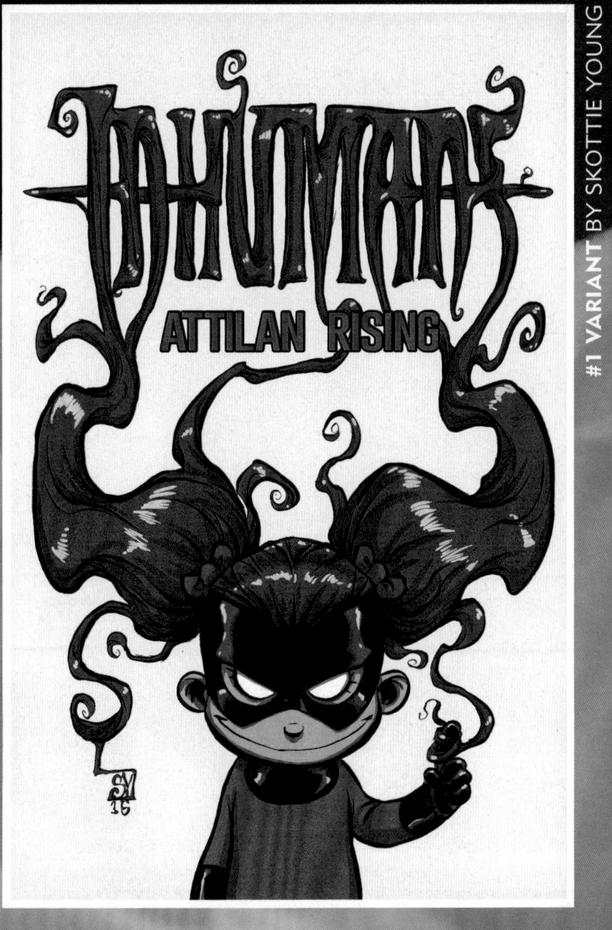

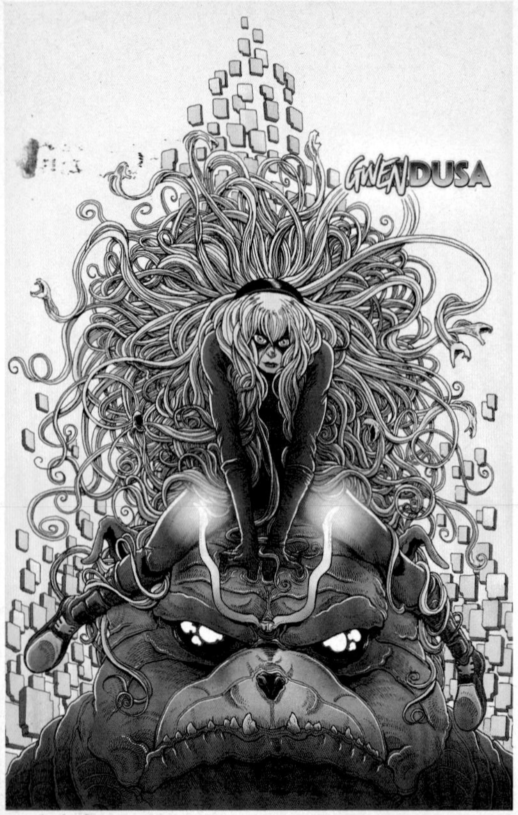
GWENDUSA

#2 GWENDUSA VARIANT BY JAMES STOKOE

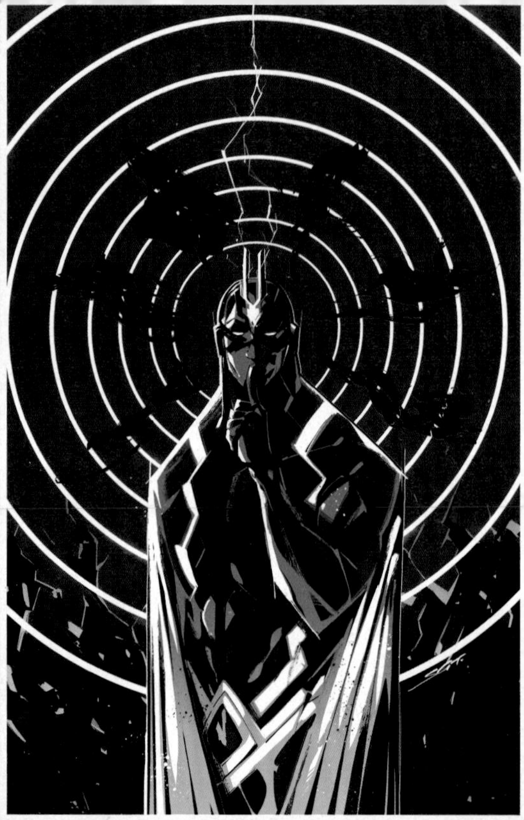

#2 MANGA VARIANT BY SHIGETO KOYAMA

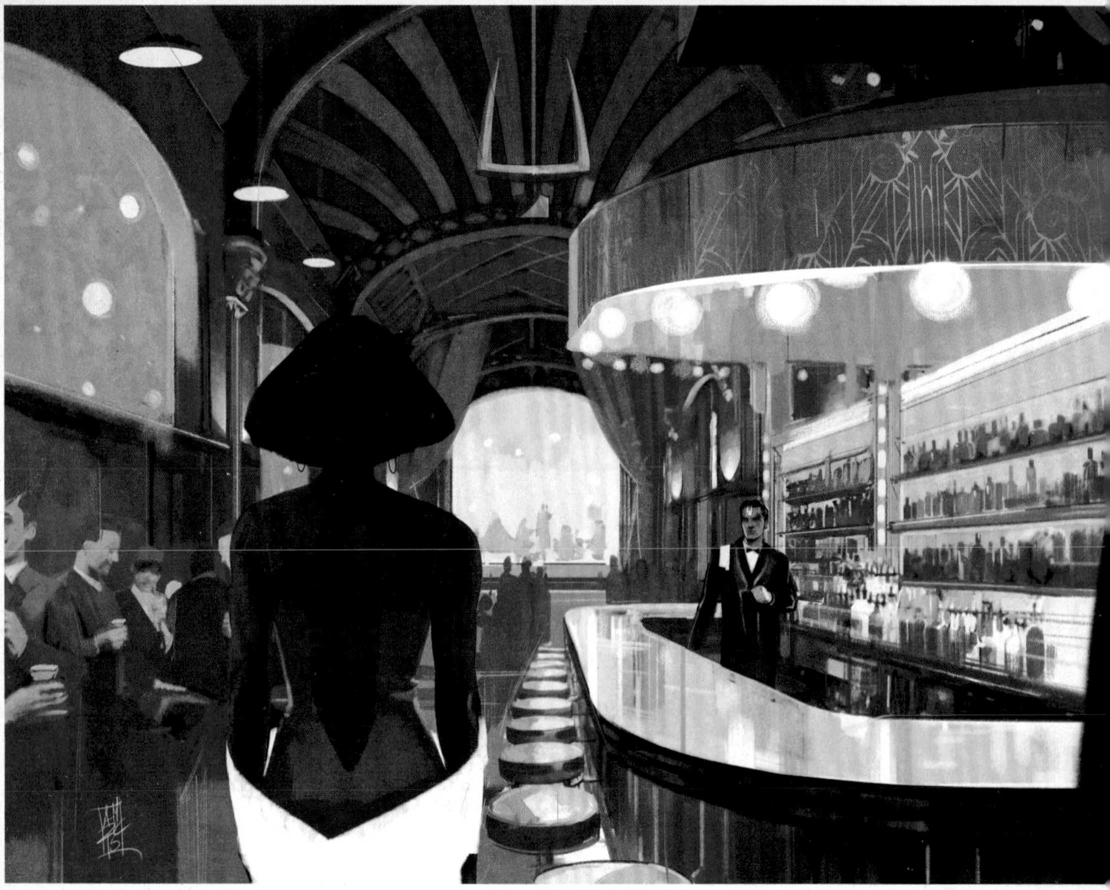

#3 LANDSCAPE VARIANT BY ALEX MALEEV